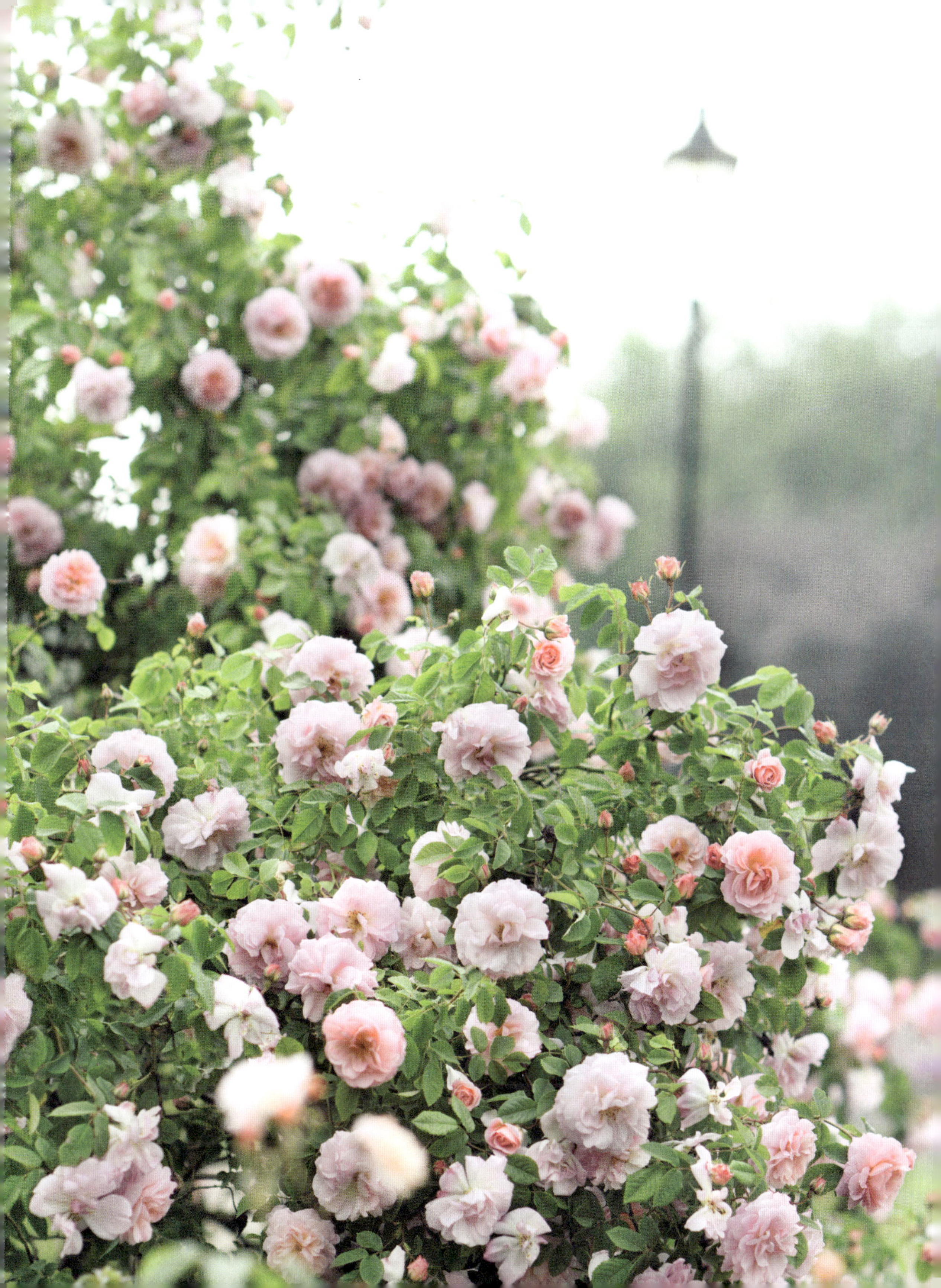

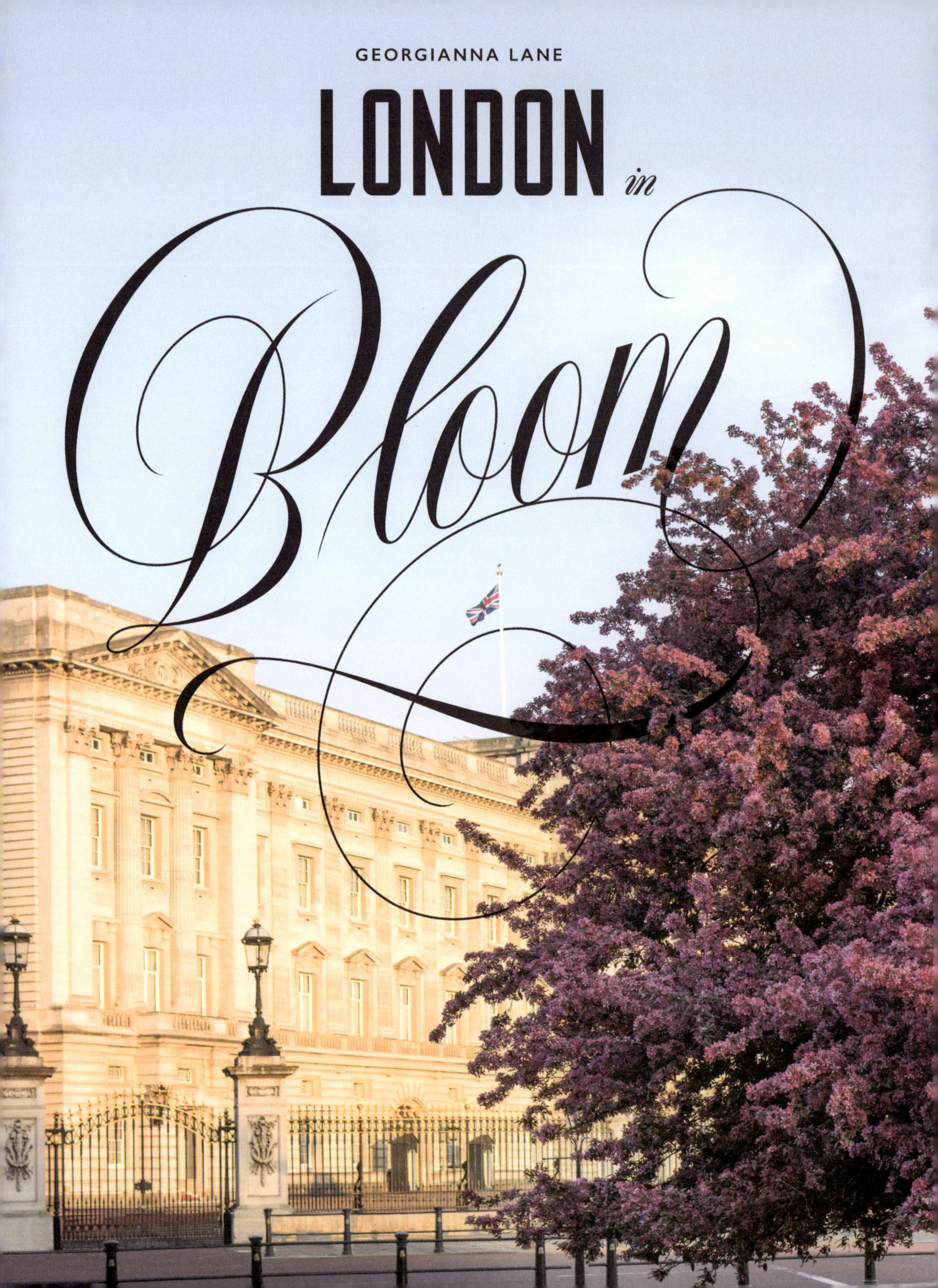

GEORGIANNA LANE
LONDON in
Bloom

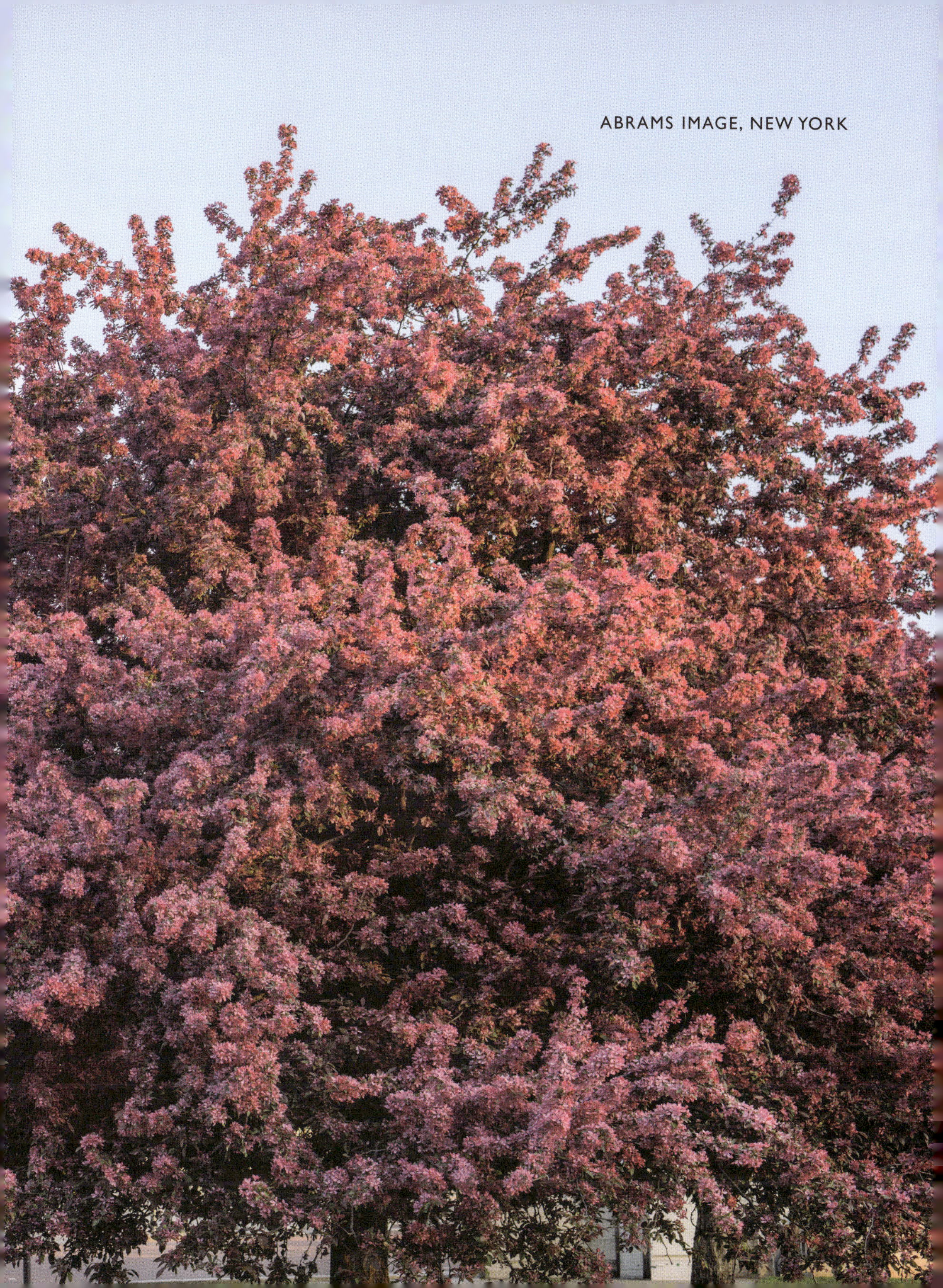

ABRAMS IMAGE, NEW YORK

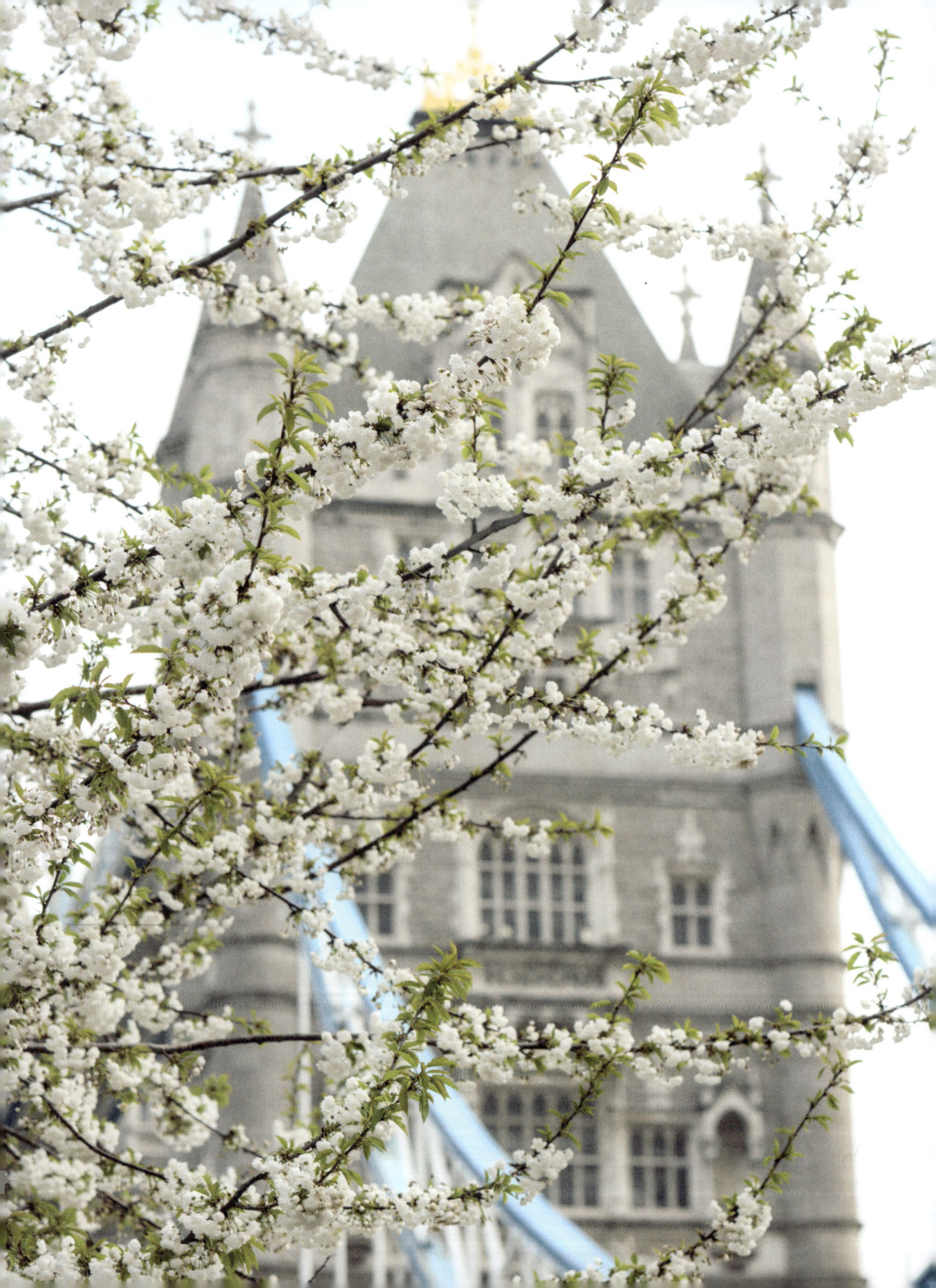

CONTENTS

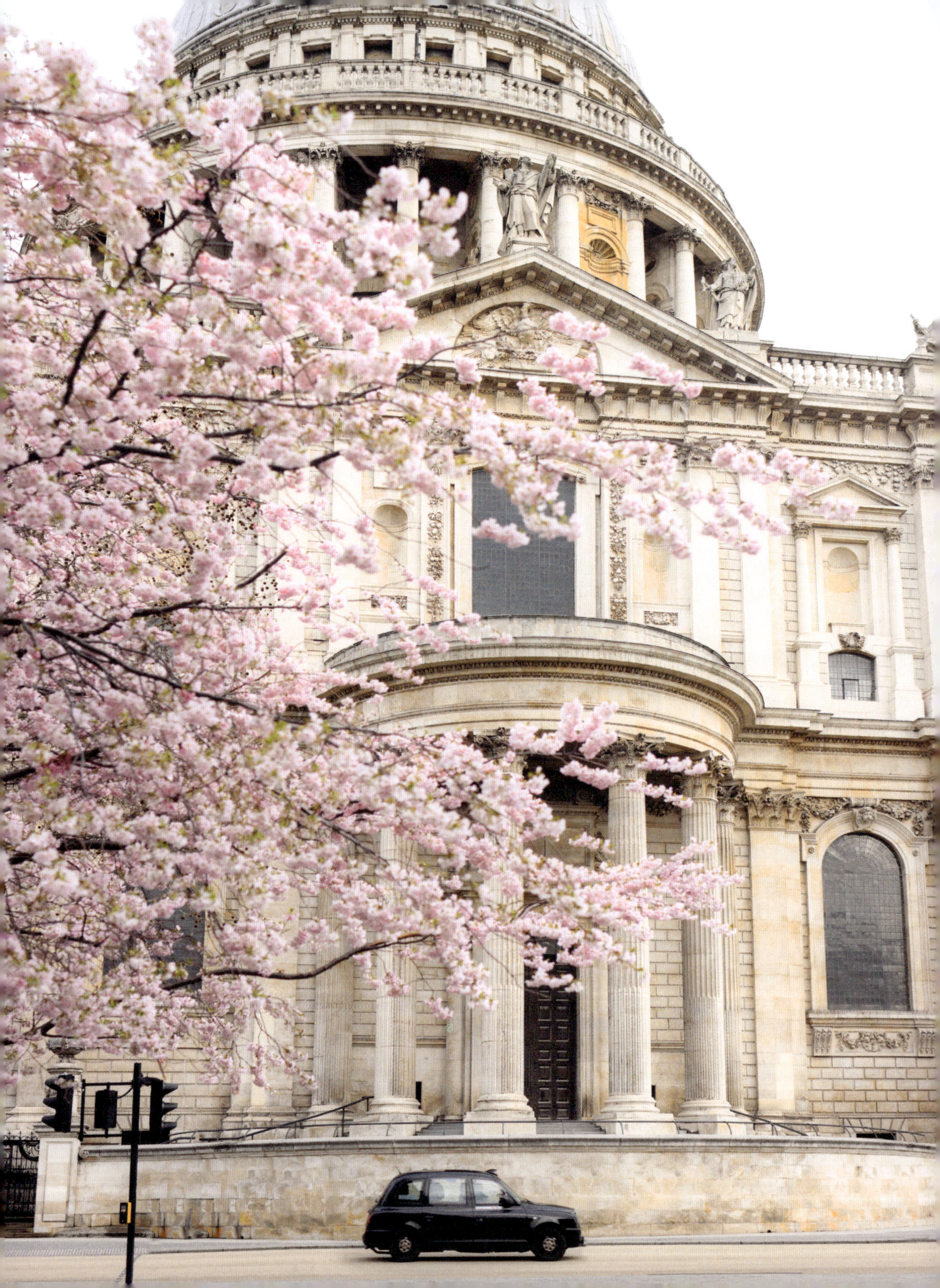

INTRODUCTION

CELEBRATING LONDON'S FLORAL HERITAGE

London captivated me well before I meandered along its ancient cobblestoned alleyways or marveled at its historic structures. From the air, circling Heathrow one long-ago summer, I discerned, at first, the bright-green patchwork fields of the countryside, and then the breathtakingly grand expanses of the Royal Parks, and finally, closer in, a multitude of row houses with their tiny gardens of pinks and purples, all lush and welcoming.

Subsequently, I fell deeply in love with the irresistibly complex bouquet of tradition and trendsetting, whimsy and pageantry, playfulness and propriety that is this magnificent city.

Perhaps not surprisingly, my most memorable London experiences have been inextricably interwoven with gardens. Whether I was rambling through nearby Richmond Park from our Sheen cottage the first summer I visited in my teens, or sitting in Russell Square in my early twenties, memorizing Shakespeare for my acting courses at the Royal Academy of Dramatic Art, the open spaces of London have seeped into my consciousness, awakened my imagination, and become part of me.

My dual passions for nature's flowers and mankind's resplendent buildings form the basis of much of my photography and writing. Thus, as in the creation of the previous volumes in this series, *Paris in Bloom* and *New York in Bloom*, I've drawn inspiration for this book not only from the botanical bounty found in the city but also from its floral-inspired architecture, and the juxtaposition of the two.

Throughout, I've been continually fascinated by the distinctive London details that make up its unique visual language, inscribed with quintessential English eloquence: the blacks of taxis, iron railings, lampposts, and checkered tiles; the reds of buses, phone booths, post boxes, and the Union Jack; the yellows of daffodils and mews cottages.

To those I would add gilded ceiling medallions, spiral staircases that mirror the whorled petals of an unfolding flower, painted panels in stately homes, designer fabrics, vintage cars, flowery china teacups, pubs festooned with flowers that are echoed in their etched and frosted windows, the rose gates at the National Portrait Gallery, imposing white Mayfair mansions that take themselves seriously, and pastel-painted Notting Hill houses that don't. I'll never tire of wandering, observing, and collecting images of this evolving panorama.

I adore chatting with London taxi drivers, especially when, upon inquiring about my profession as a floral photographer, they invariably share particulars of their own cherished gardens, which are an essential element of their existence. These simple conversations exemplify the nearly universal passion that Londoners have for gardening, on glorious display everywhere in the city.

Photographing the floral abundance of London is a joy and a privilege. But equally, I like the rare days when I leave my camera behind and amble through a park with only a pen and notebook, scribbling down details about the emerging plants and flowers, gathering field notes and memories.

These past few months, while completing this volume, I've been fortunate to reside in an elegant Kensington house on an exceptionally quiet and pretty street that must be one of the city's most floriferous. Flanked at either end by two residences extravagantly embellished with wisteria, the lane has since early March offered an astonishing procession of spring beauty: ornamental plum trees, magnolias, camellias, cherries, lilac, wisteria, jasmine, roses, and, soon to come, lavender. Each week brings new and fragrant wonders outside my front door.

At this moment, as I write from a curvy iron bench in Kensington Gardens on a warm April morning, with the heavy scent of lilac entwined in my hair, all the magic of that first London summer comes rushing back: the thrill of arriving, the anticipation of exploring, the jubilance of discovering a land of enchantment.

So, if the realm of England is a garden, an Elysium of blooming delights, London has always been, to me, its floral heart, a demi-paradise for flower gardeners, flower sellers, and flower lovers. My ardent wish is that you may also discover, through these pages, that glorious wonderland beckoning to you.

Georgianna Lane
London, April 2019

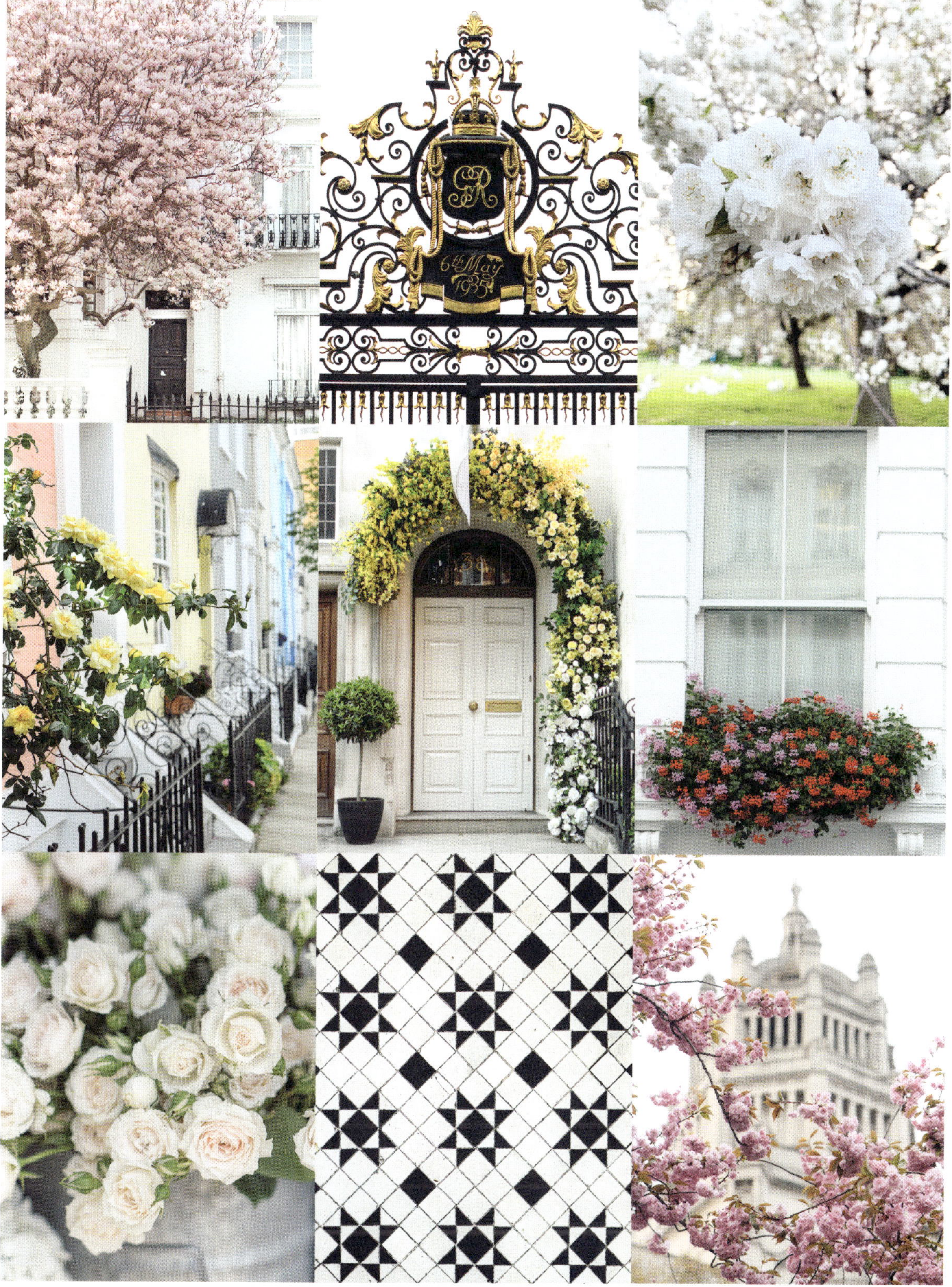

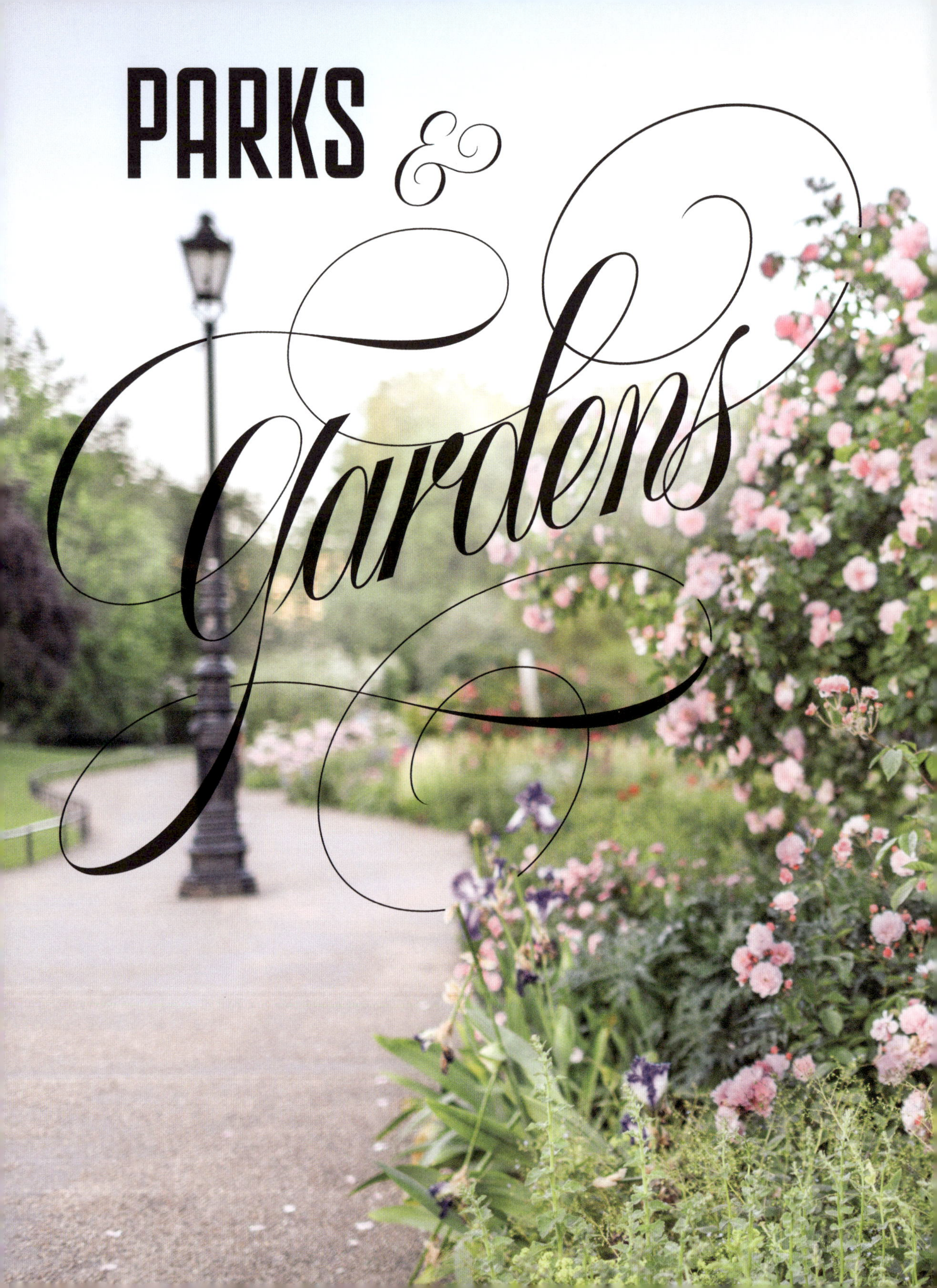

PARKS
&
Gardens

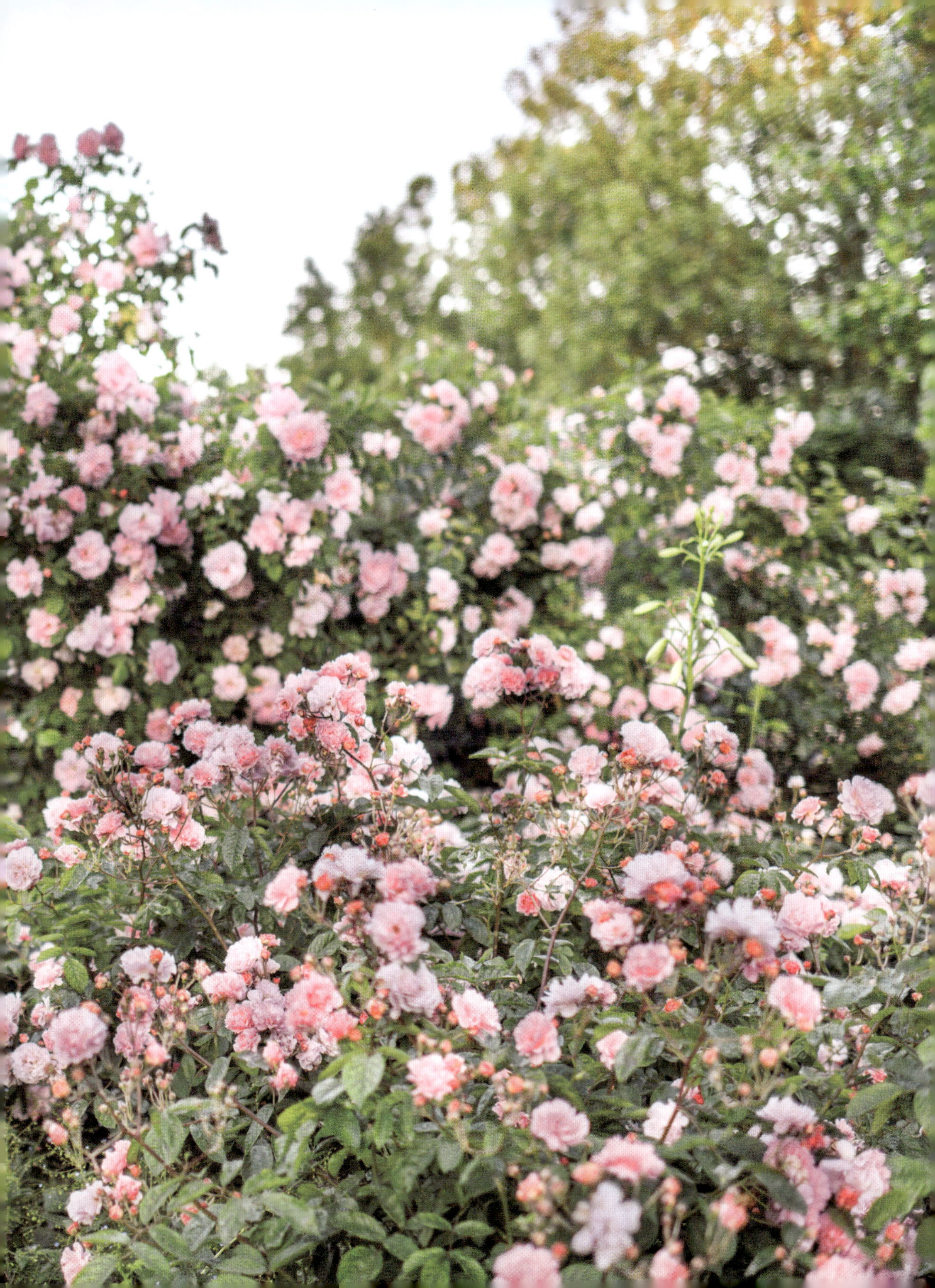

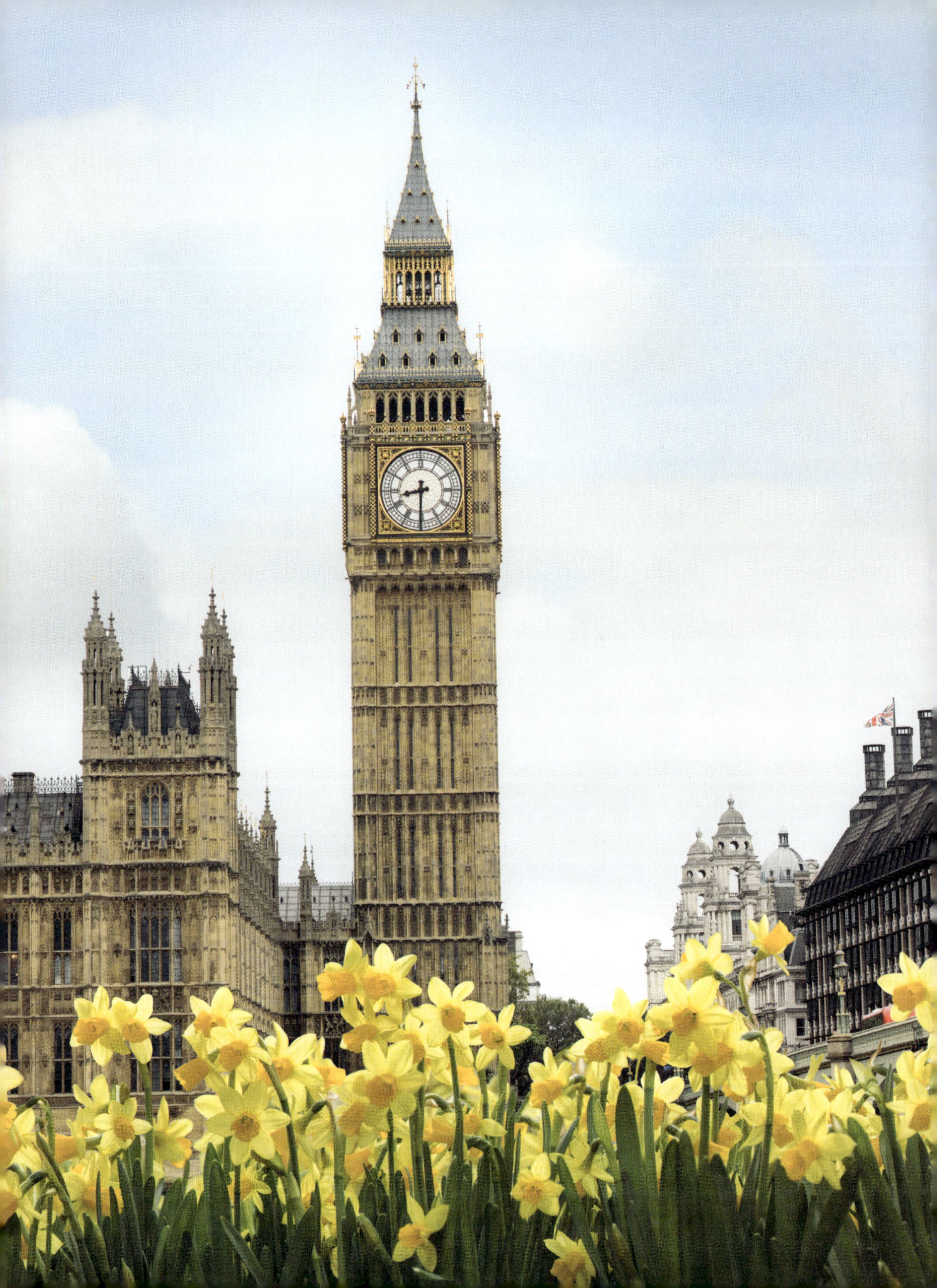

No place, real or imagined, enchants quite like an English garden. The ornate gates, the tumbling roses, the winding paths, and the sunlight winking through branches of delicate blossoms have long inspired poetry and romance.

True to this heritage, the vast topography of London flourishes on a dual plane: a dense urban network of dignified squares, sumptuous palaces, and modern structures all harmoniously interwoven with nature by the pastoral havens of its magnificent parks and gardens.

Some are intimate and secret, with secluded corners and mysterious pools where dragonflies hover or fantastic creatures might even dwell. Others are impressive and majestic, their rolling parklands reminiscent of an eighteenth-century landscape painting, dotted with follies and sculptures and conjuring scenes of horse-drawn carriages and duels fought at dawn.

Among them, the famous eight Royal Parks, once the hunting grounds of kings, have witnessed as much pageantry and history, intrigue and drama as nearby castles. Their broad promenades that fade into the distance and idyllic water features are punctuated with formal fountains and classical statues.

A favorite is Kensington Gardens, deeply associated, through centuries of literary references, with magic, pixie dust, and fairies. Reclining on the lawn in quiet contemplation, a visitor might be given to conjuring childhood fantasies and imagining an enticing land of adventurous possibilities. This lovely oasis is, after all, the home of Peter Pan.

Wandering into the shelter of a London park, one can experience a palpable embrace of soothing calm, a tranquil sanctuary and respite from the sustained velocity of city life. The pace immediately slows, and the cacophony of traffic and sirens diminishes, replaced by the rustle of leaves and gentle birdsong in the milder months.

As a new year advances, spring nudges London out of winter's bleakness with variegated carpets of white snowdrops, mauve and pink crocuses, and nodding bluebells. Hundreds of thousands of daffodils paint the lawns of Green Park with undulating bands of golden yellow, while deep-vermilion tulips spread a regal mantle before the entrance to Buckingham Palace.

Reveling in the return of light and the joyous explosion of blooms, Londoners flock to the parks, little caring about the still-chilly temperatures. The rush of city life may be invigorating, but March in a London green space offers a more natural form of exhilaration.

On wooden benches beneath blossoming trees, office workers, investment bankers, and high-street clerks balance takeaway lunches and books on their laps, indulging for an hour in a novel that promises a rewarding escape. Others, relaxing in the iconic green-striped deck chairs, might fondly recall impromptu picnics, cloud gazing, tree climbing, and the twirling-around-barefoot-in-the-grass kind of giddiness of childhood.

Before long, the early-blooming camellias, magnolias, and ornamental trees are daubing the scene with pinks and crimsons and pale-blush tones. In St. James's Park, branches of early-flowering Accolade cherry trees shed faded petals onto the lake with a graceful flourish, as swans glide underneath with a coy tilt of their heads, as if subtly aware of the picturesque scene they create. Directly opposite Ranger's House at Greenwich, another Royal Park, a double row of frilly, deep-pink Kwanzan cherry trees creates a petaled canopy, with sunbeams dappling the path below.

The countless squares and private gardens throughout the city extend the floral show with billowy crab apple trees, fragrant shrubs, and endless climbing roses and peonies. Pale-purple wisteria cascades over windows and railings with grapelike bunches of delicately scented blossoms. In neighborhoods such as Notting Hill and Chelsea, the pinks, mauves, and pale yellows of the residents' gardens visually echo their whimsical, pastel-painted houses.

By late May, the superb rose gardens, especially at Kew, Hyde Park, and Regent's Park, are flush with blooms that clamber up and around pillars and drape romantically in swags between them. Myriad varieties in rich hues overflow winding walkways and cascade over the borders of informal beds interspersed with irises, foxgloves, and delphiniums. At the base of the magnificent ornate gates of the Queen's Garden, an extravagance of coral floribunda roses welcomes all who enter.

Plantings of purple allium at Kew in early June harmoniously counterpoint the yellow-green new growth of the sheltering willows near the lake. And all through the warm months, well into September, the city's continuously blooming roses endure as the crowning triumph of summer.

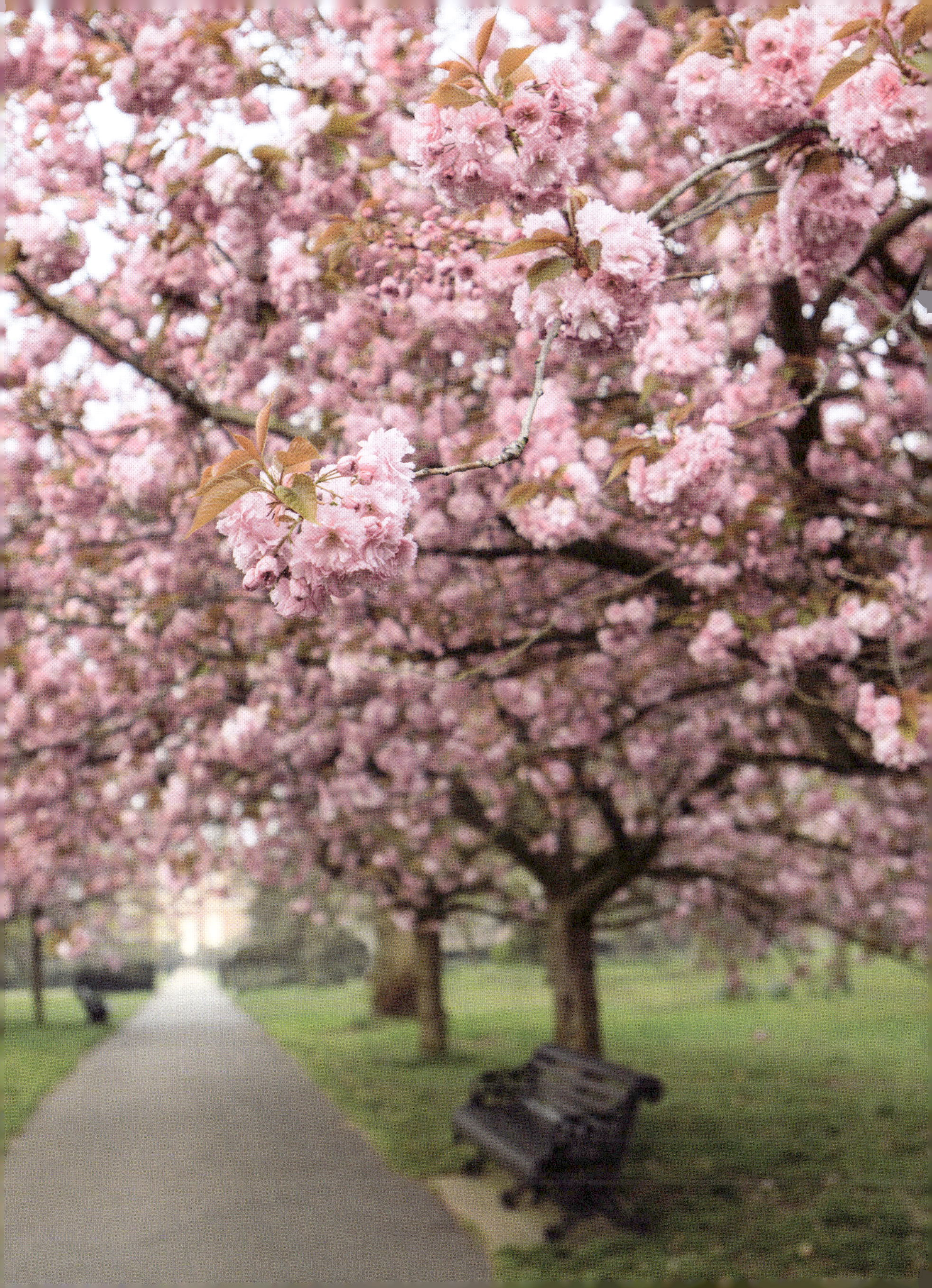

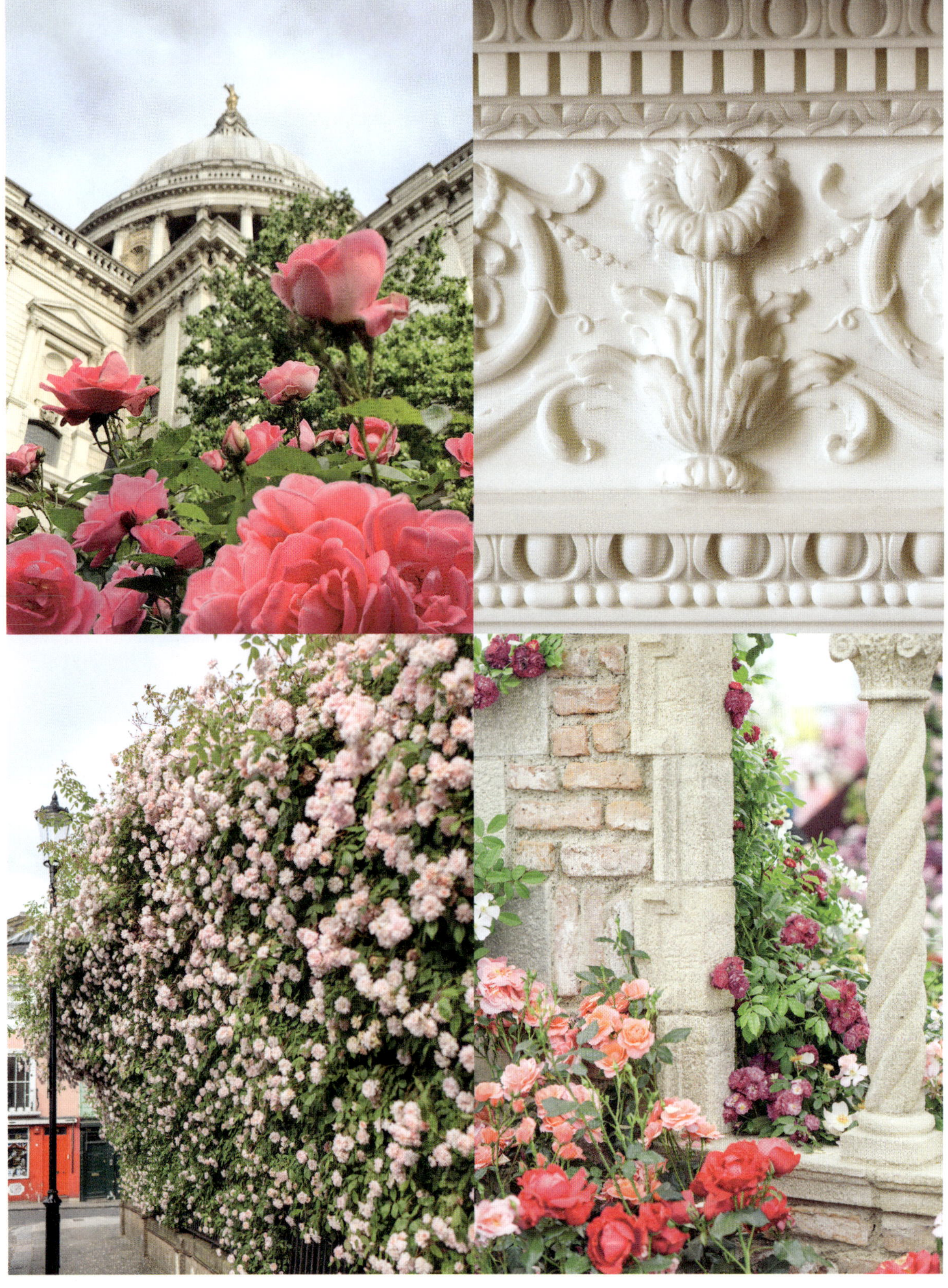

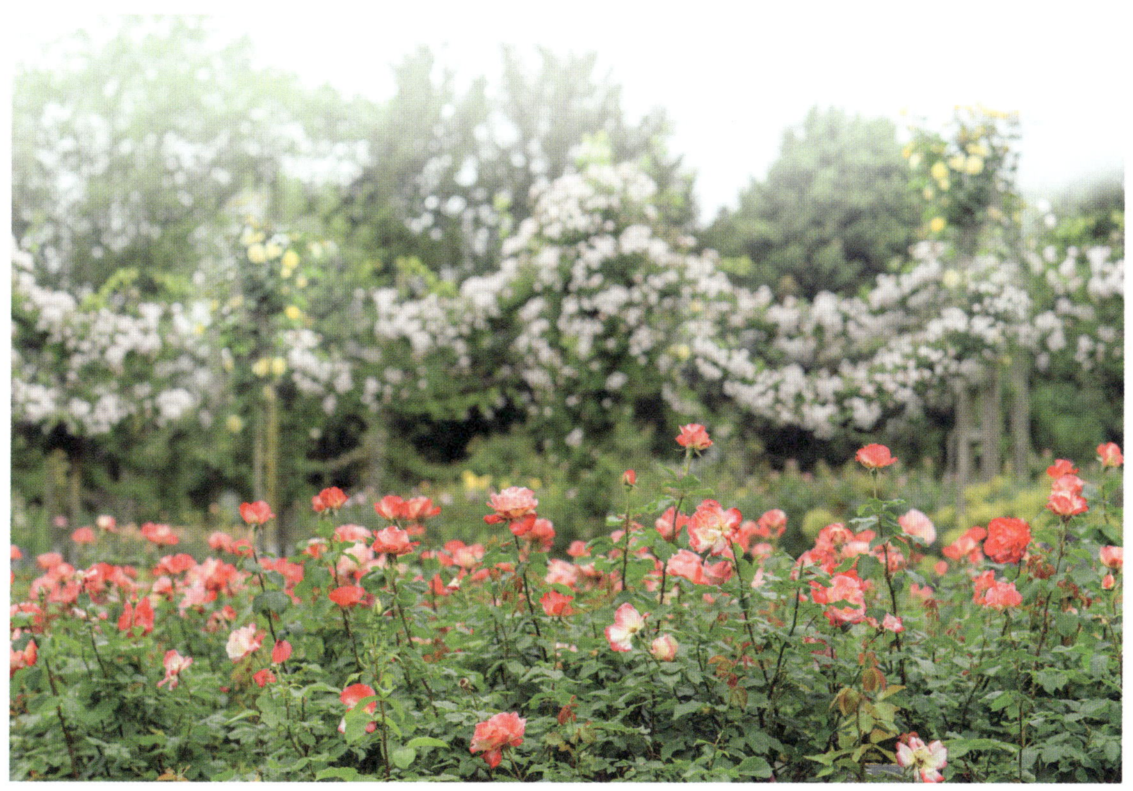

In autumn, a gentler mood pervades when jewel-colored dahlias and cosmos dominate the plantings, accented by the first of the fallen leaves. The exuberance of golden days may be waning, but the parks are entering their most peaceful season, before winter once again descends.

A reflective afternoon in a garden can provide a reminder of what is most important in life, an affirmation of the good and right and beautiful in the world. One can gather scattered thoughts, reconnect with dreams, and rejuvenate one's outlook.

Approach with a sense of wonder and a London park can be a gateway to another world, a land of time suspended, where one can feel as ageless as Peter Pan and, if the light is just right, perhaps even glimpse fairy dust glittering on the morning breeze.

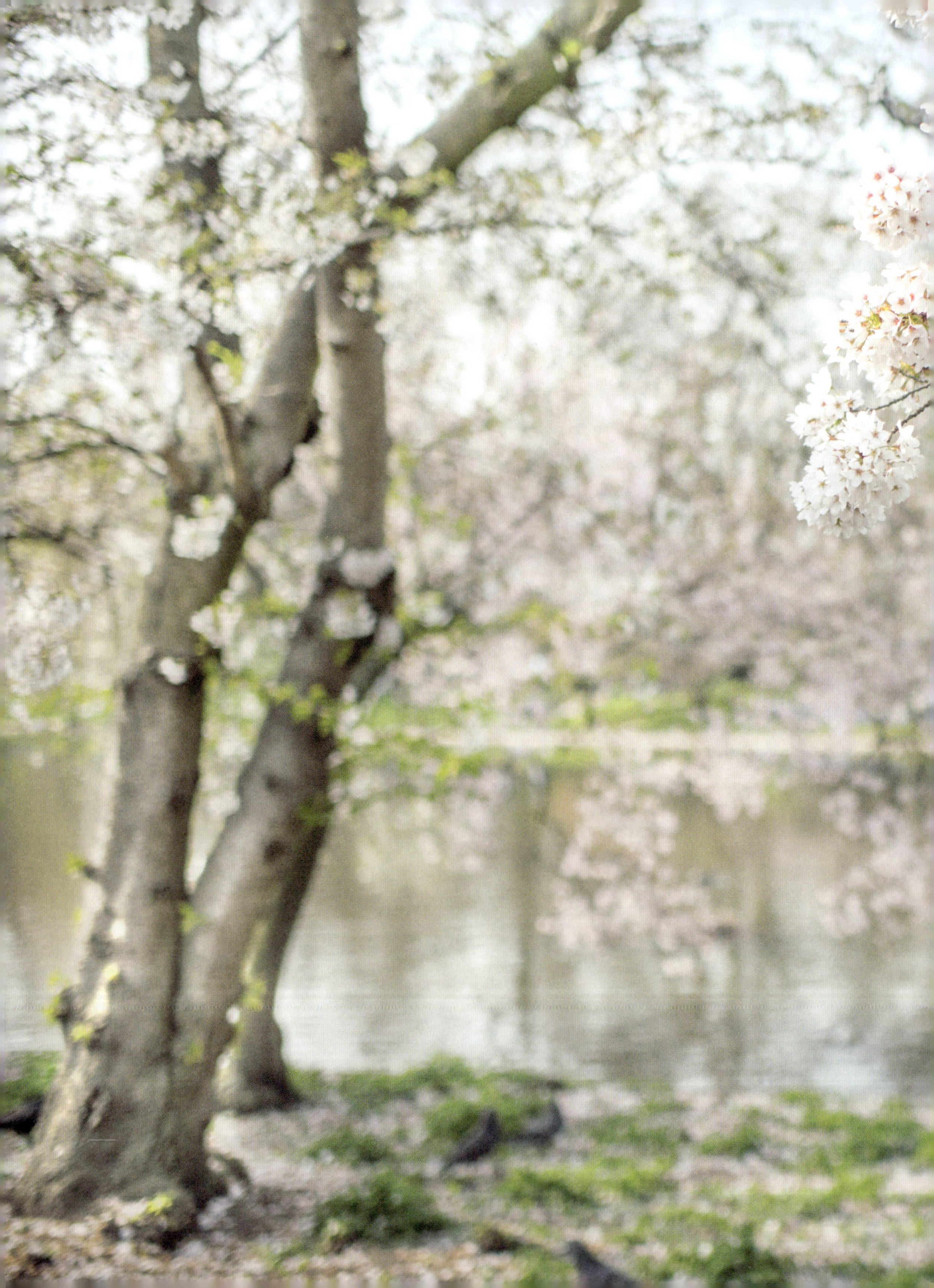

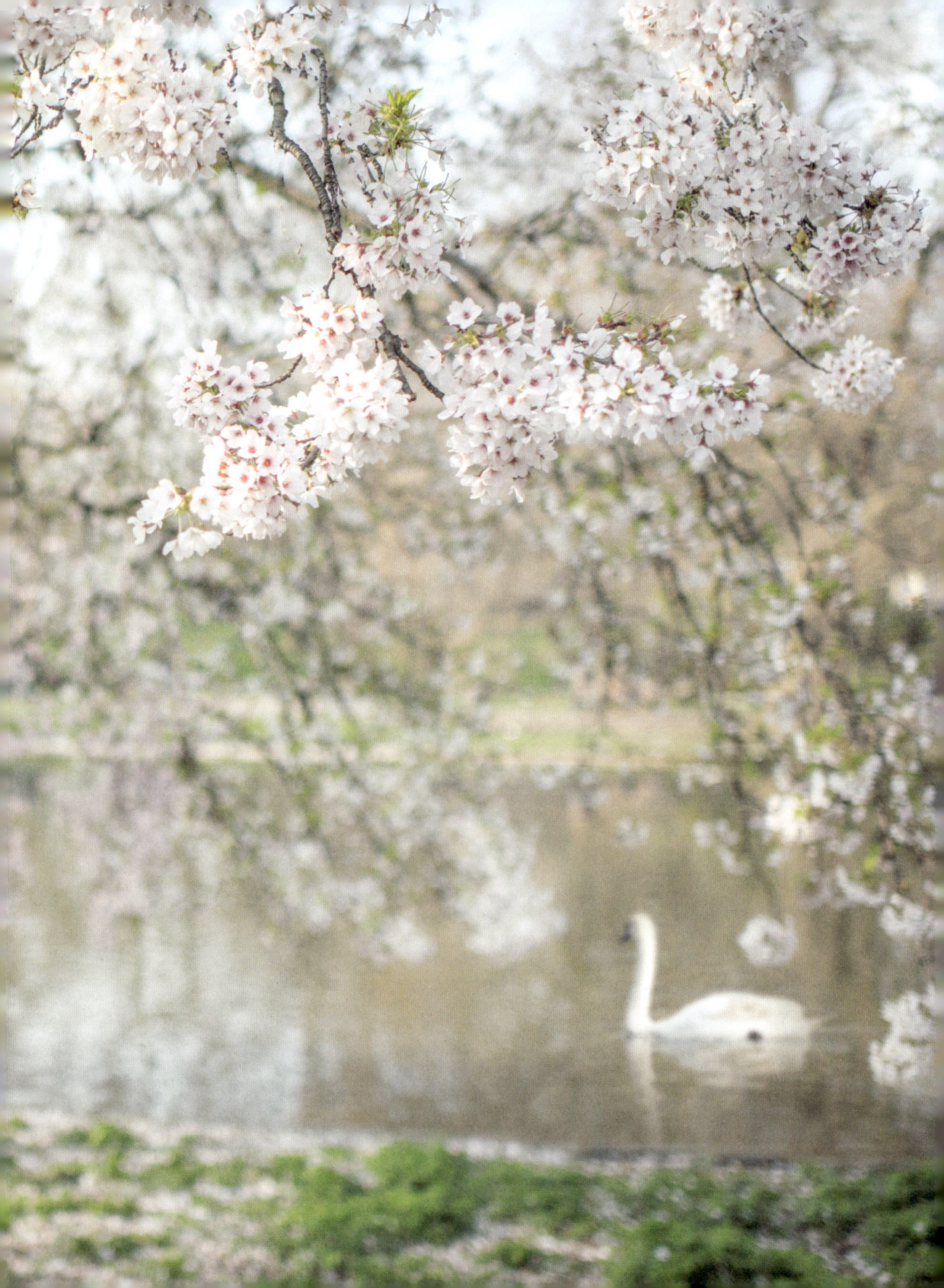

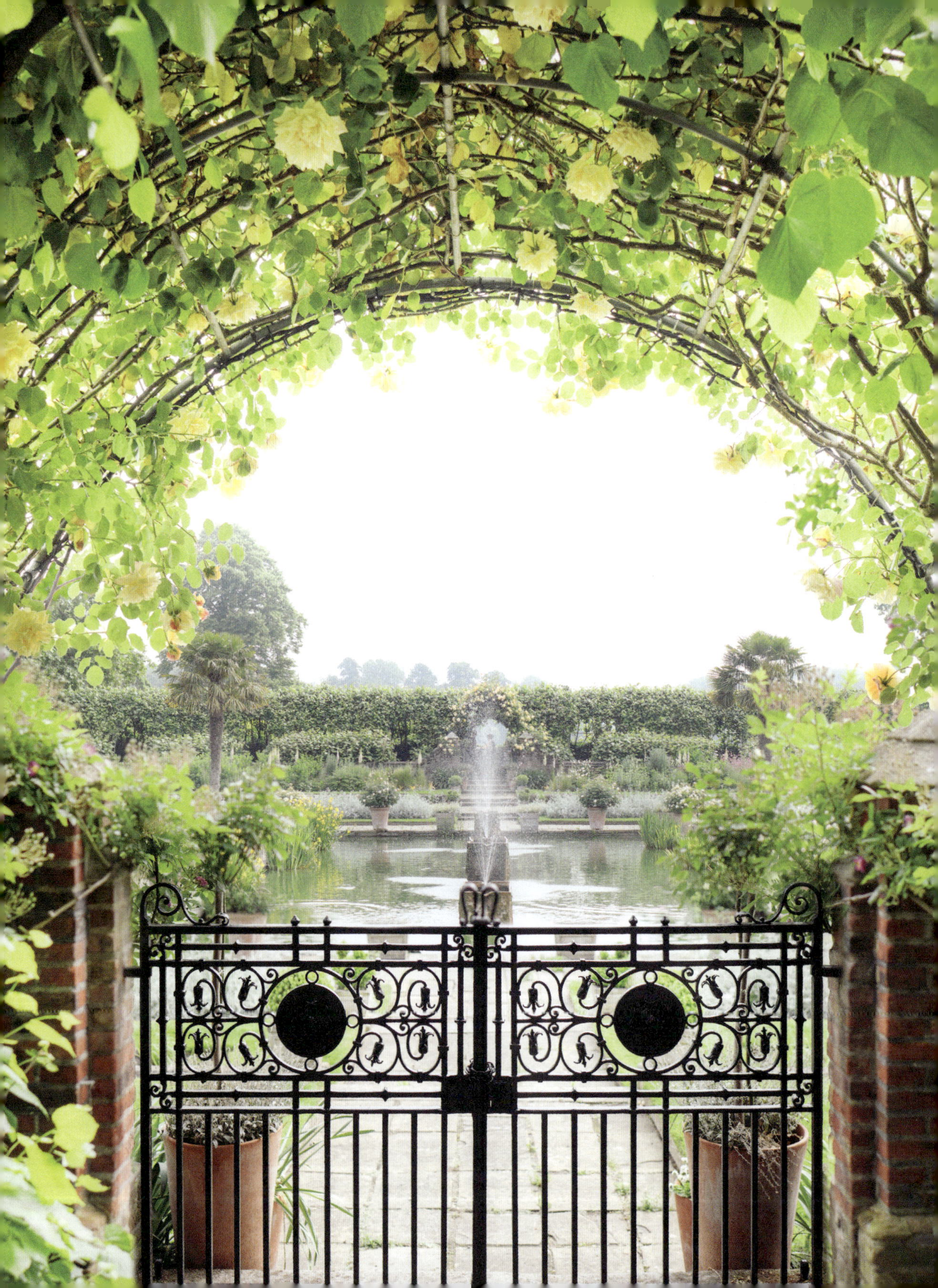

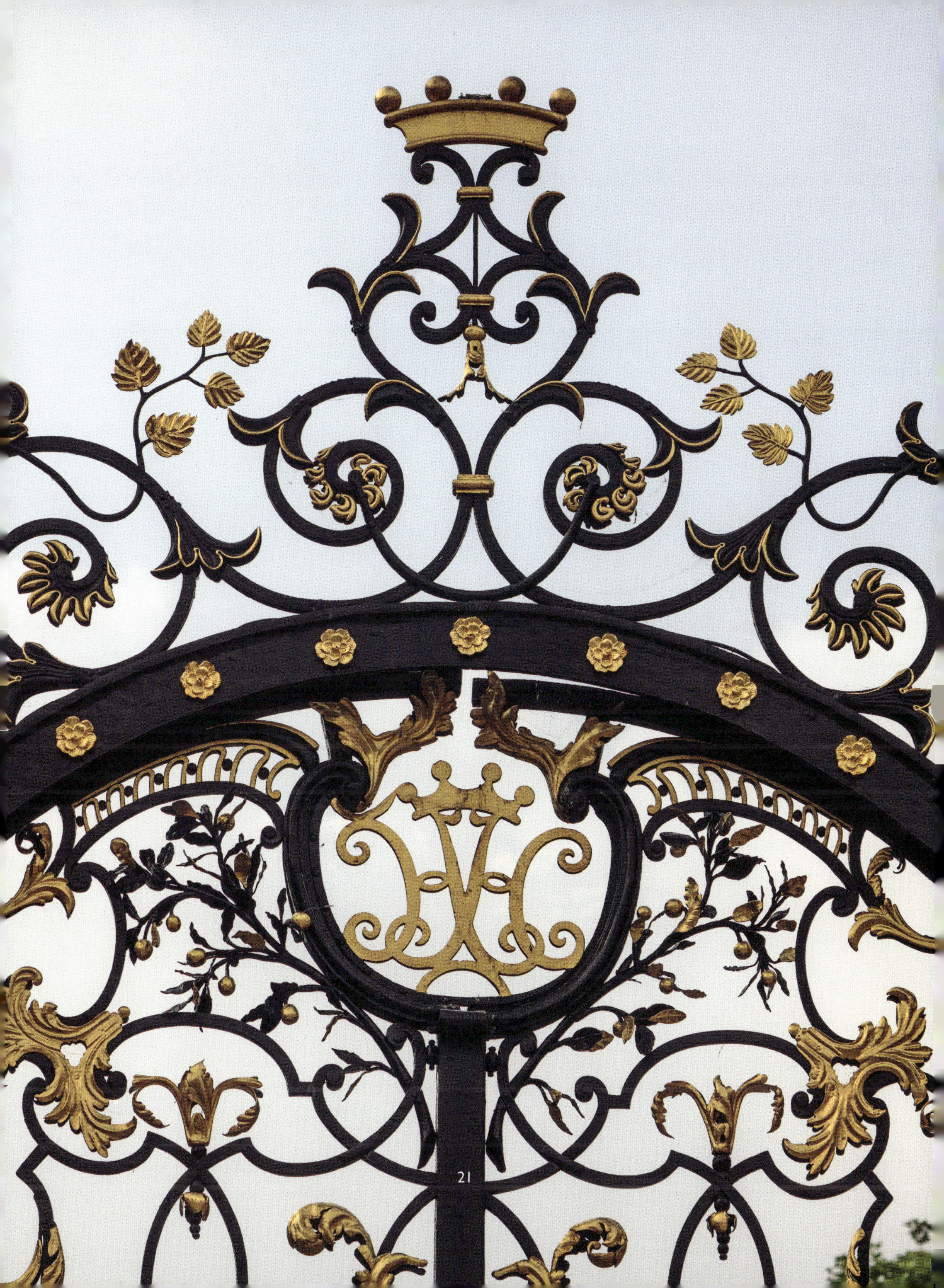

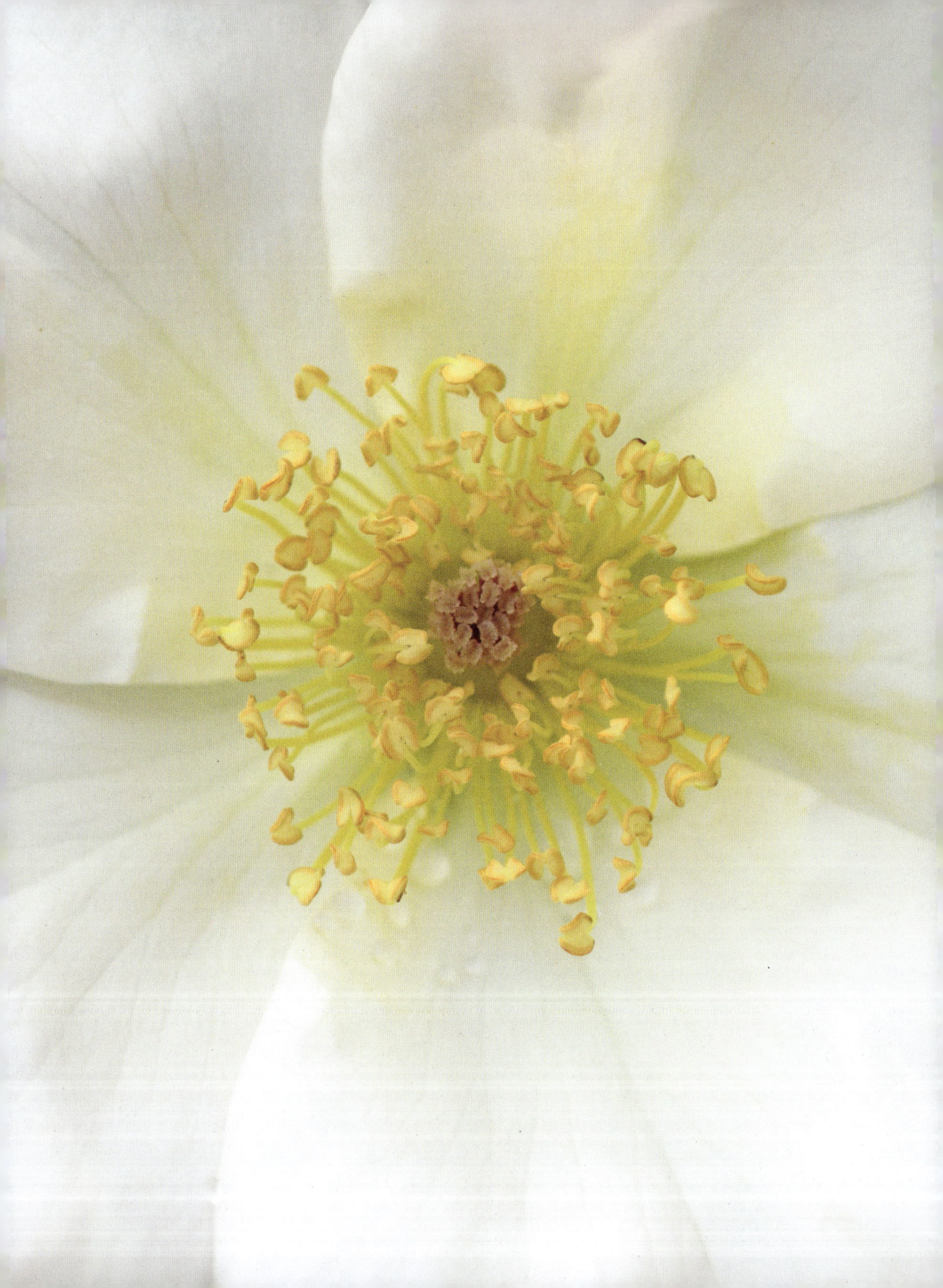

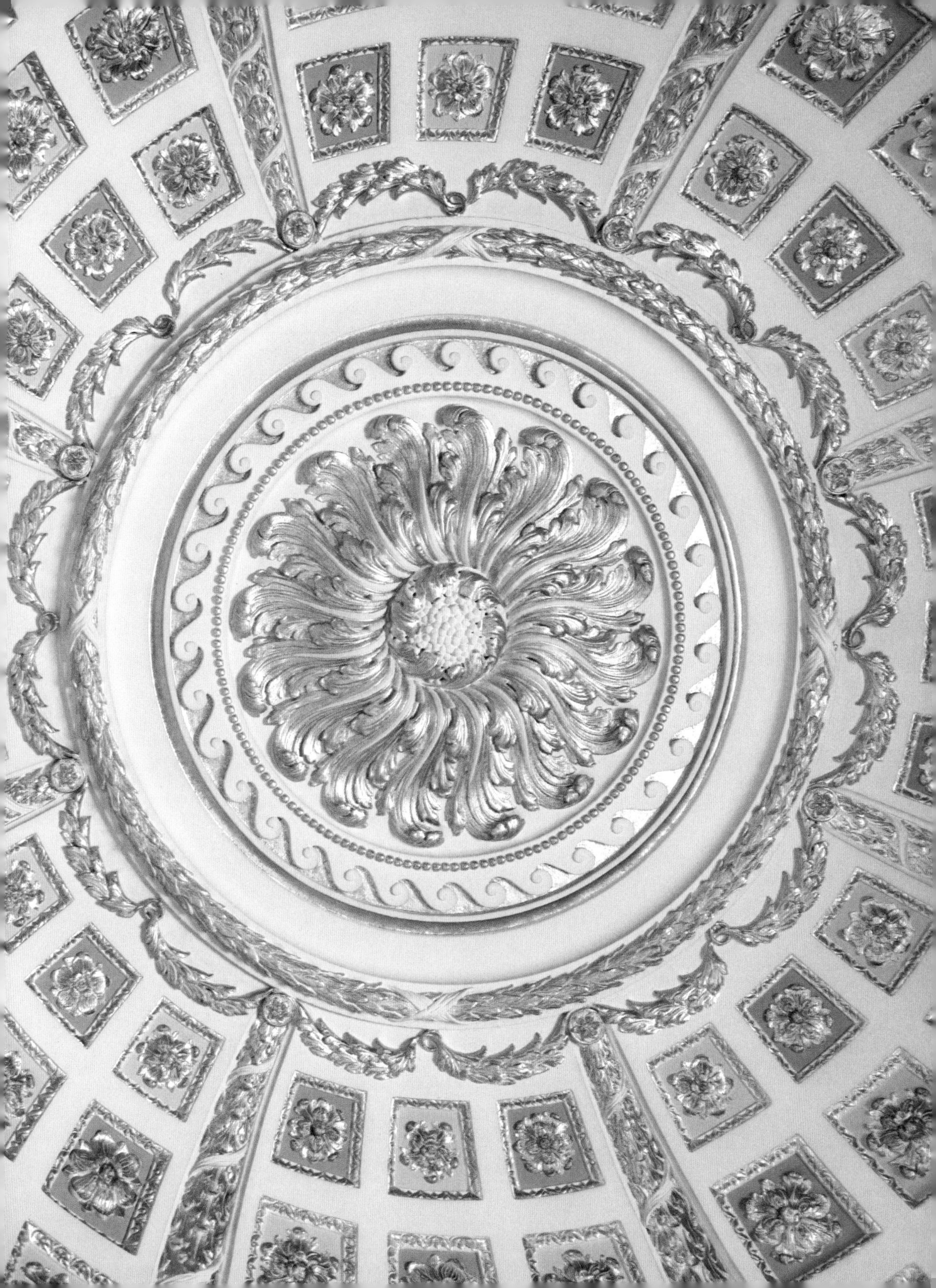

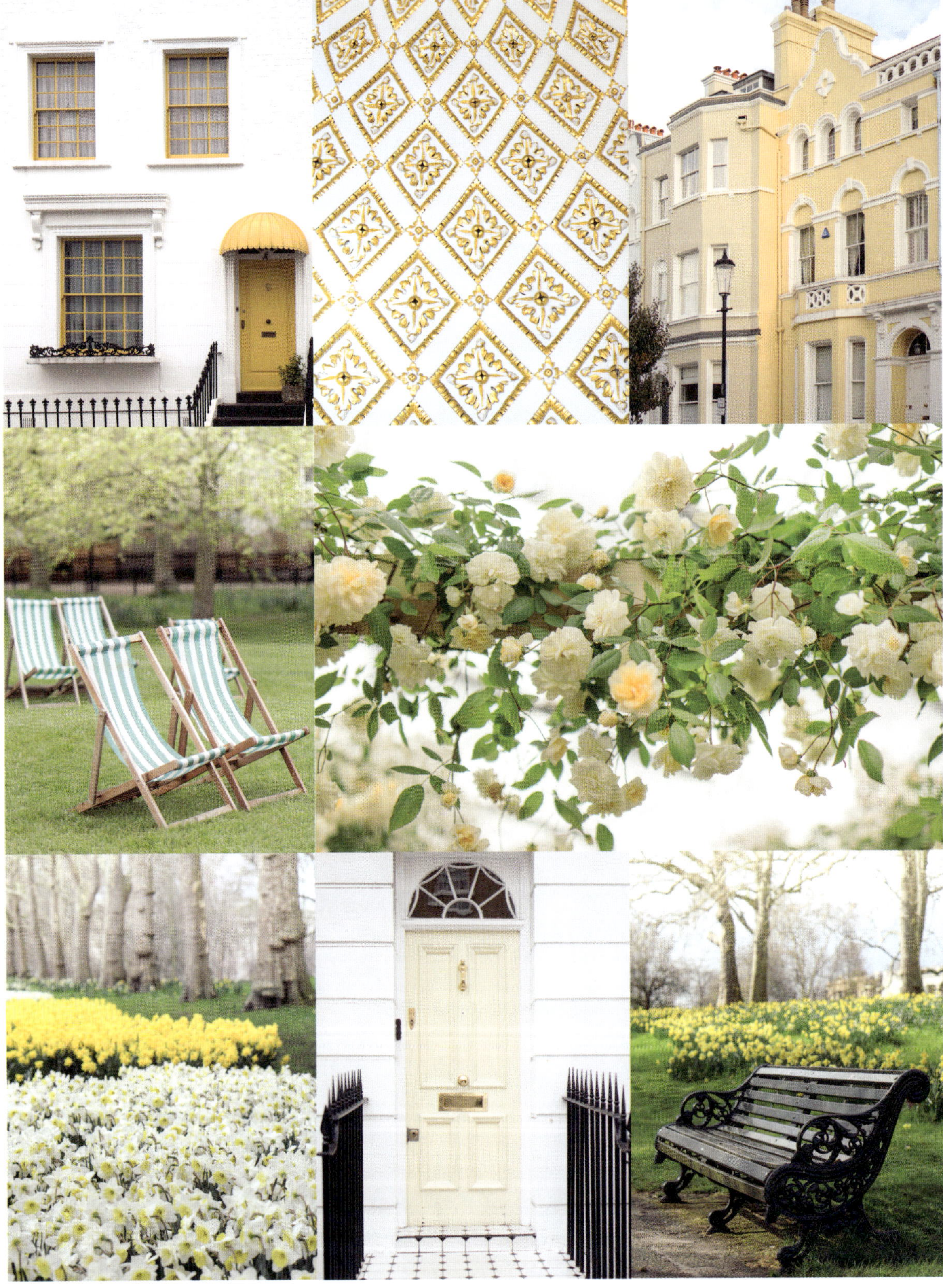

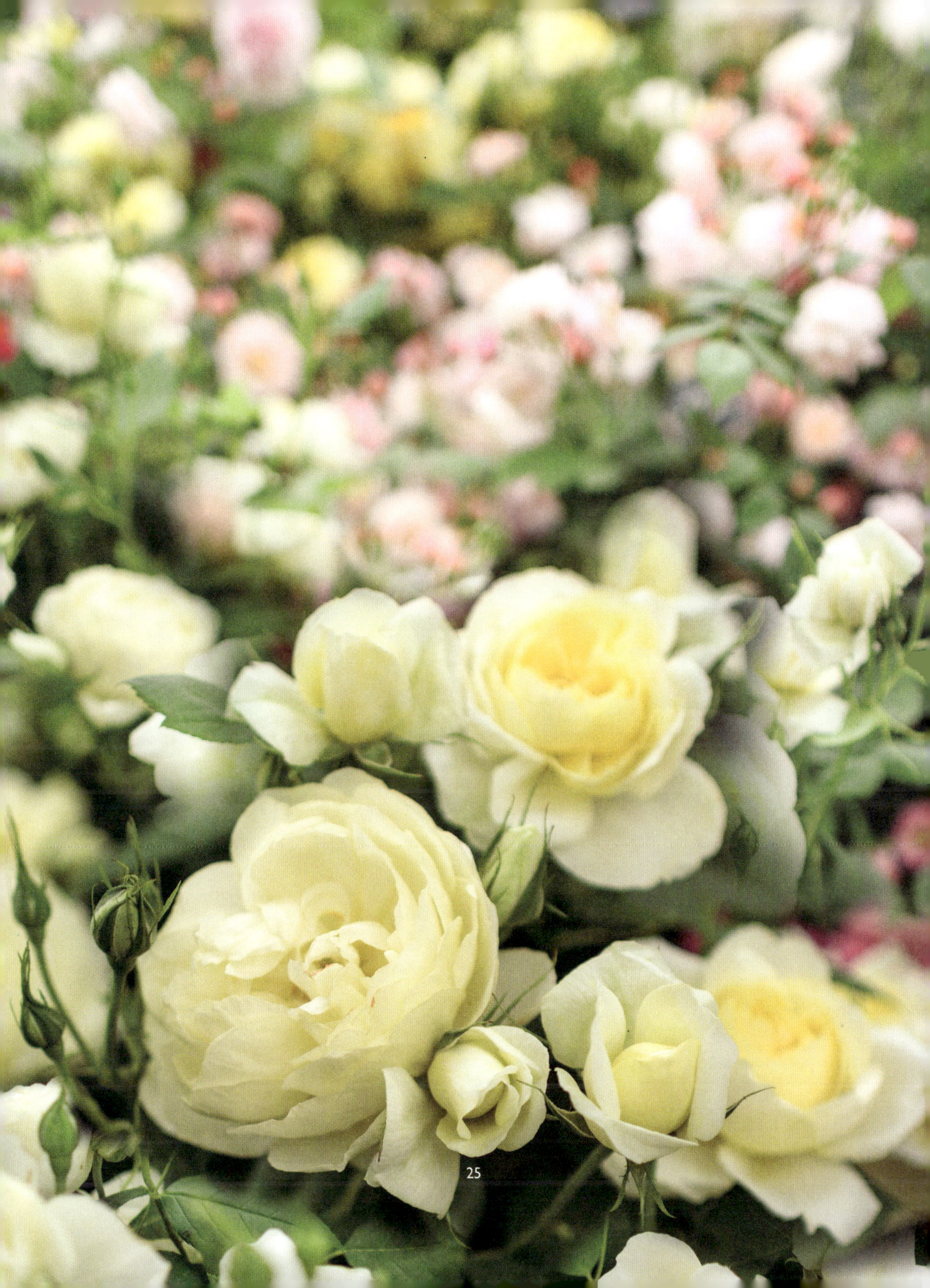

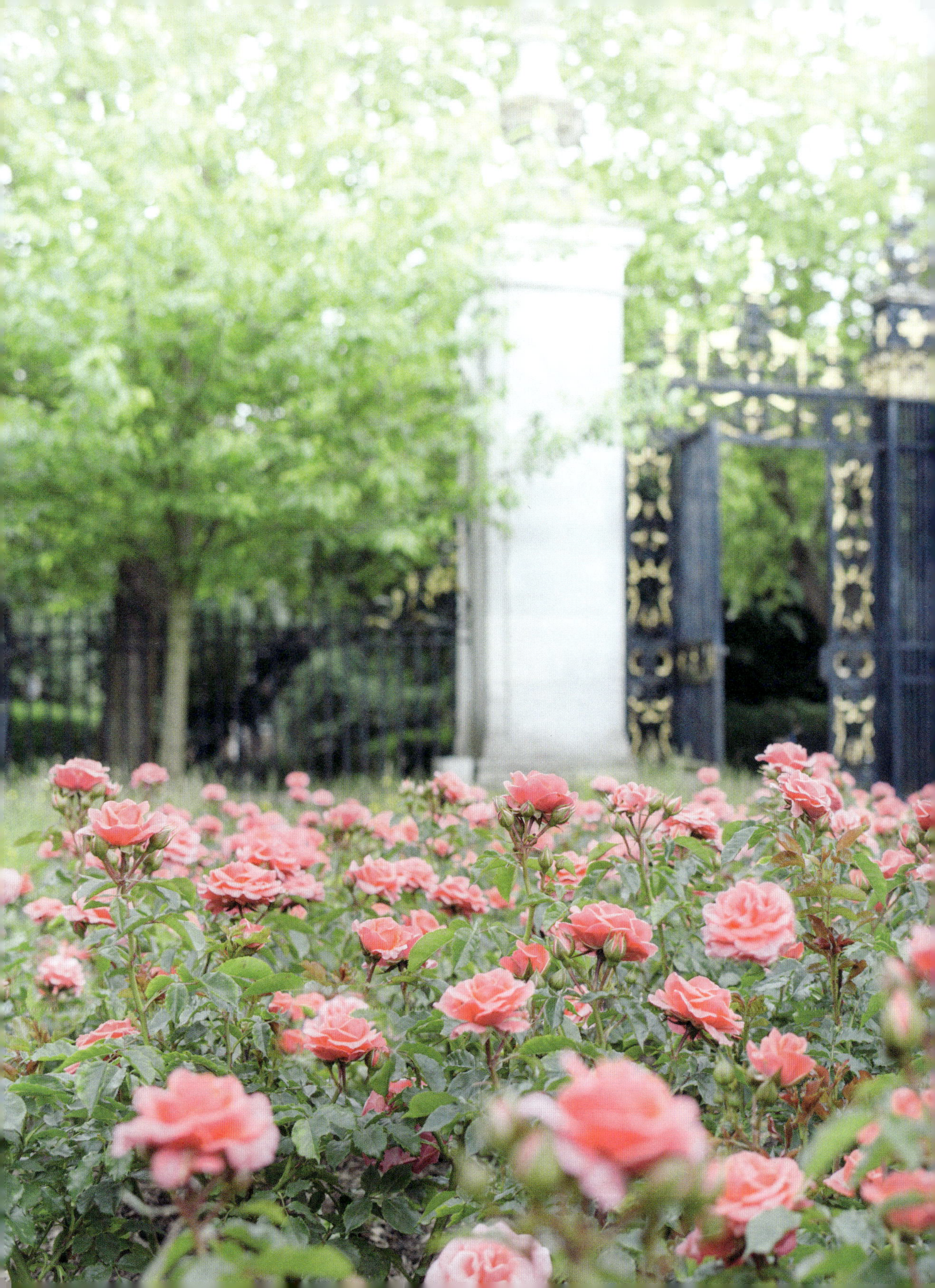

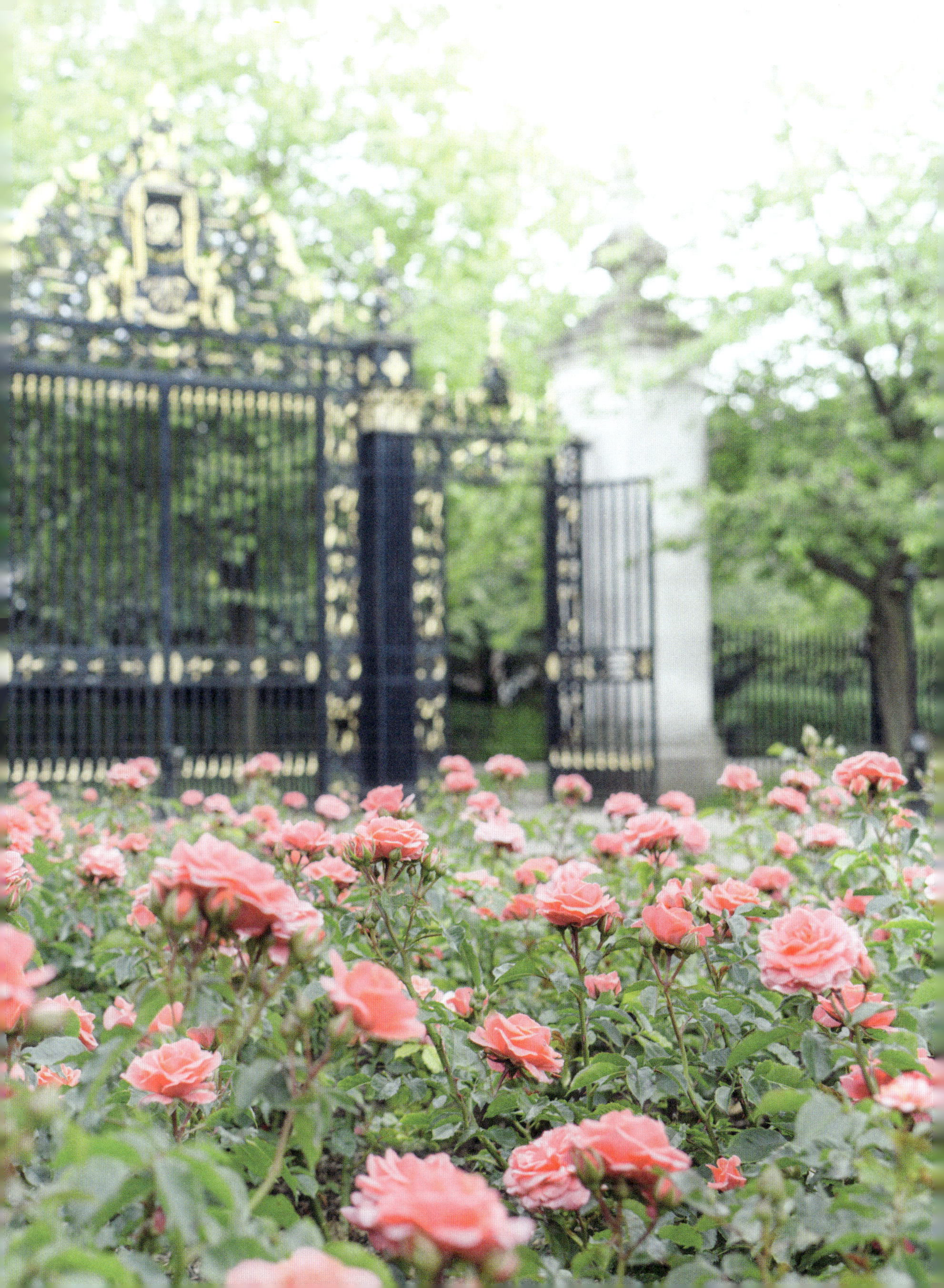

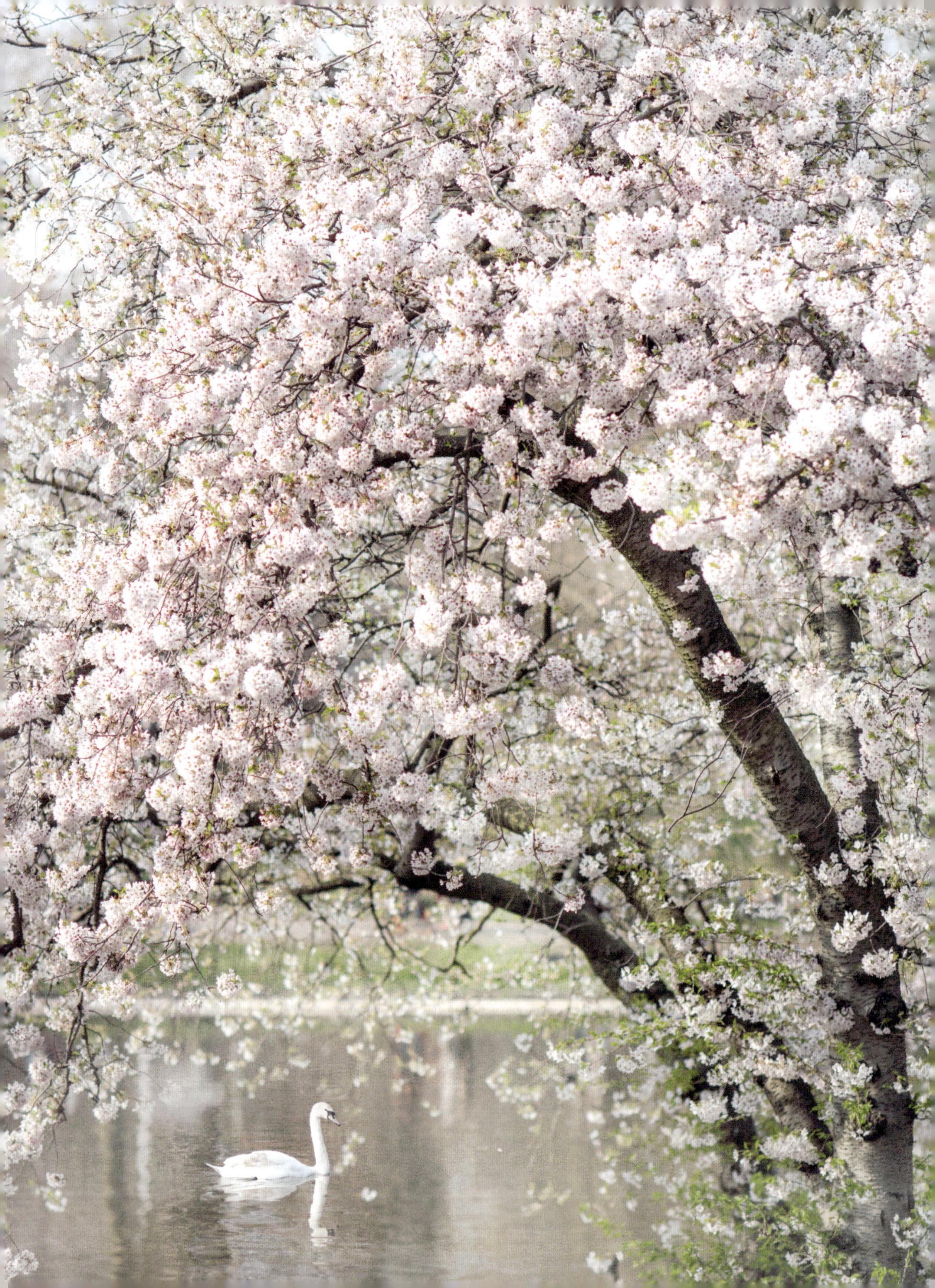

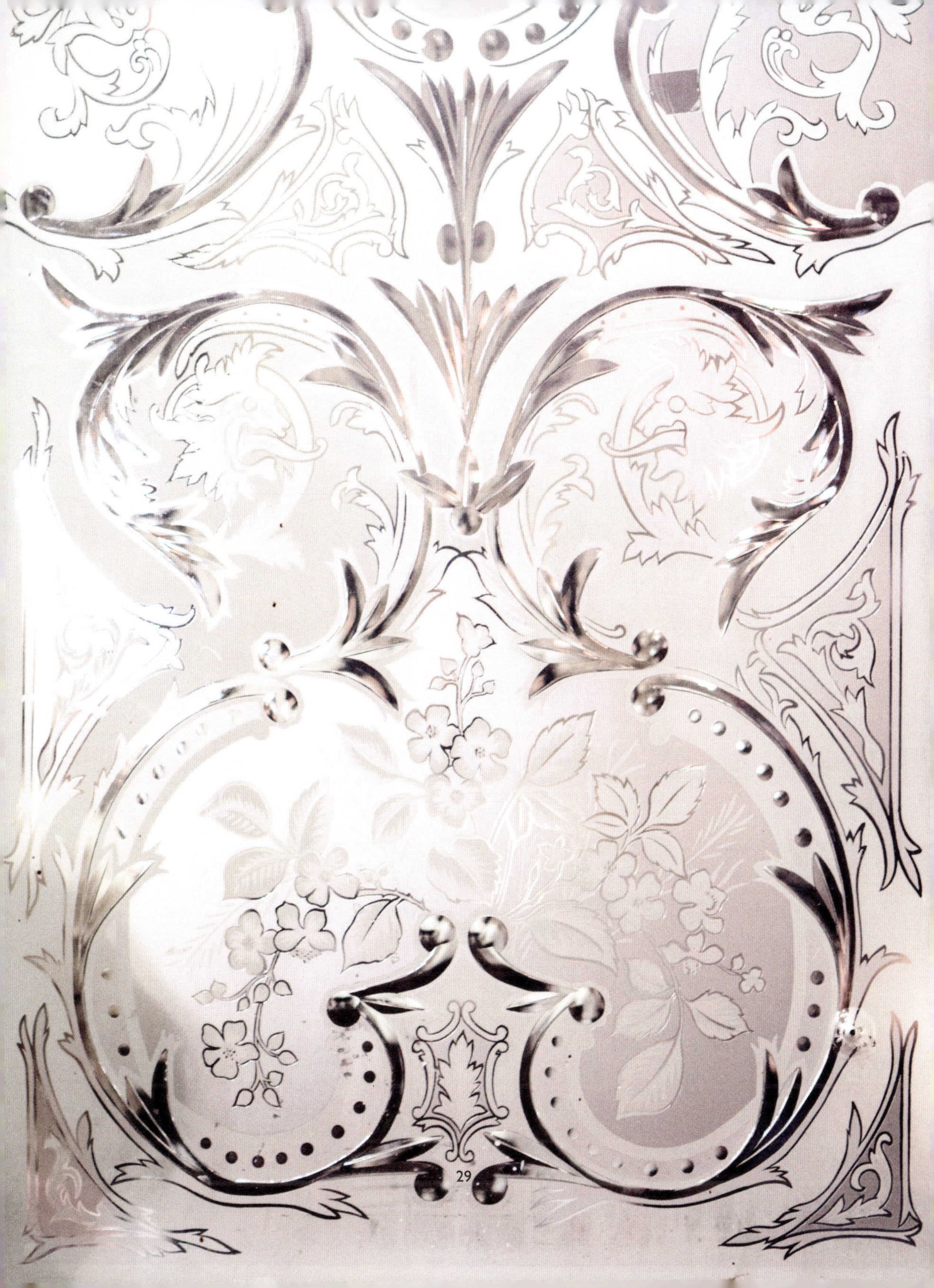

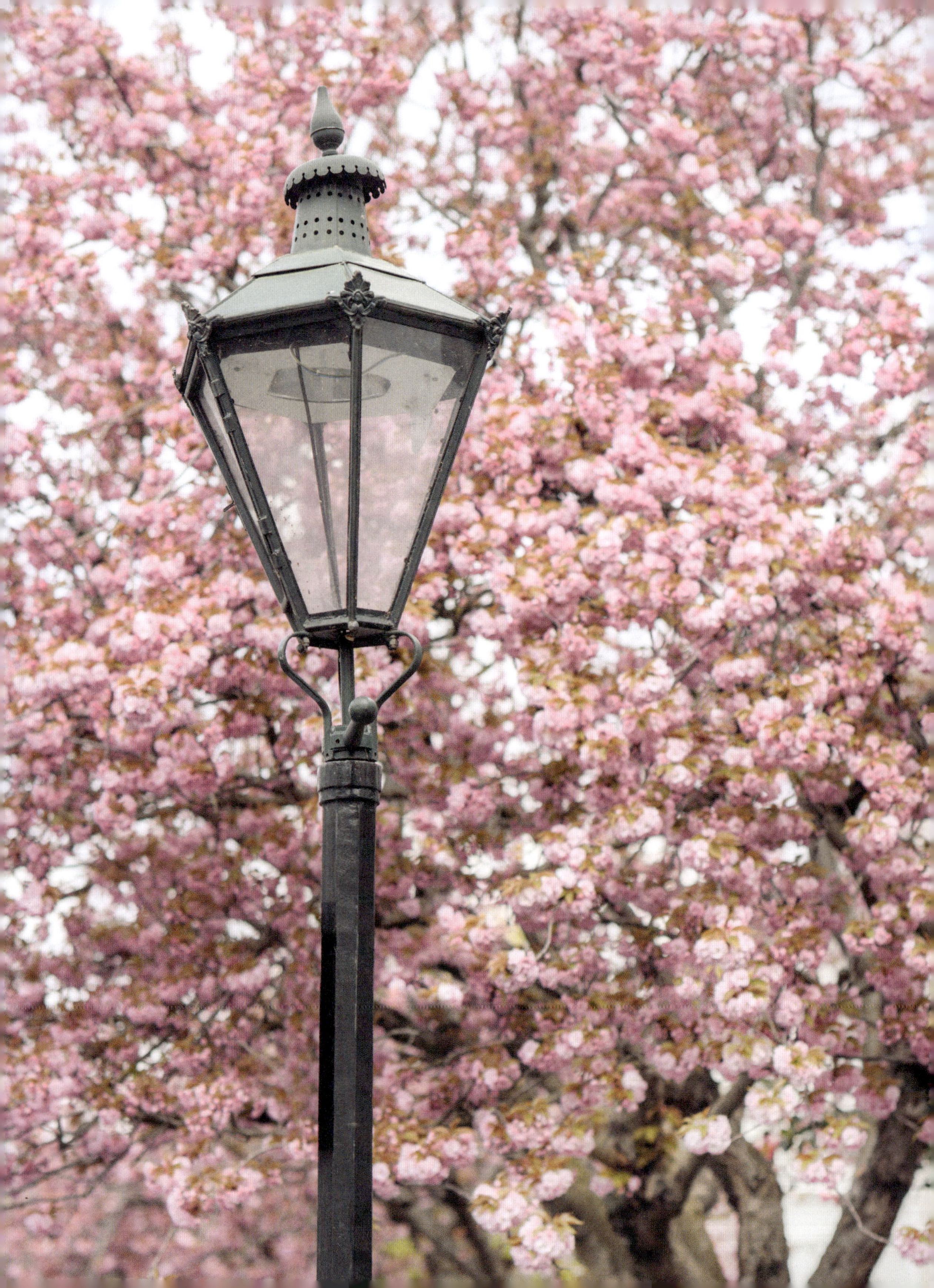

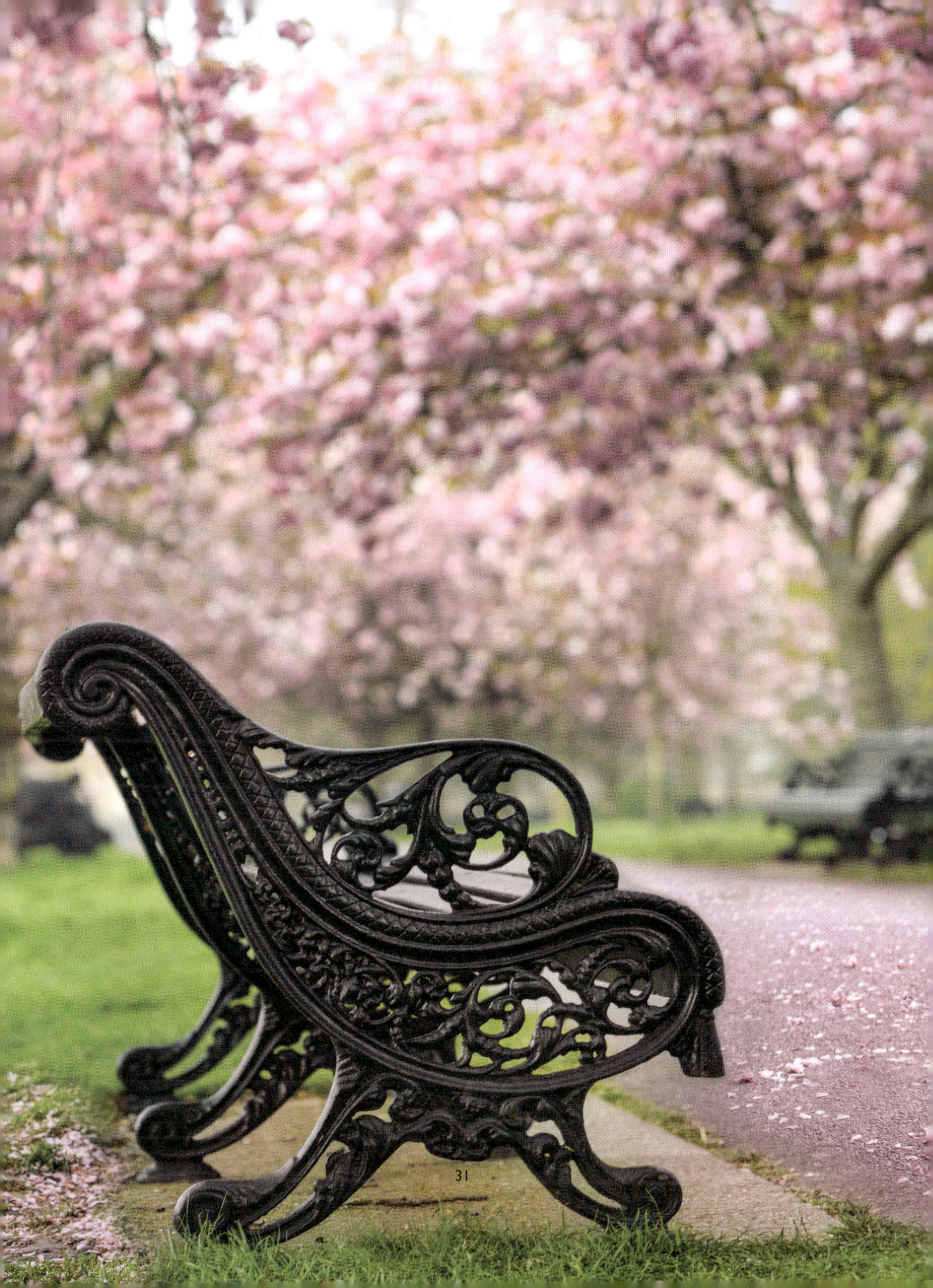

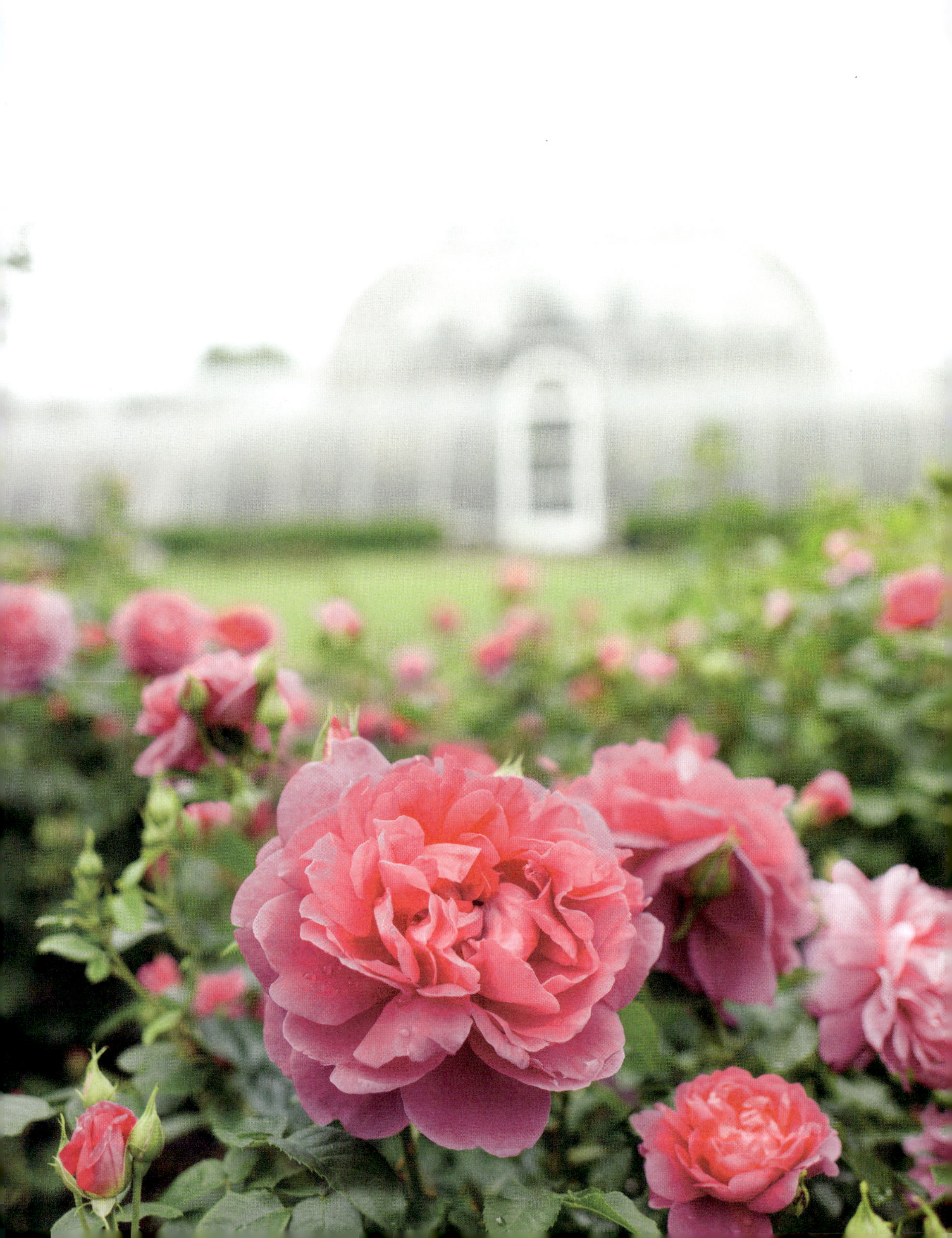

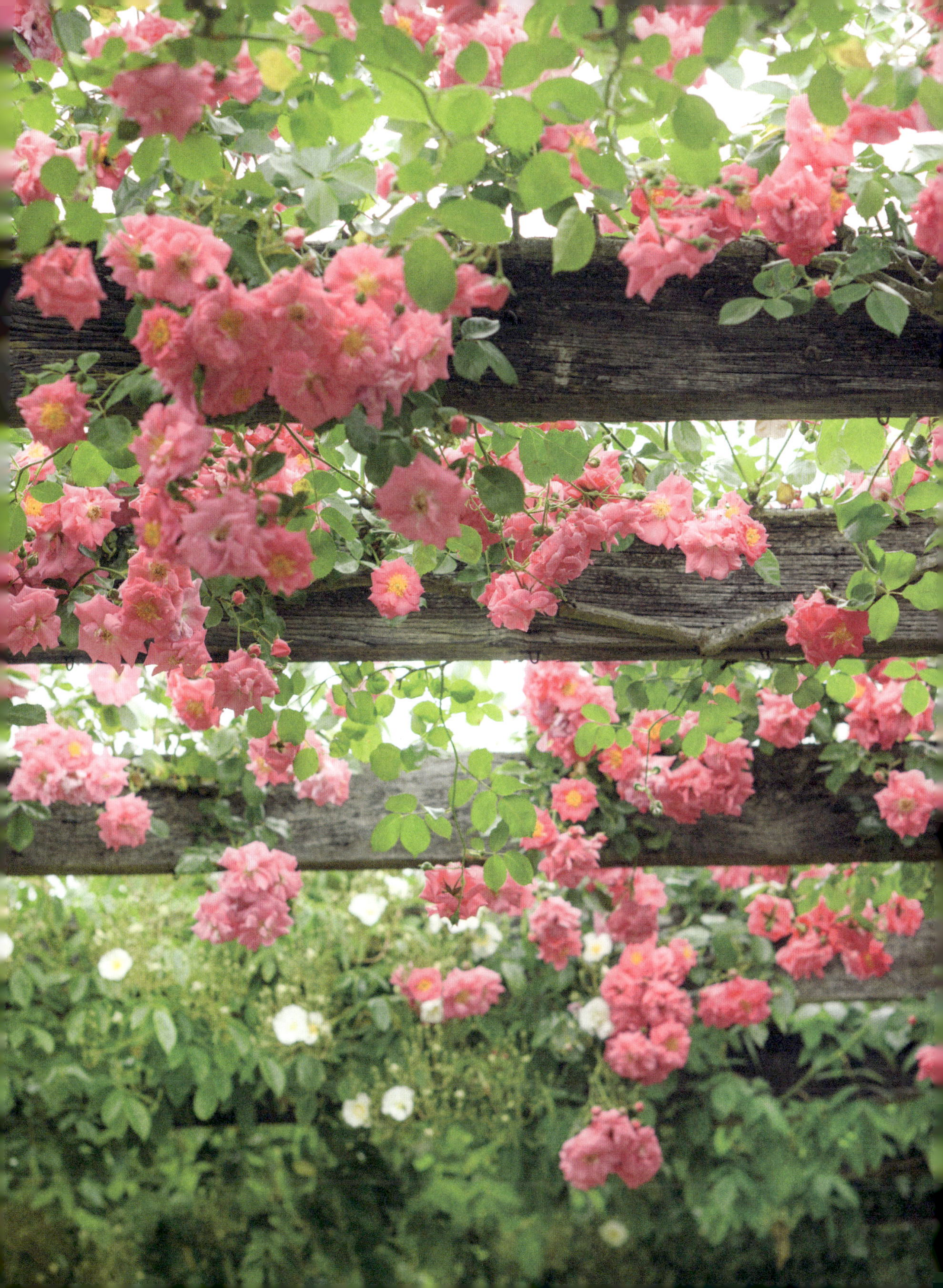

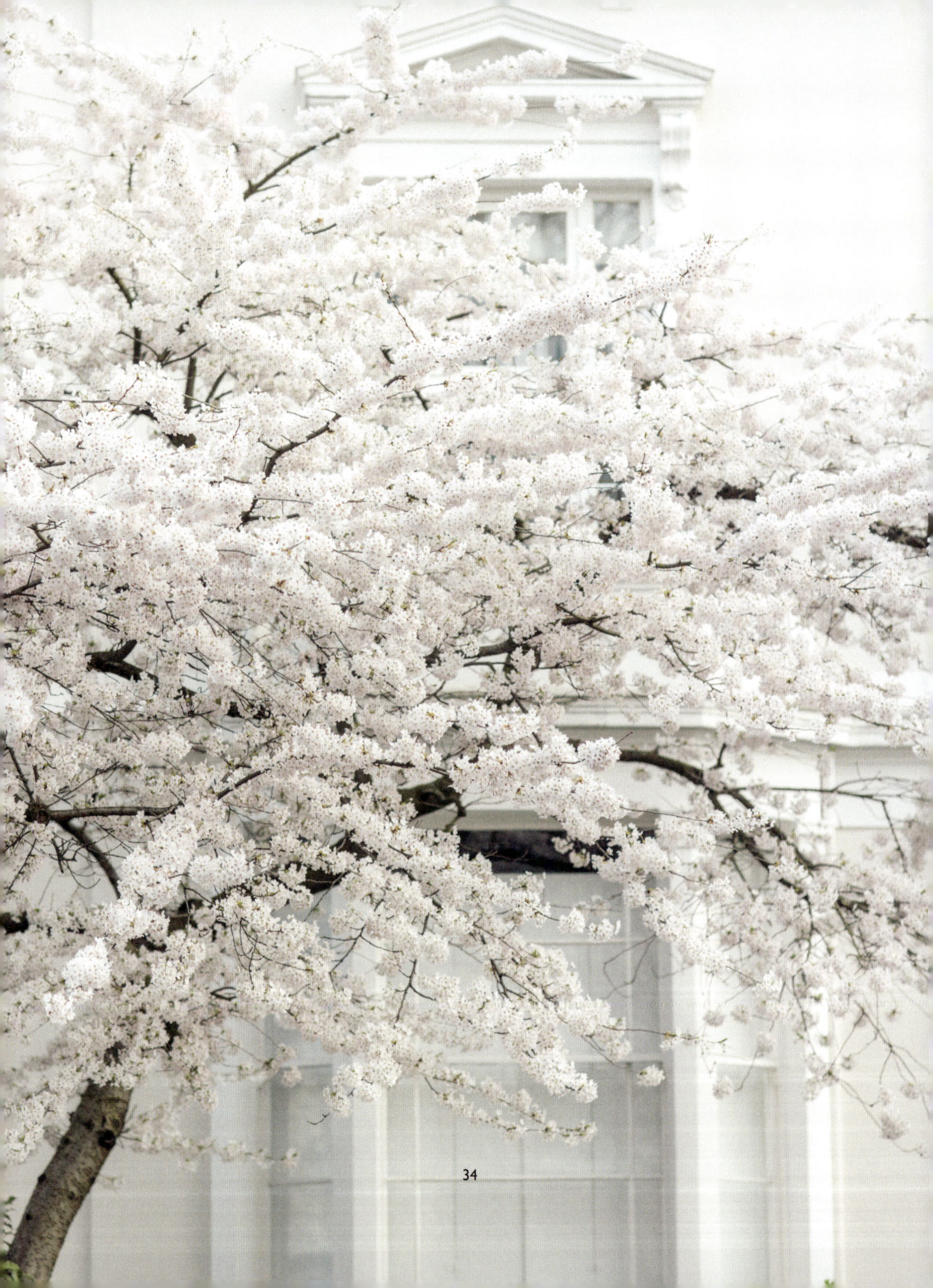

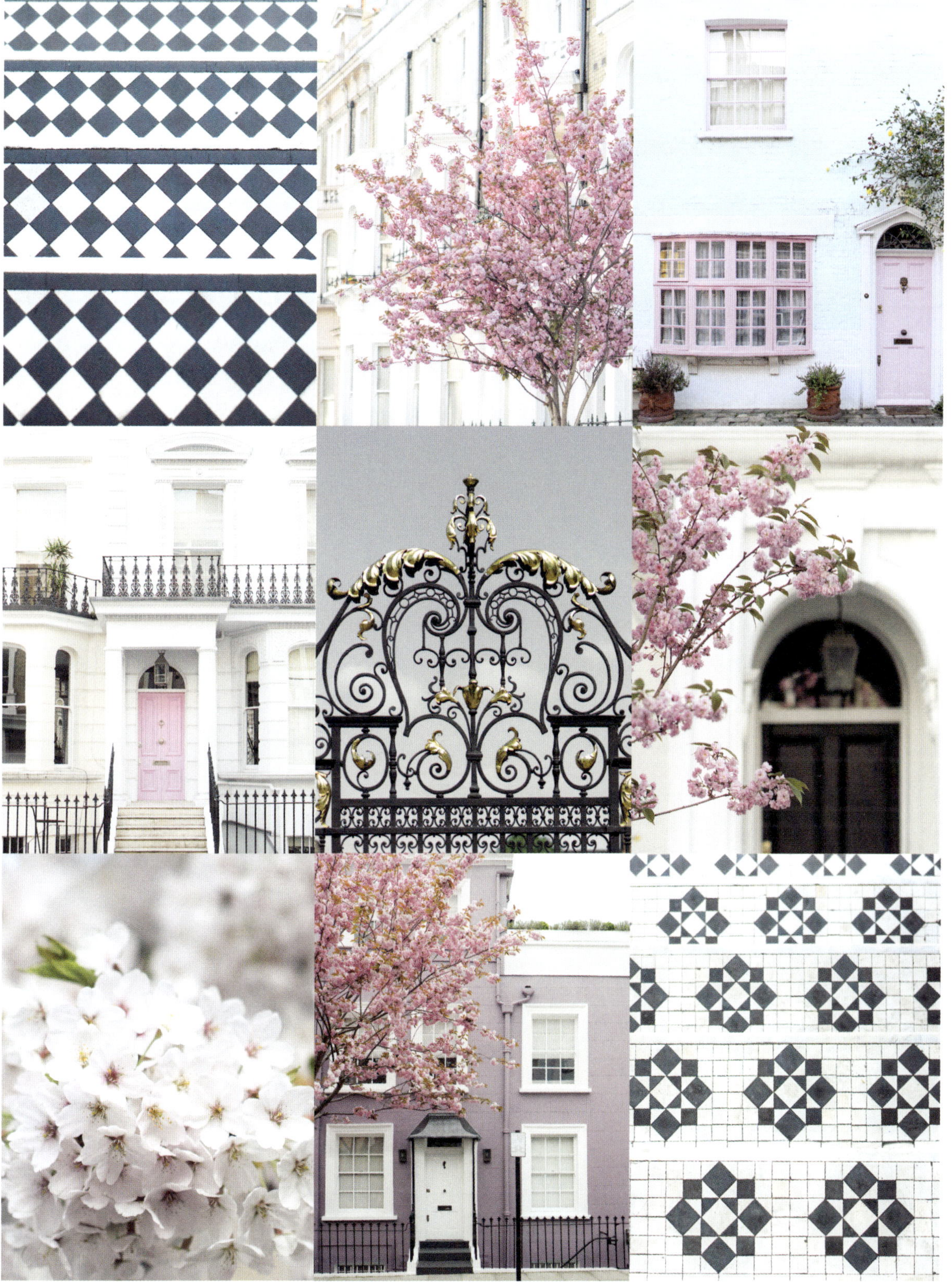

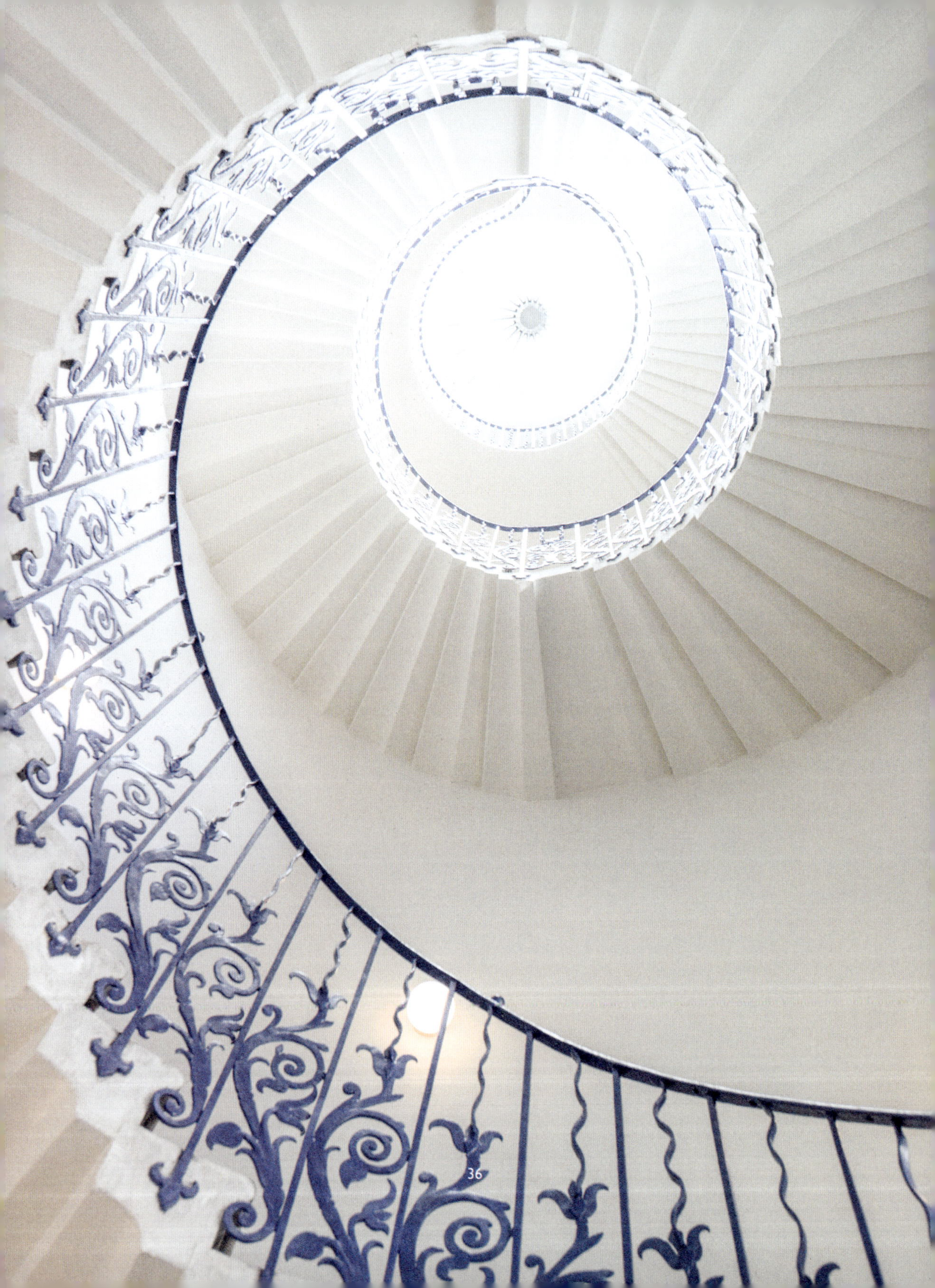

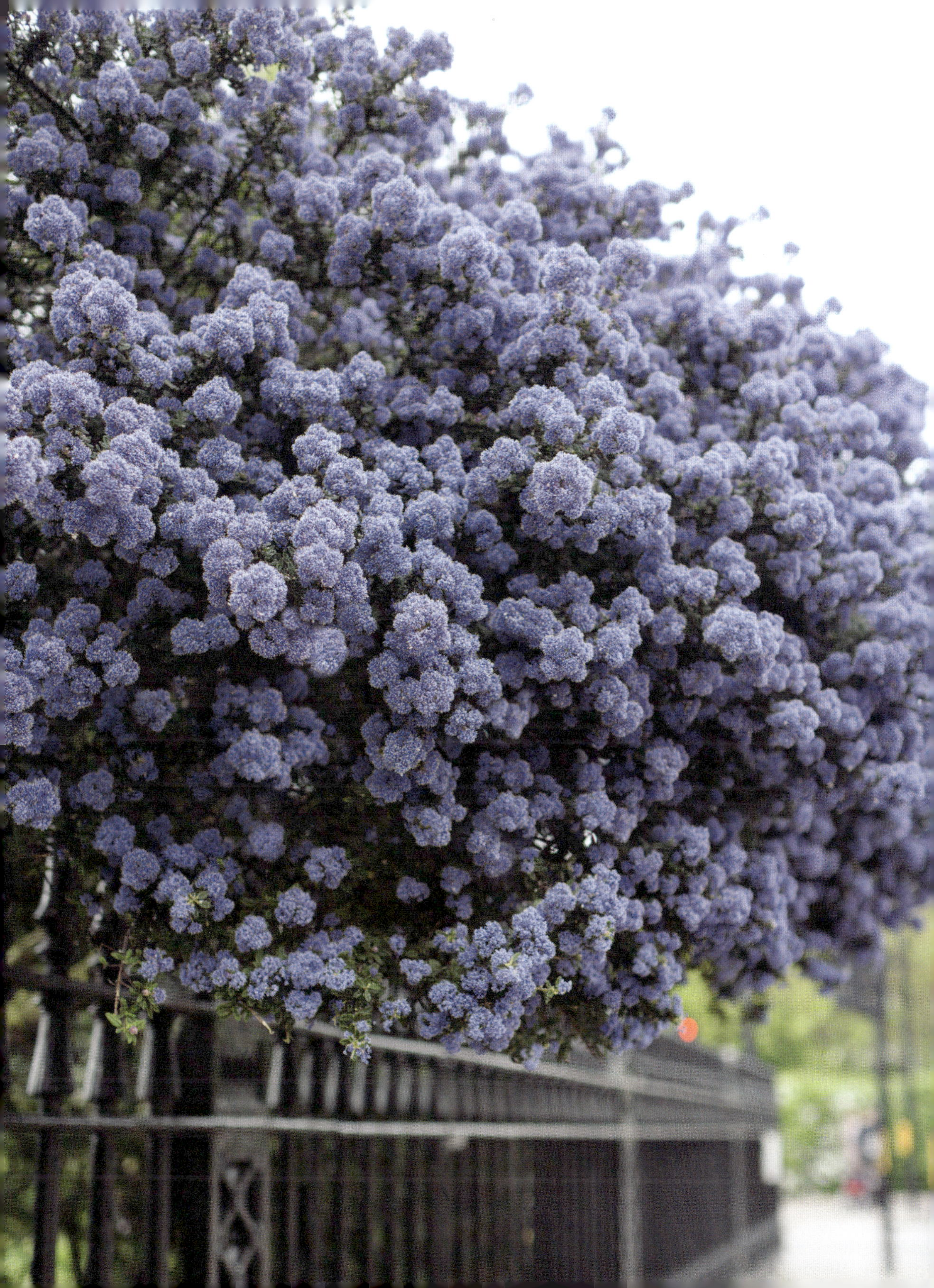

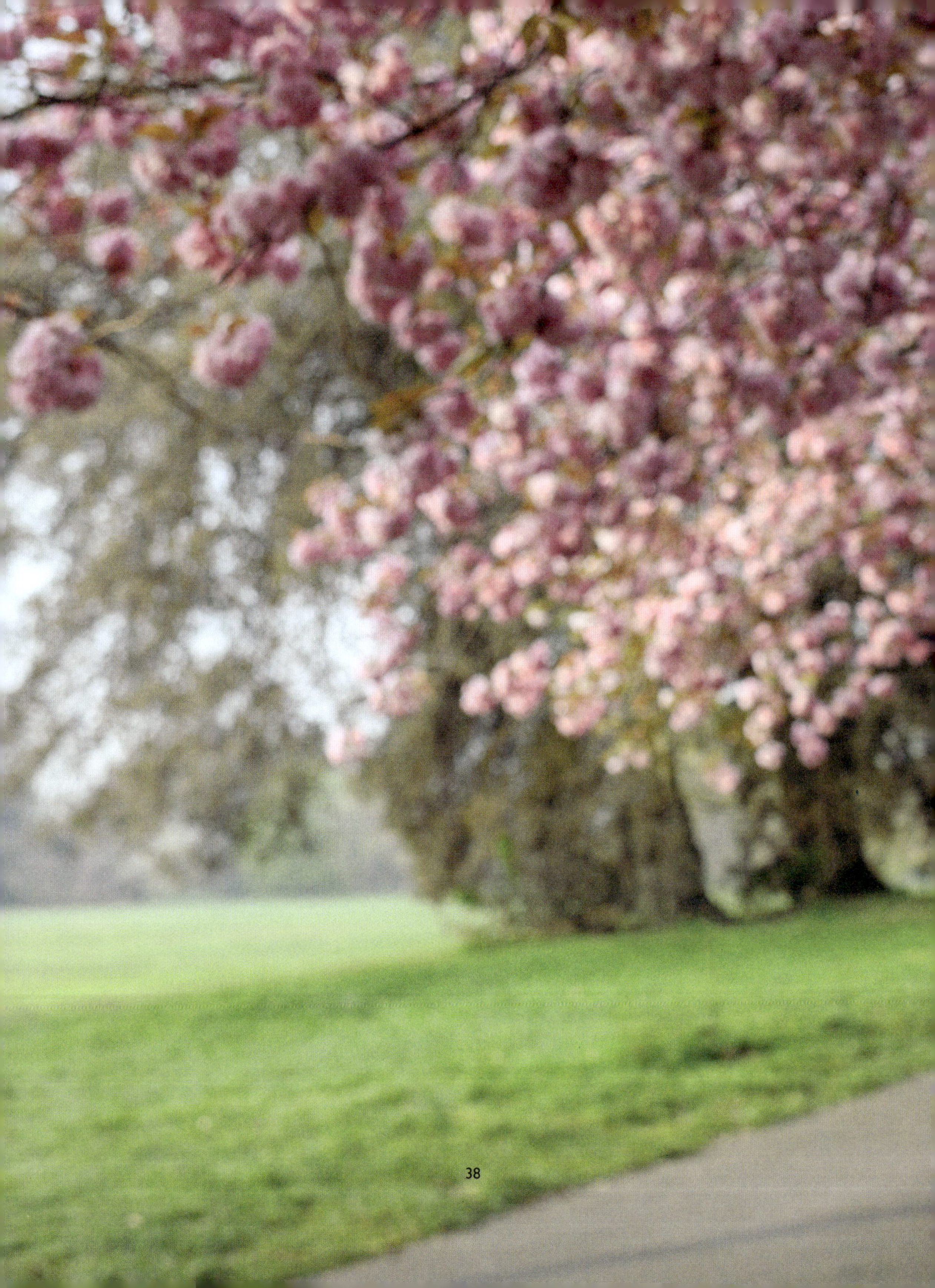

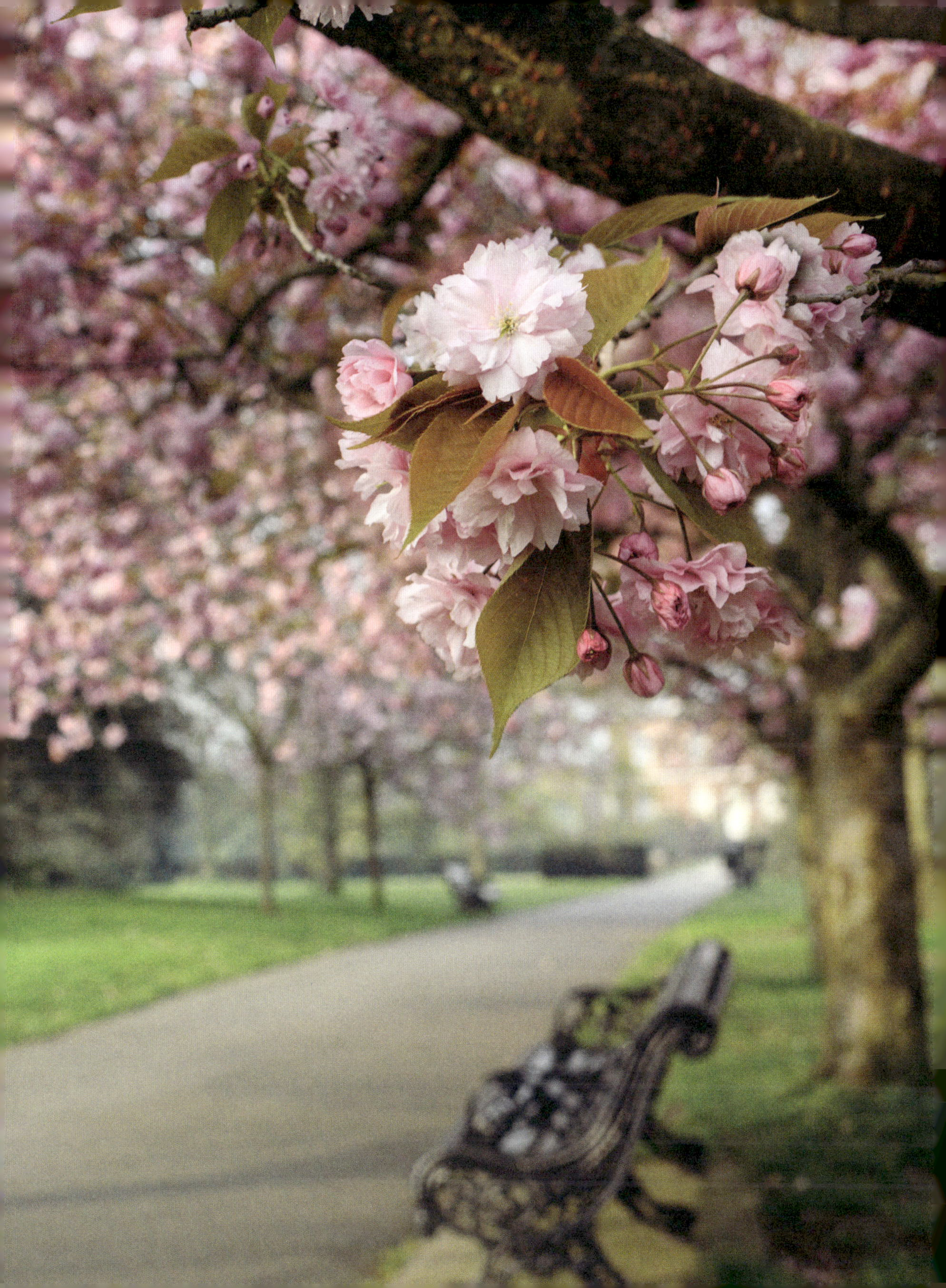

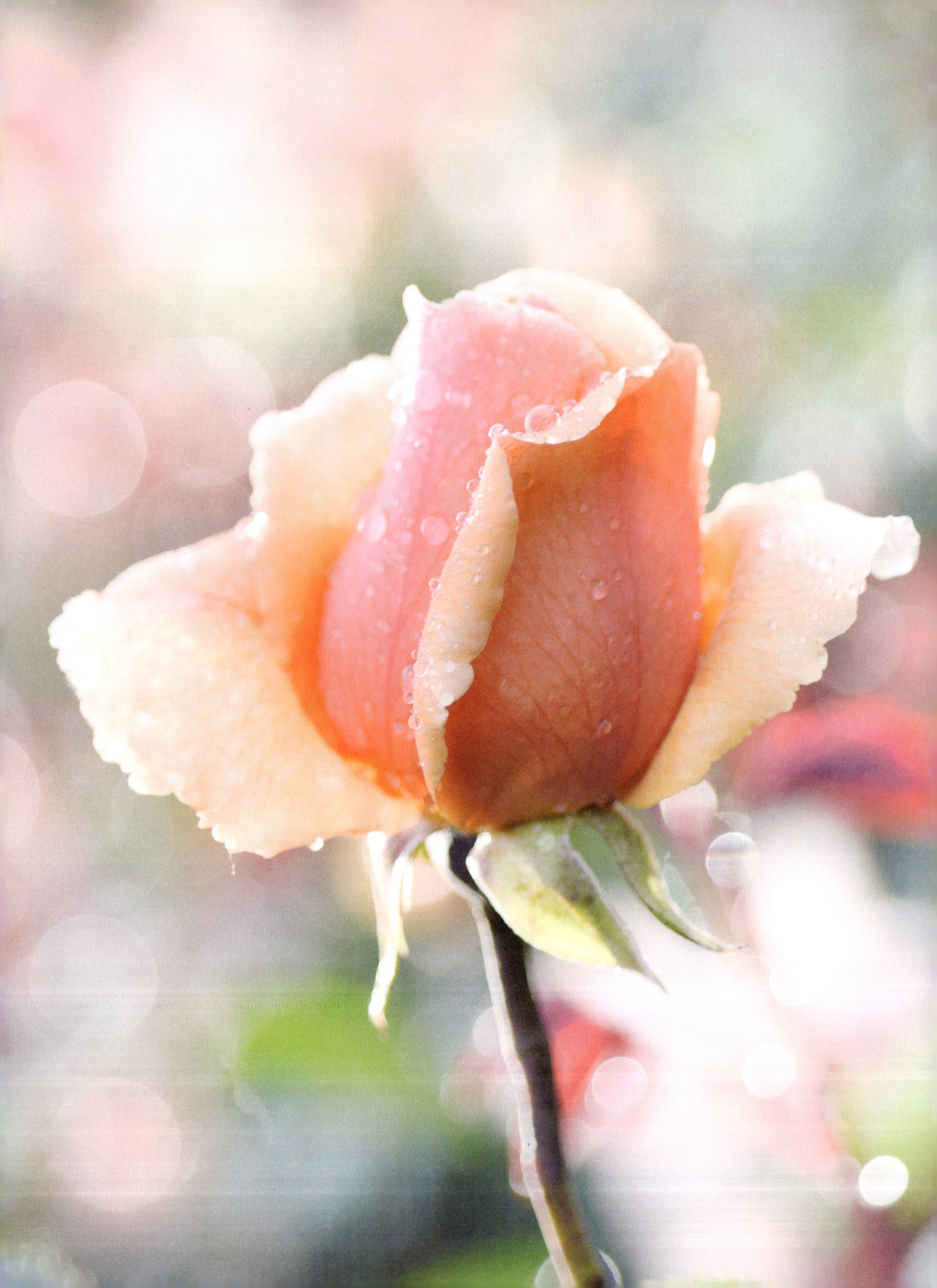

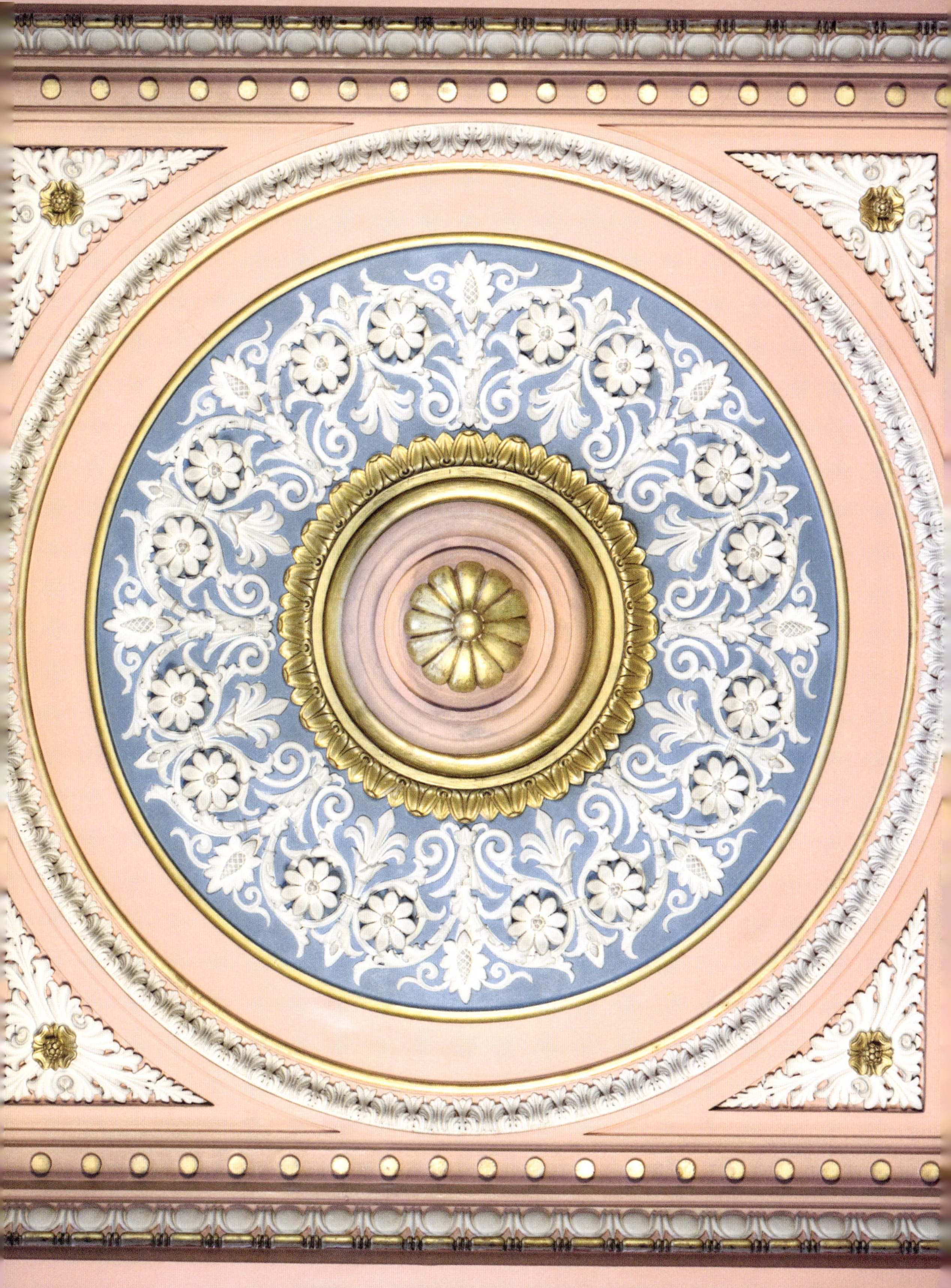

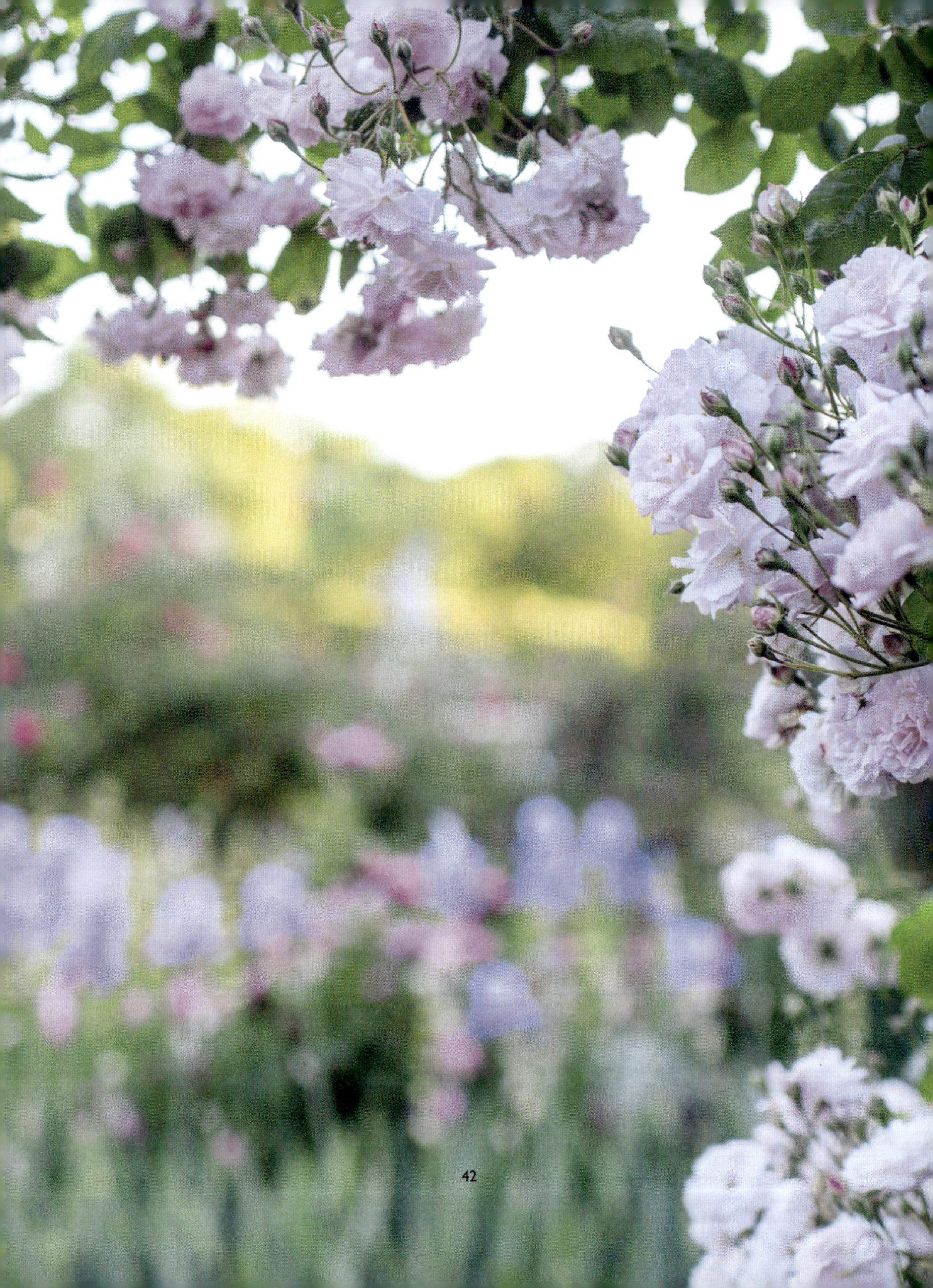

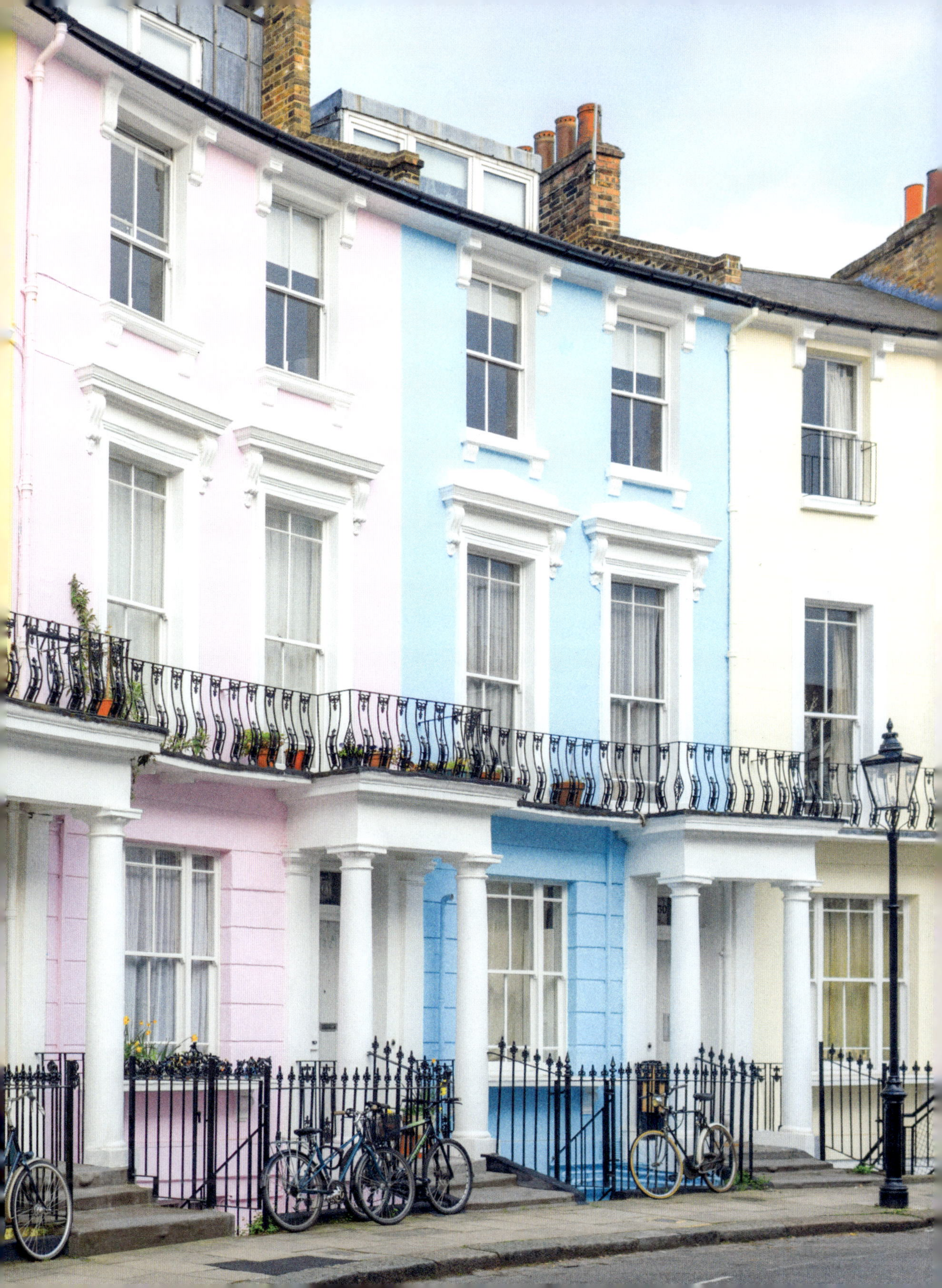

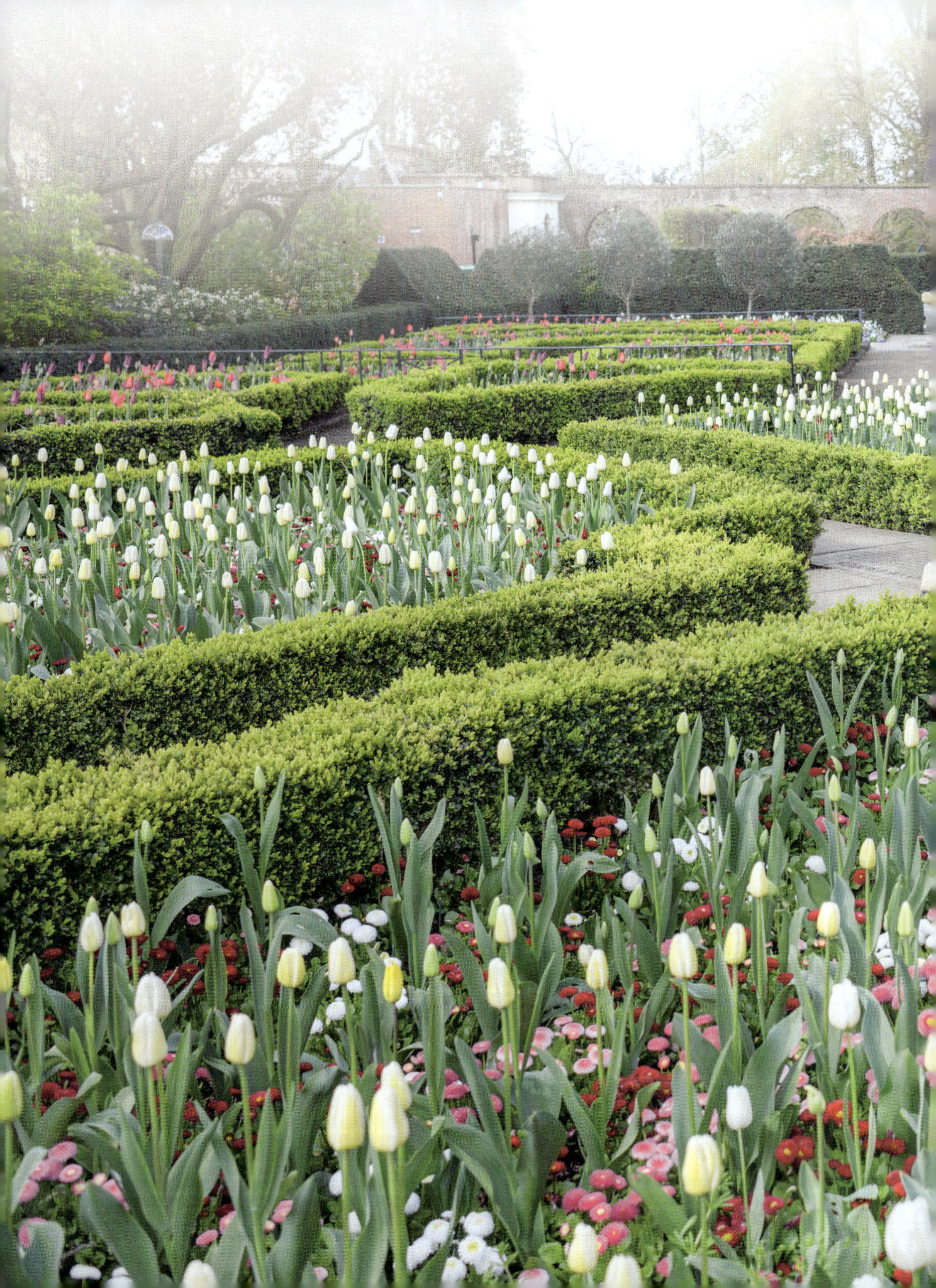

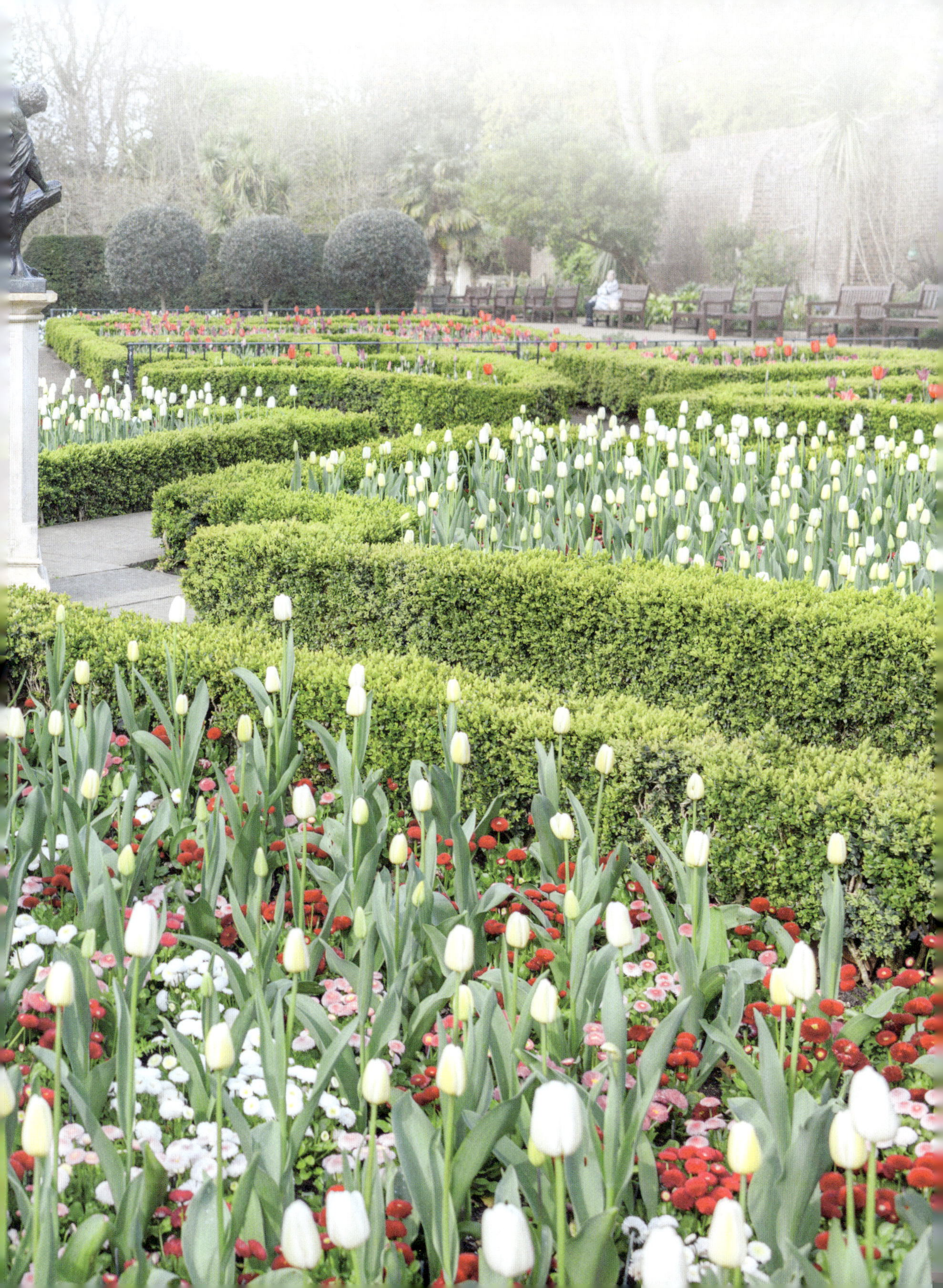

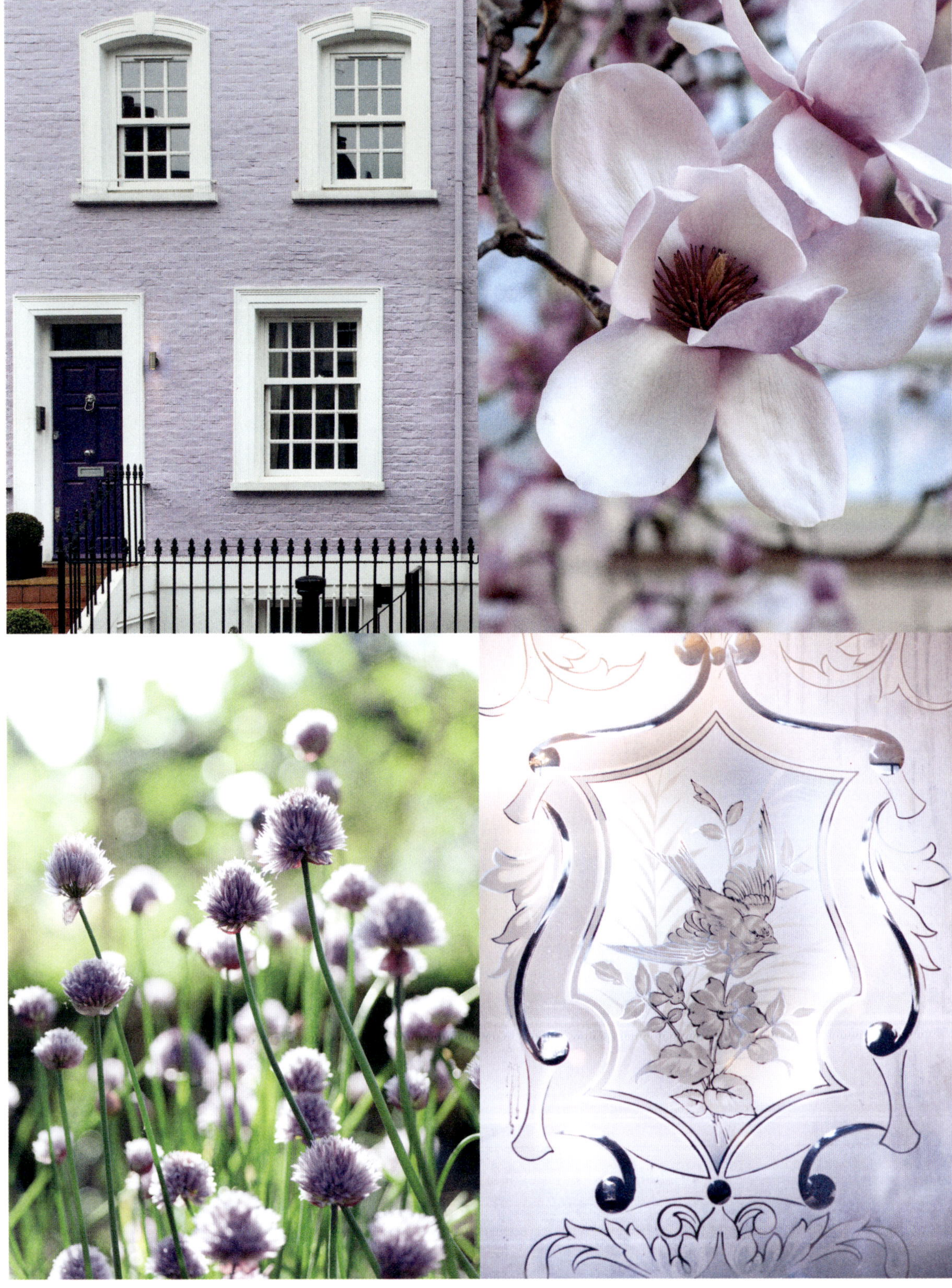

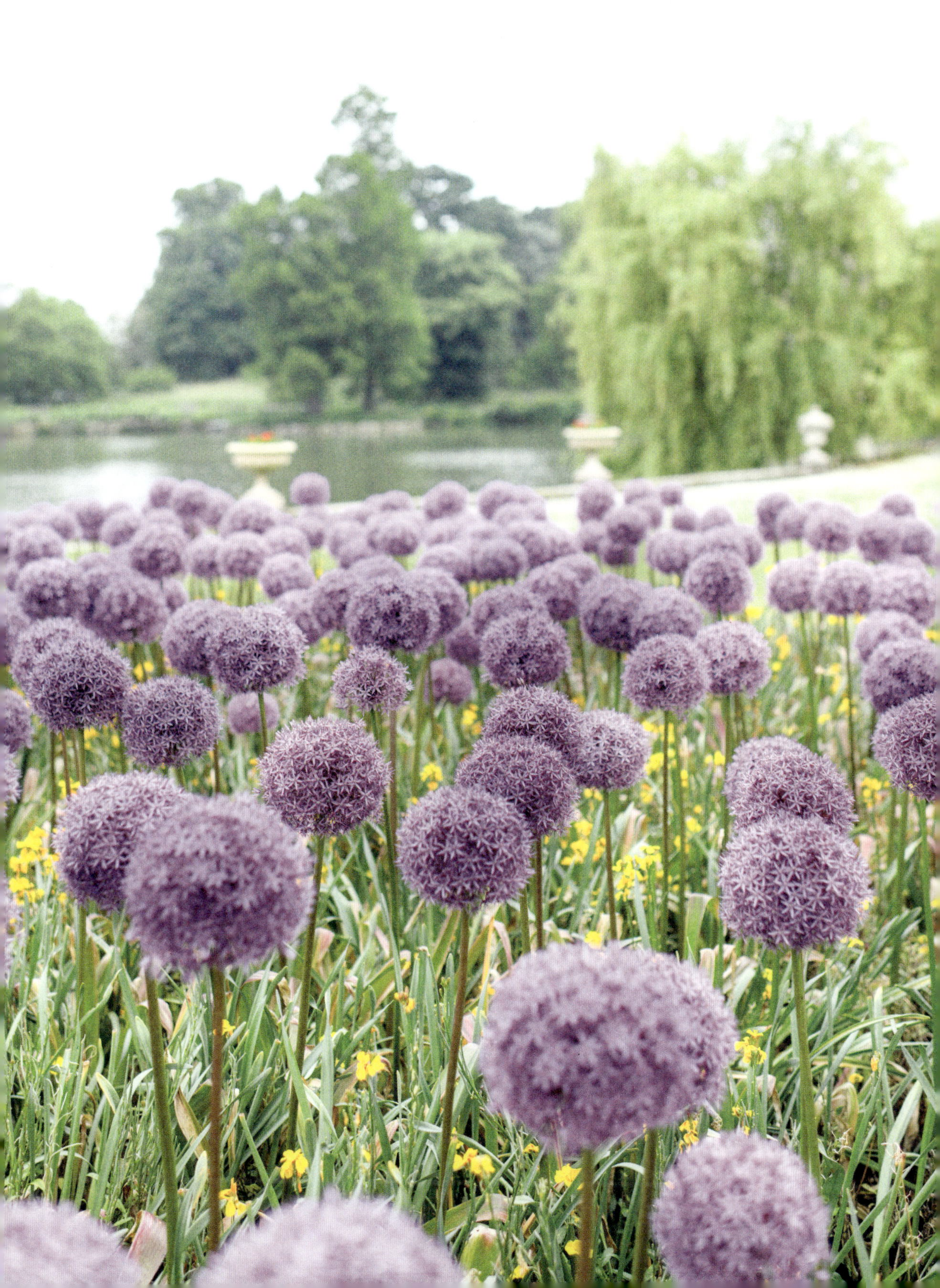

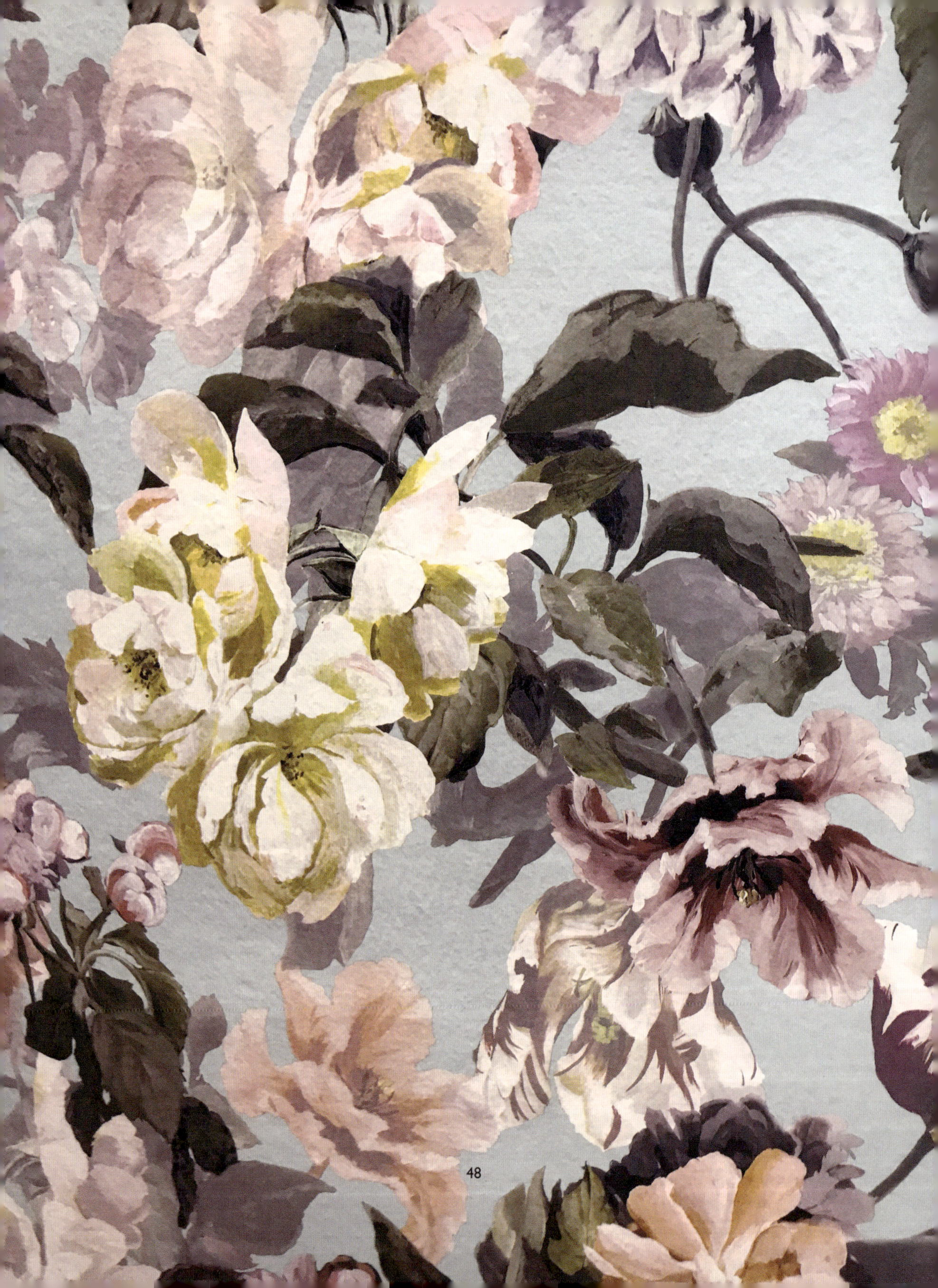

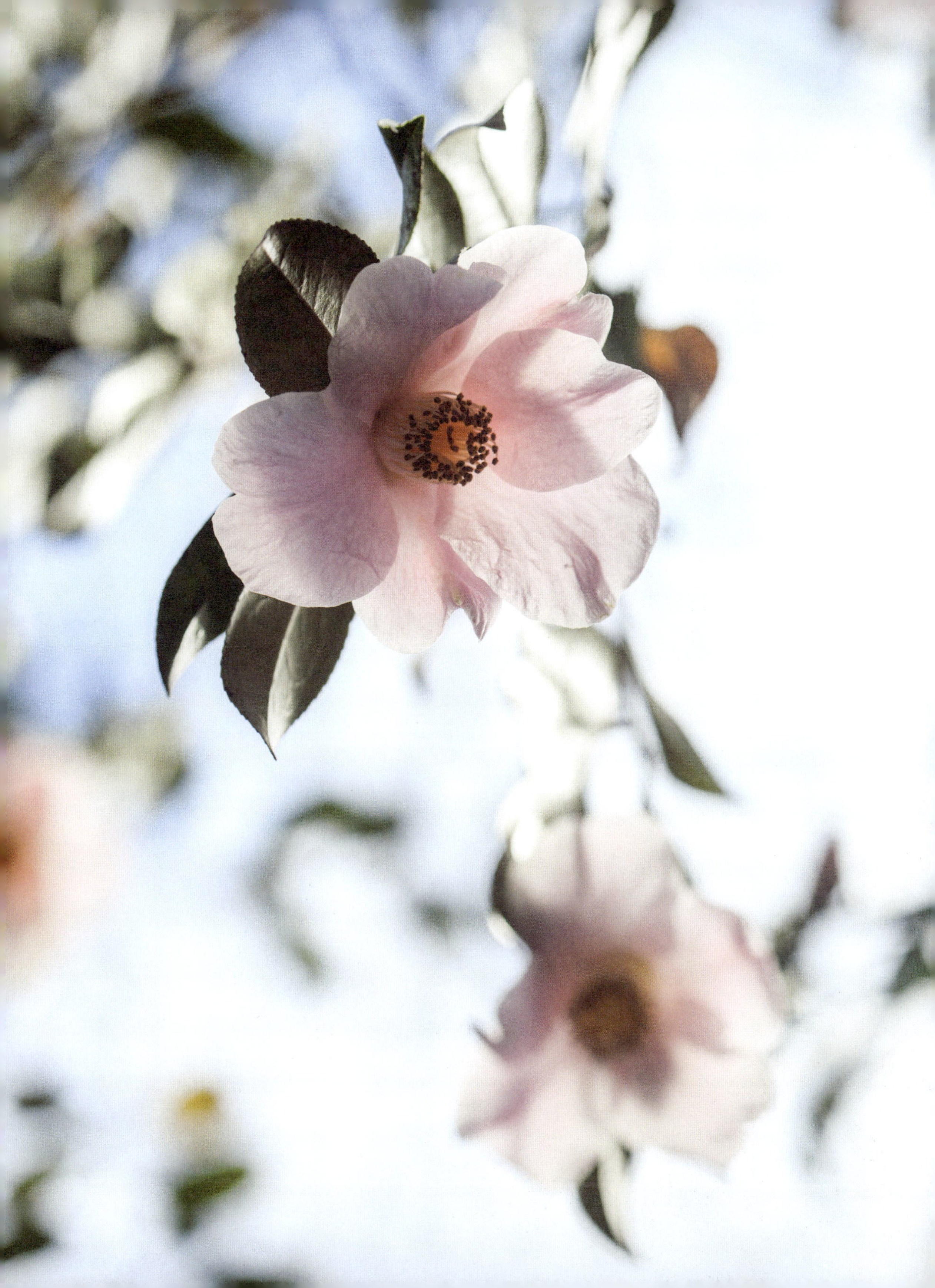

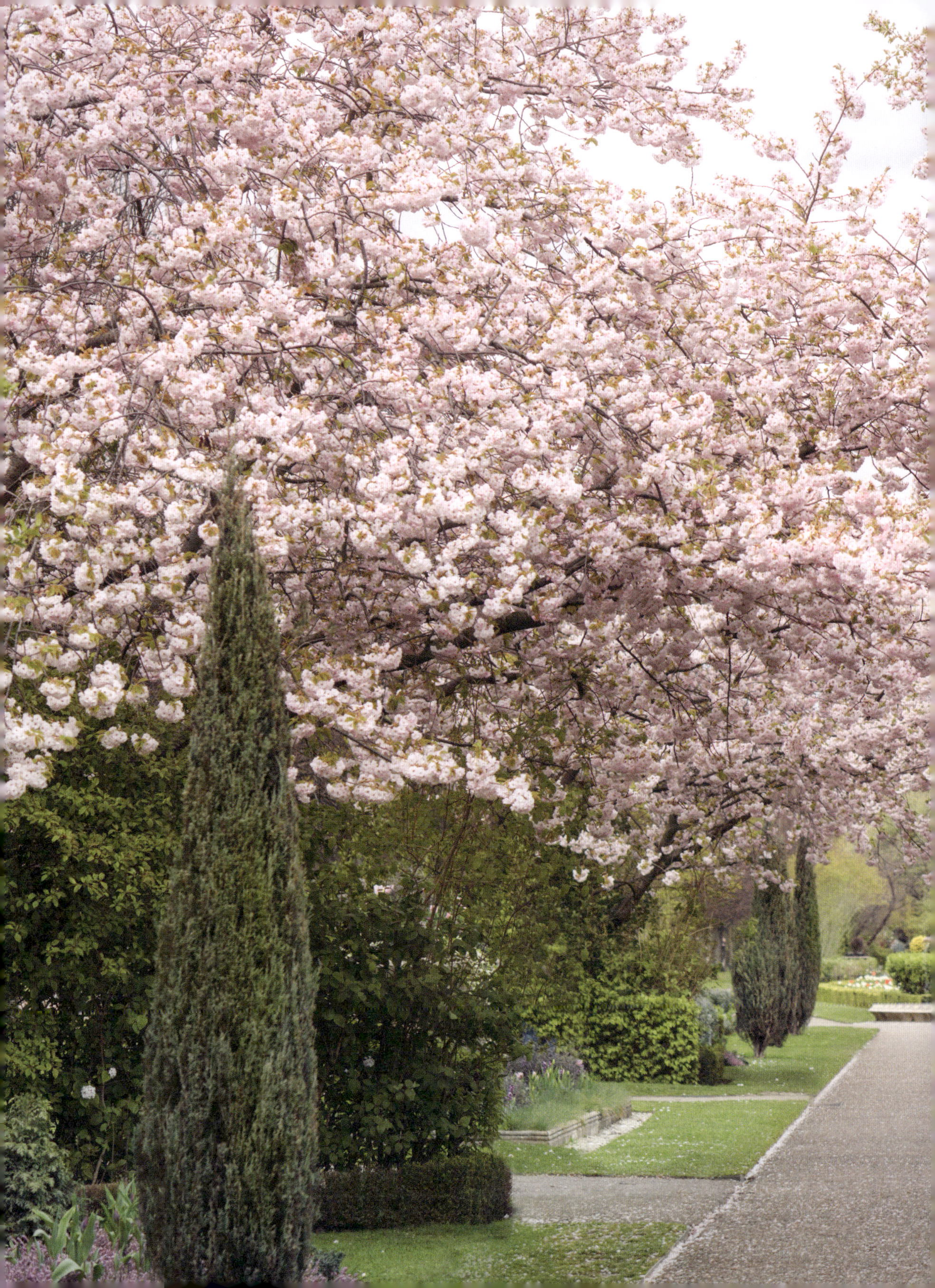

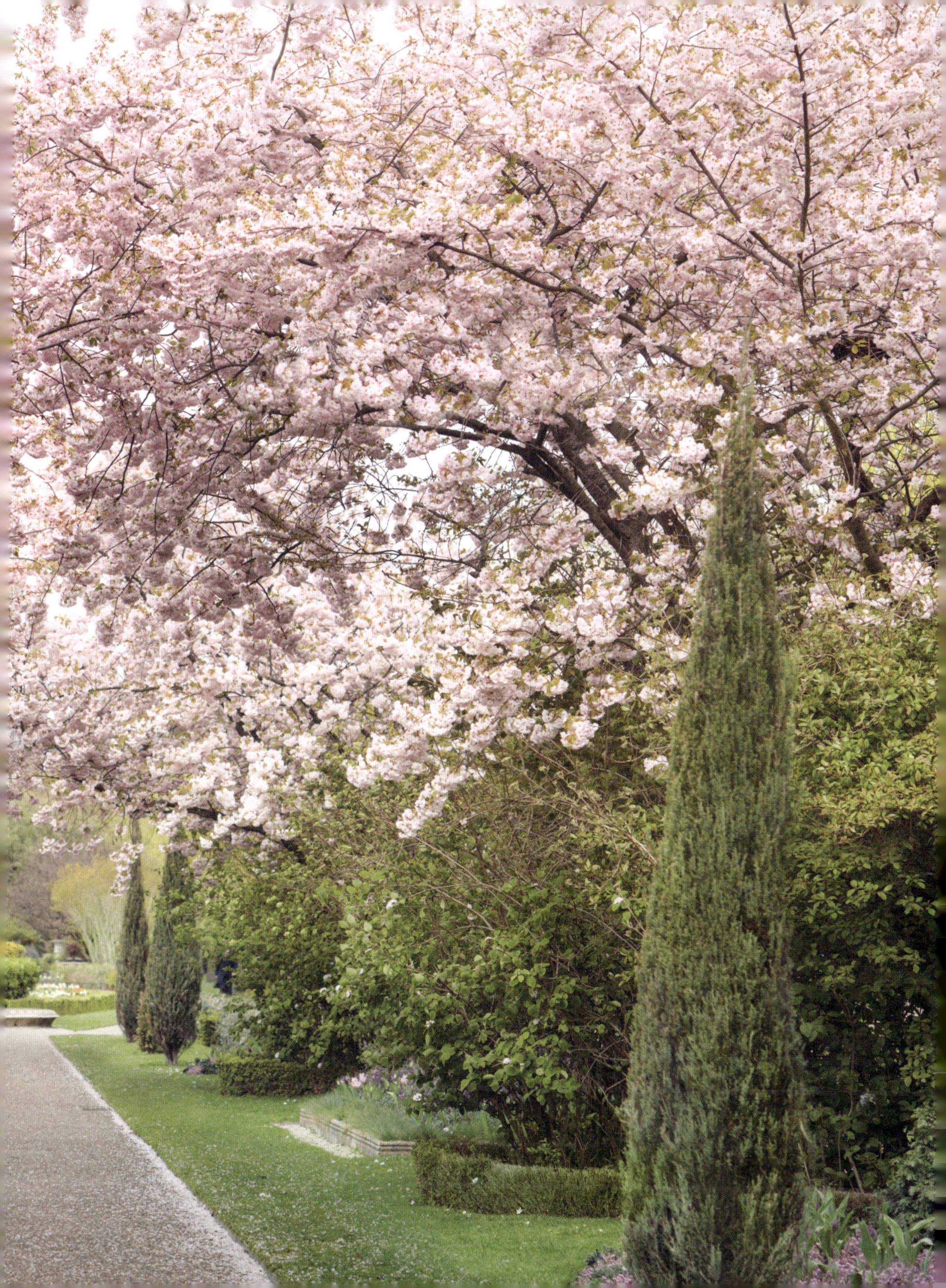

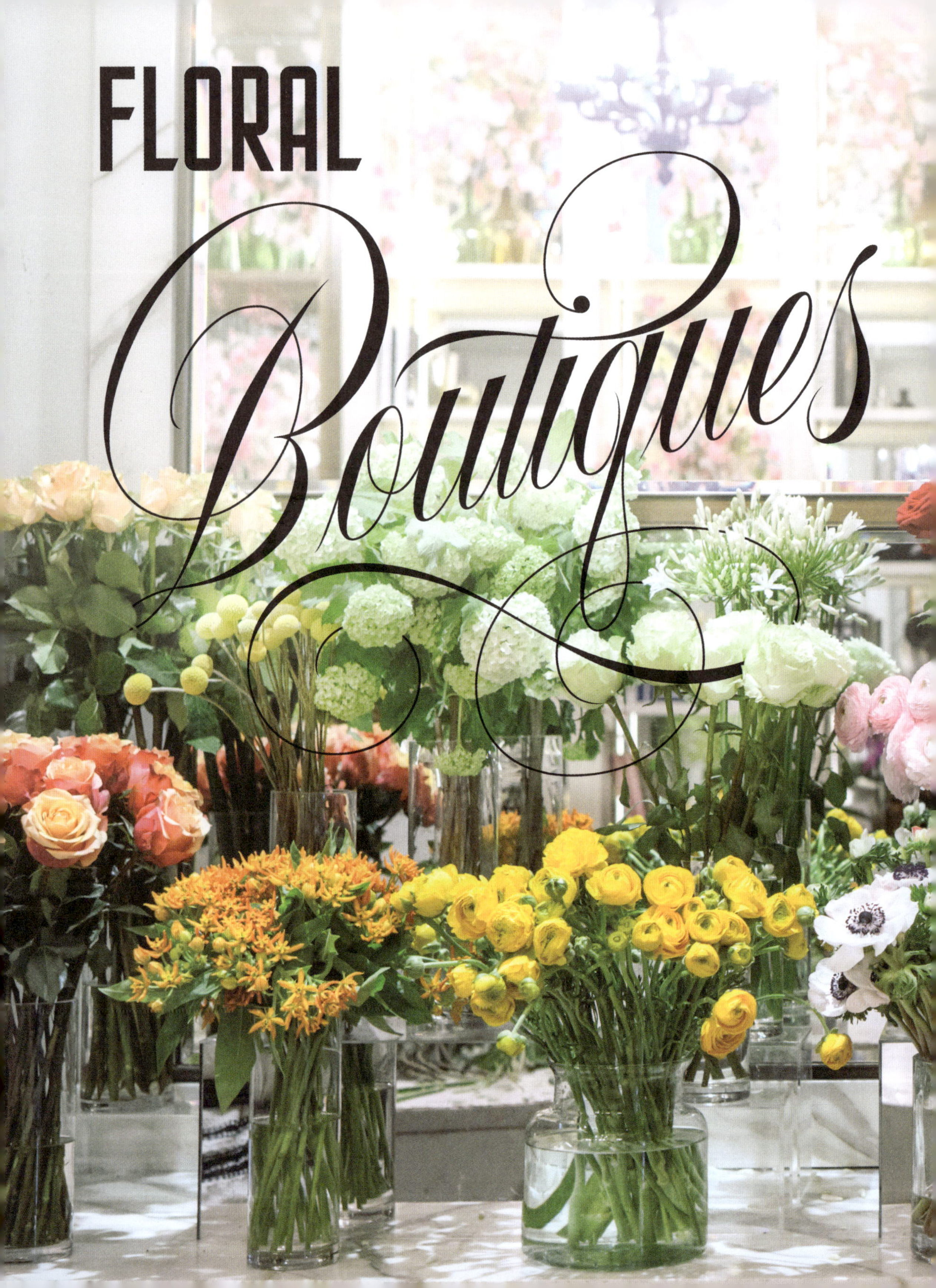

FLORAL
Boutiques

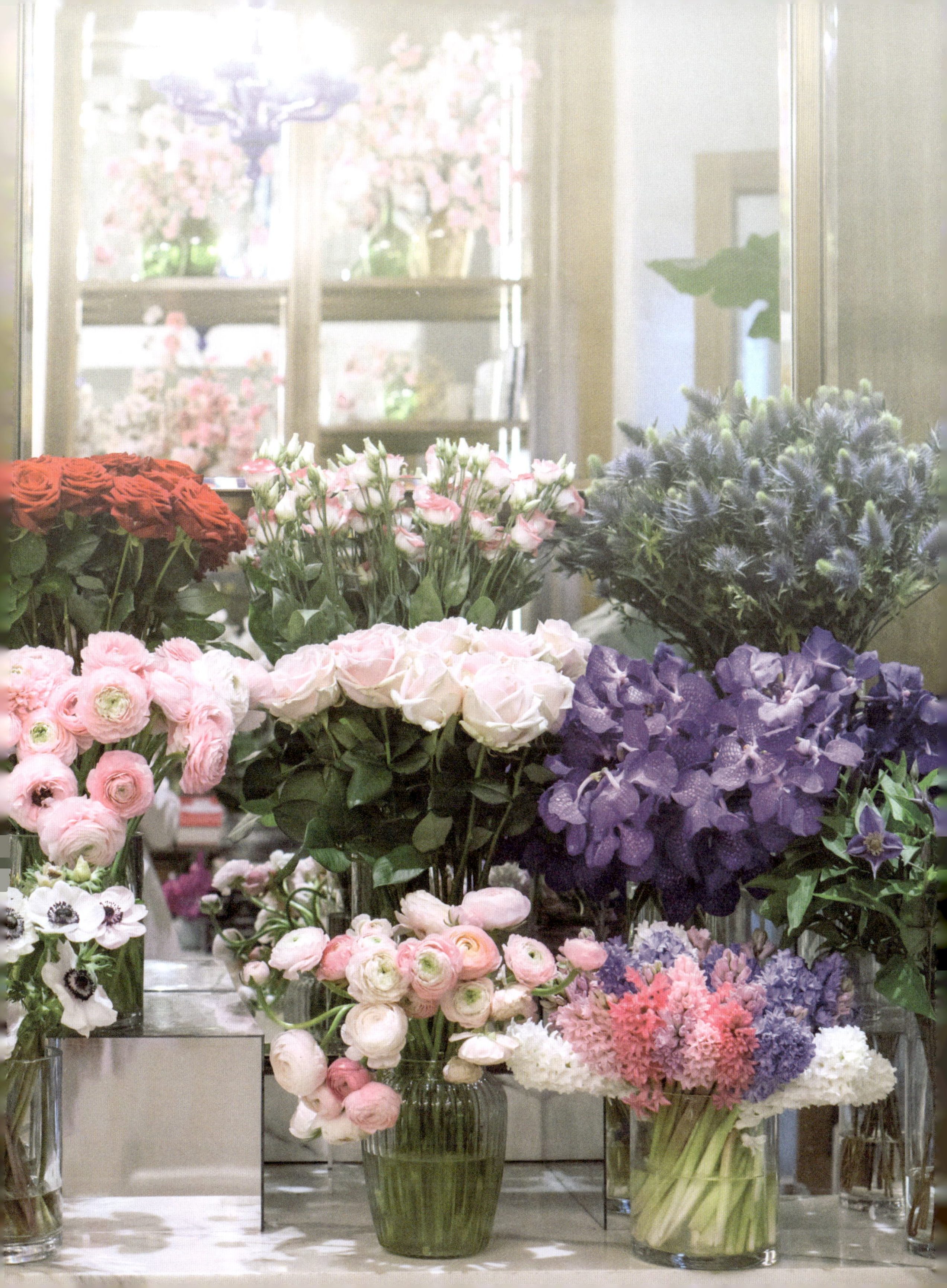

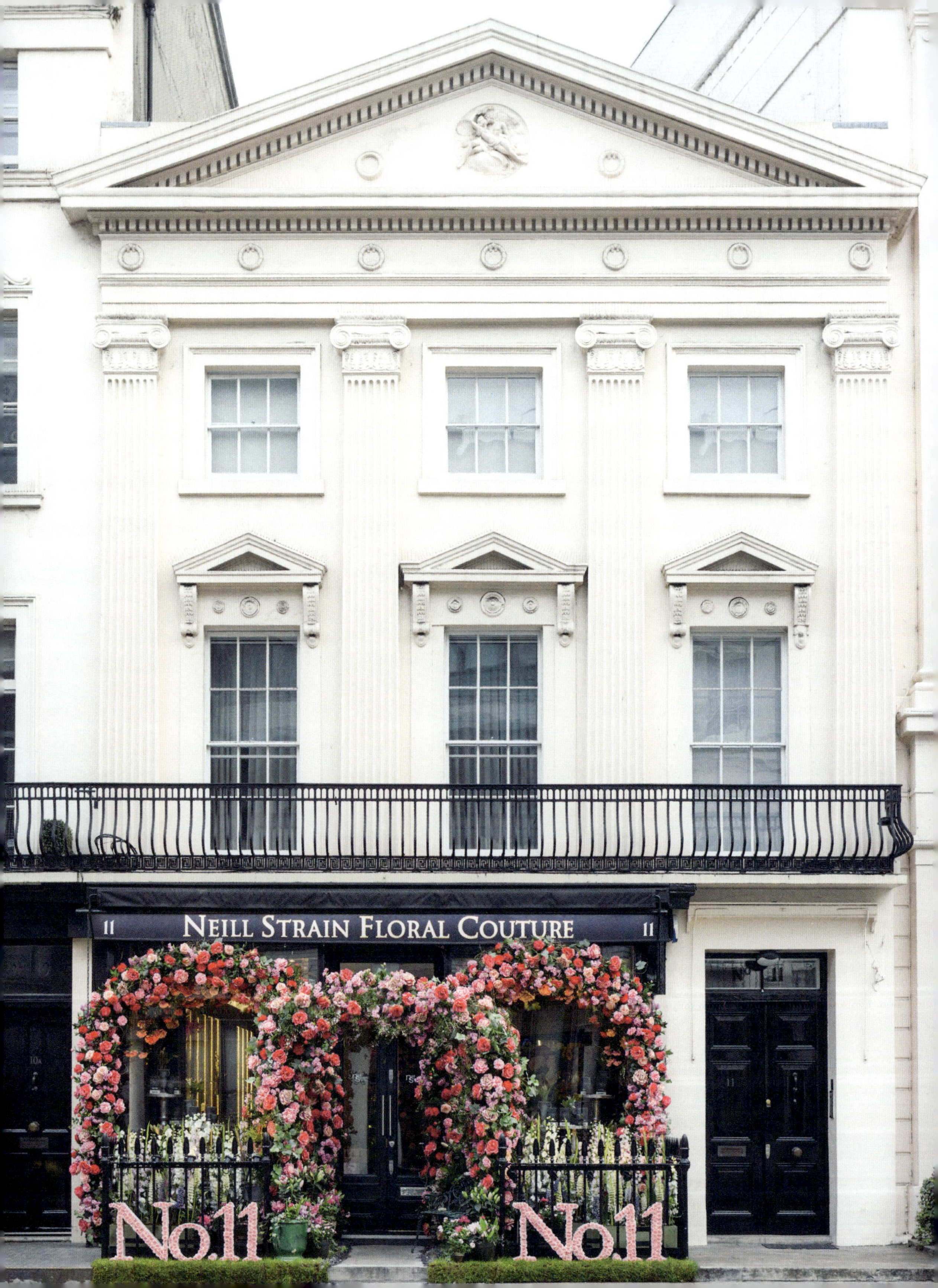

11
NEILL STRAIN FLORAL COUTURE
11
No.11
No.11

If a poem can be written in flowers, then the floral storytellers of London's boutiques and shops daily create visual verses, composing flowering sonnets of color and texture. With custom arrangements, bouquets, and installations, they deliver lyrical works of botanical beauty to convey emotions and messages that words alone cannot.

These enthralling ambassadors originate from an array of beautiful emporiums. Of all the cities in the world, London can rightfully claim many of the most charming and photogenic floral boutiques and shops in existence. Architecturally detailed storefronts in deep green, fashionable black awnings, leaded glass windows, and flower-garlanded exteriors grace their locations.

Inside, sparkling chandeliers, antique mirrors, glass cylinder jars, or possibly botanical charts set a romantic, almost imaginary, scene. Splendid arrangements of David Austin garden roses and Italian ranunculus may be placed in unusual containers such as hatboxes or vintage leather traveling trunks. Voluptuous all-white peonies and nostalgic sweet peas conveying purity might spill over urns, and enormous lilies perfume the air.

The dramatic outdoor decor at Neill Strain Floral Couture in Belgravia is a prelude to the bountiful displays of exotic orchids, birds-of-paradise, and long-stemmed roses in the interior. Not far away is Moyses Stevens, where floral artistry has been practiced since 1876. Their work, including hand-tied bouquets of nearly overwhelming beauty, has earned them a Royal Warrant from the Prince of Wales.

The well-loved zinc "ponds" on the pavement outside Wild Things Flowers in Mayfair are filled with ever-changing, floating displays of roses, dahlias, and hydrangeas, creating an irresistible photo op for all who pass.

Combine a visit to the Royal Botanical Gardens at Kew with a stop at the unique Zita Elze, a chic shop a few blocks from the garden. Established by the award-winning floral artist, designer, and teacher Zita Elze, the company also offers courses in flower design.

In nearby Richmond, you'll find Bramble & Moss in a vintage, forest-green-tiled building with curved windows, decorated with stained glass and intricate architectural details. Specializing in classic British flowers in season, it often features arrangements with unusual ingredients, such as miniature orchids, designed with a personal touch.

With distinctive gold lettering on its black shop front, John & Jessie in Notting Hill sits just off busy Kensington Church Street. Potted geraniums and miniature citrus trees, cyclamen, and annuals can be purchased, as well as custom florals for any occasion.

Scarlet & Violet's signature style is that just-gathered-from-the-garden look, using country flowers often presented in colorful enamel pitchers. Established in 2006 in Kensal Green, the shop's every design portrays individual personality, frequently featuring woodland plants including narcissus, hyacinth, and fritillaria combined with airy, feathery nigella.

At luxury department stores, such as Harrods, gilded in-house stands offer spires of brilliant-blue delphinium, striking protea, deep-purple hellebores, and crimson long-stemmed roses. Fortnum & Mason, founded in 1707, assists patrons in celebrating special occasions with fabulous, ribbon-tied bouquets with its signature logo. Outside the main entrance to the Liberty department store, the Wild at Heart floral boutique is one of London's most well-known. A full spectrum of flowers in tall zinc buckets pops against the black-and-white timbered exterior of the iconic building. Small container plants are stacked on ladders, and jam jars filled with local flowers are wrapped with embroidered ribbon—little bundles of loveliness for a windowsill or desk.

In keeping with the city's literary heritage, the floral scribes of London employ petals and leaves instead of pen and paper to deliver heartfelt, poetic missives that transcend language. They elevate the ordinary conversation and add glamour to the special occasion. Even if words should fail, the sentiment will be unmistakable.

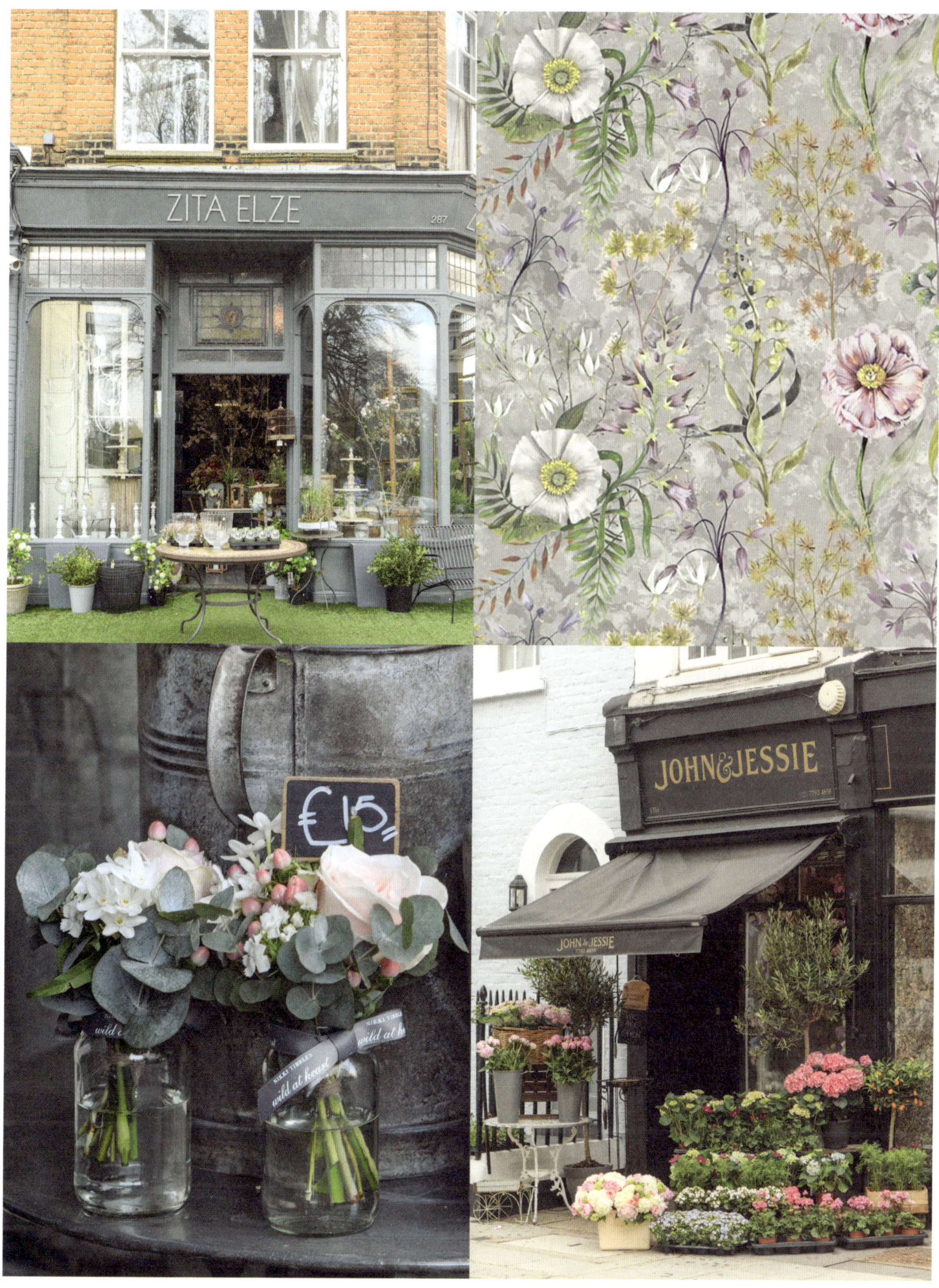

ZITA ELZE
287
€15
wild at heart
JOHN&JESSIE
JOHN & JESSIE

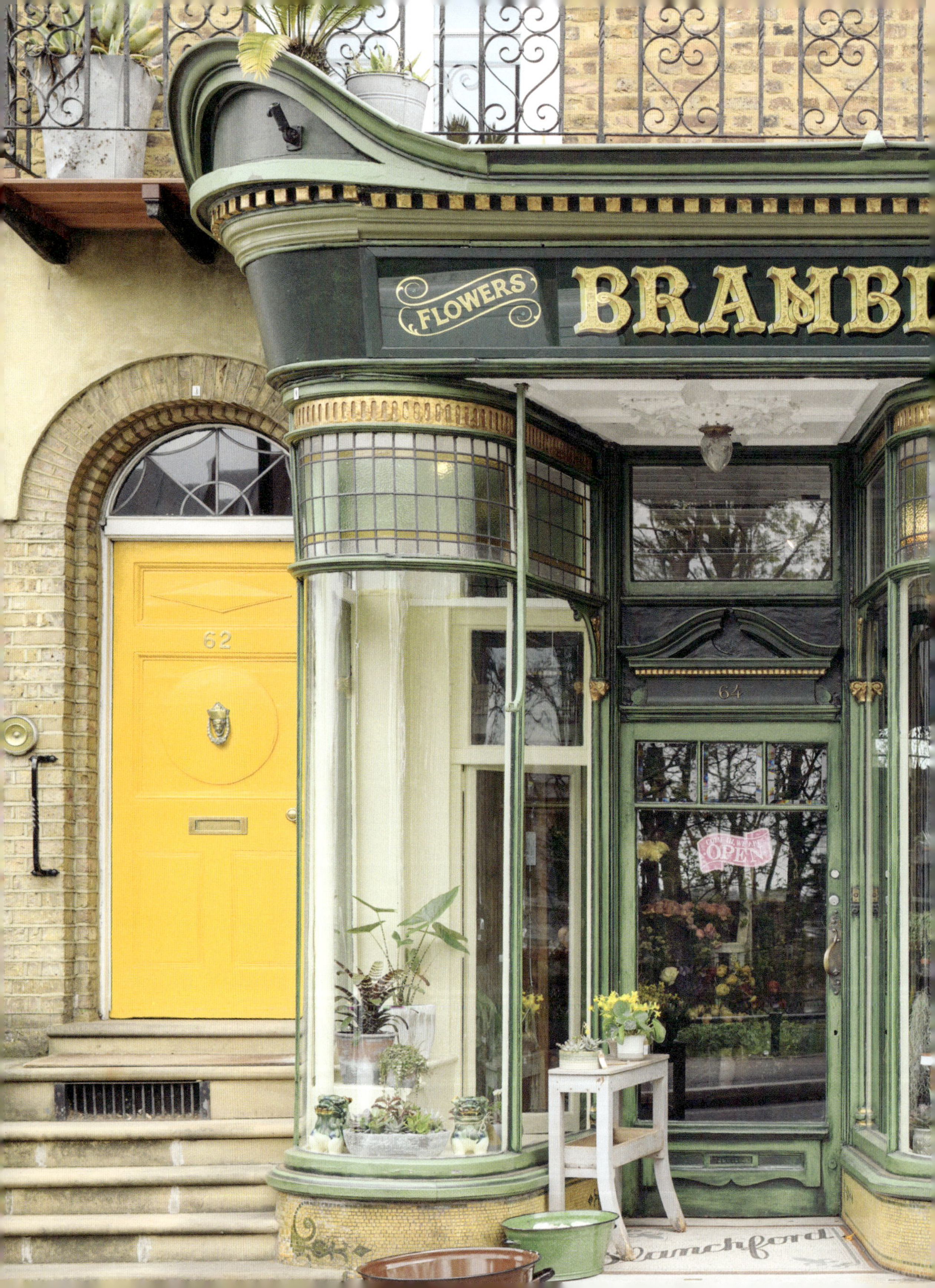

FLOWERS
BRAMBI
62
64
OPEN

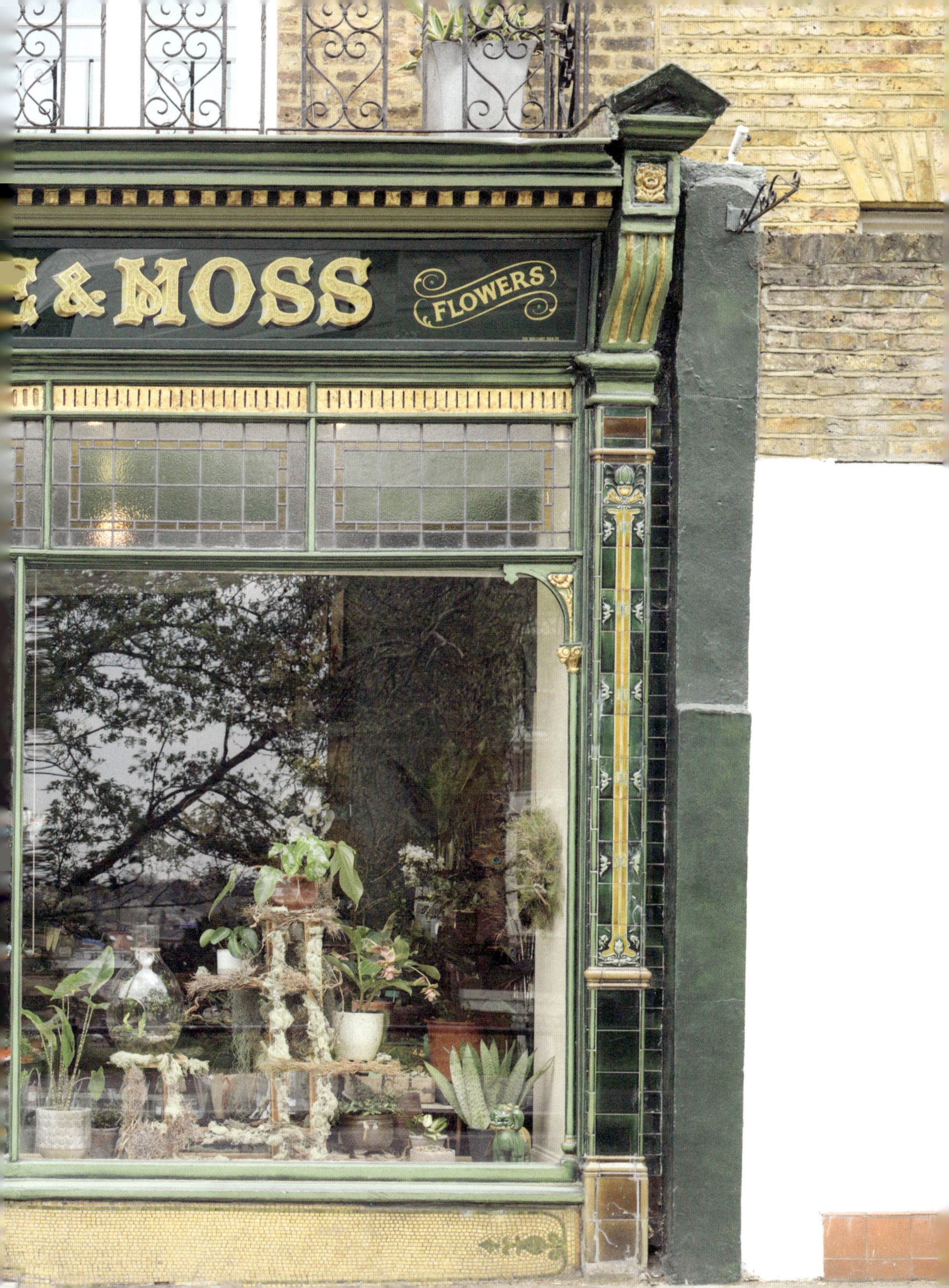
& MOSS
FLOWERS

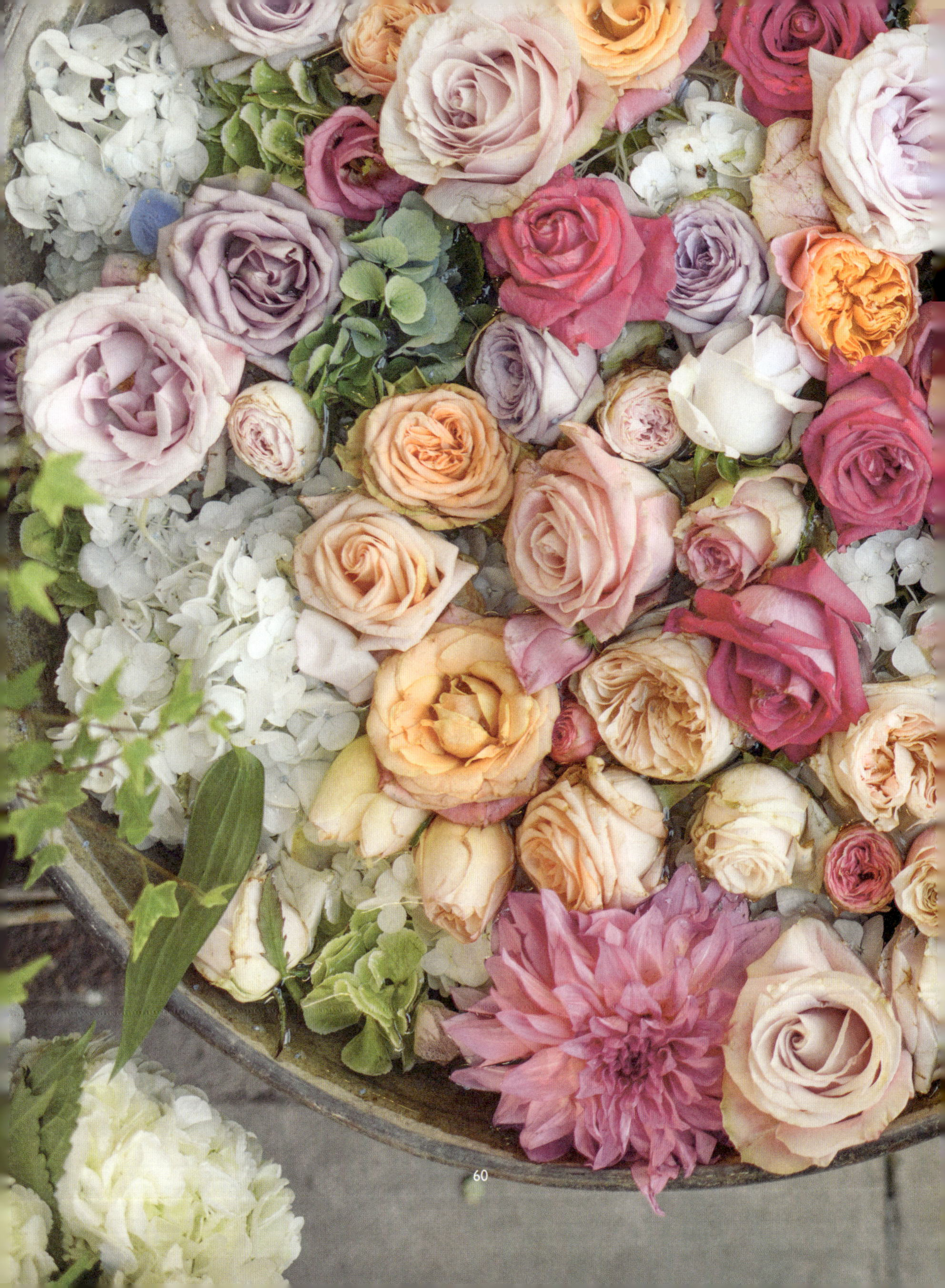

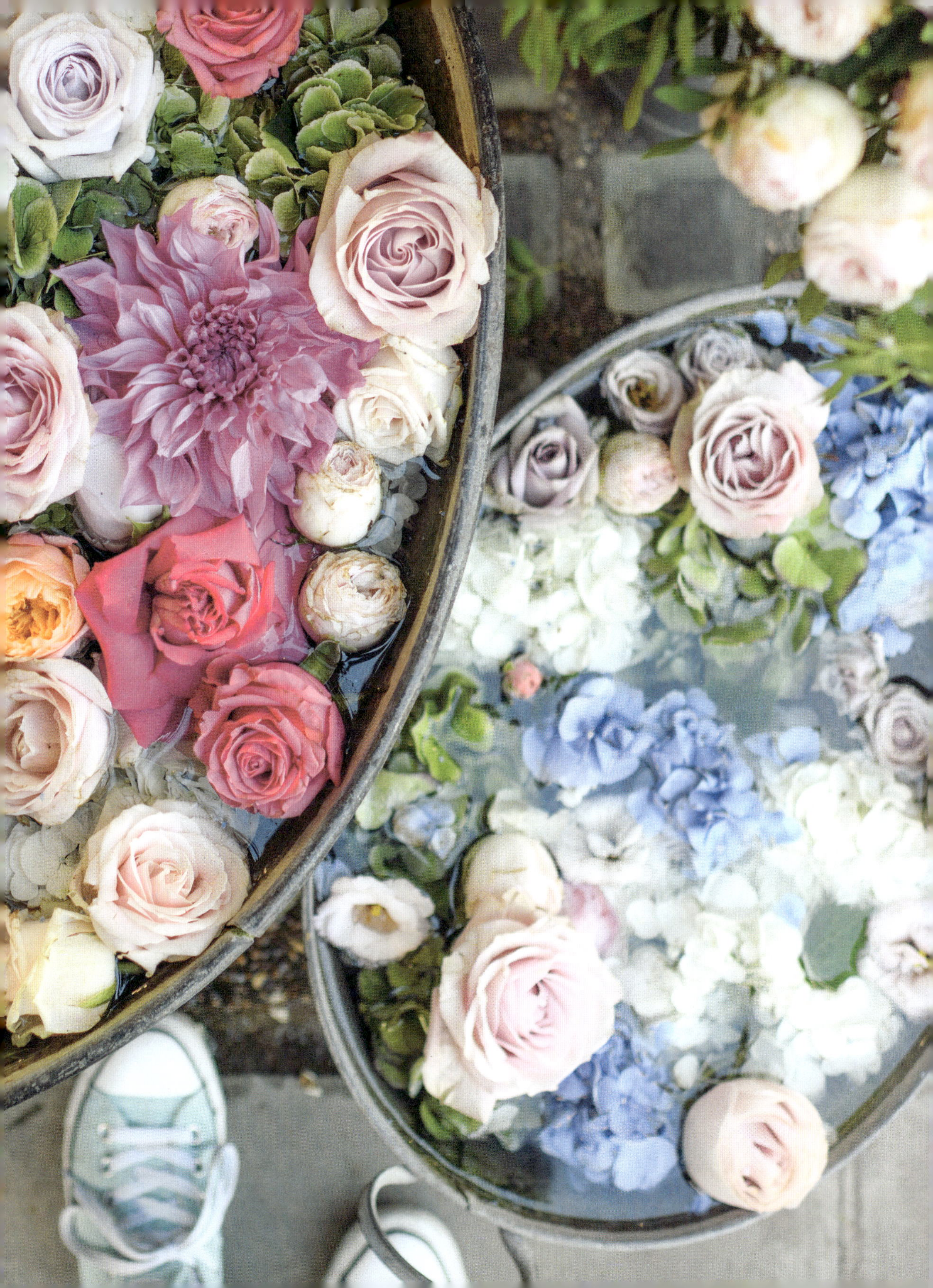

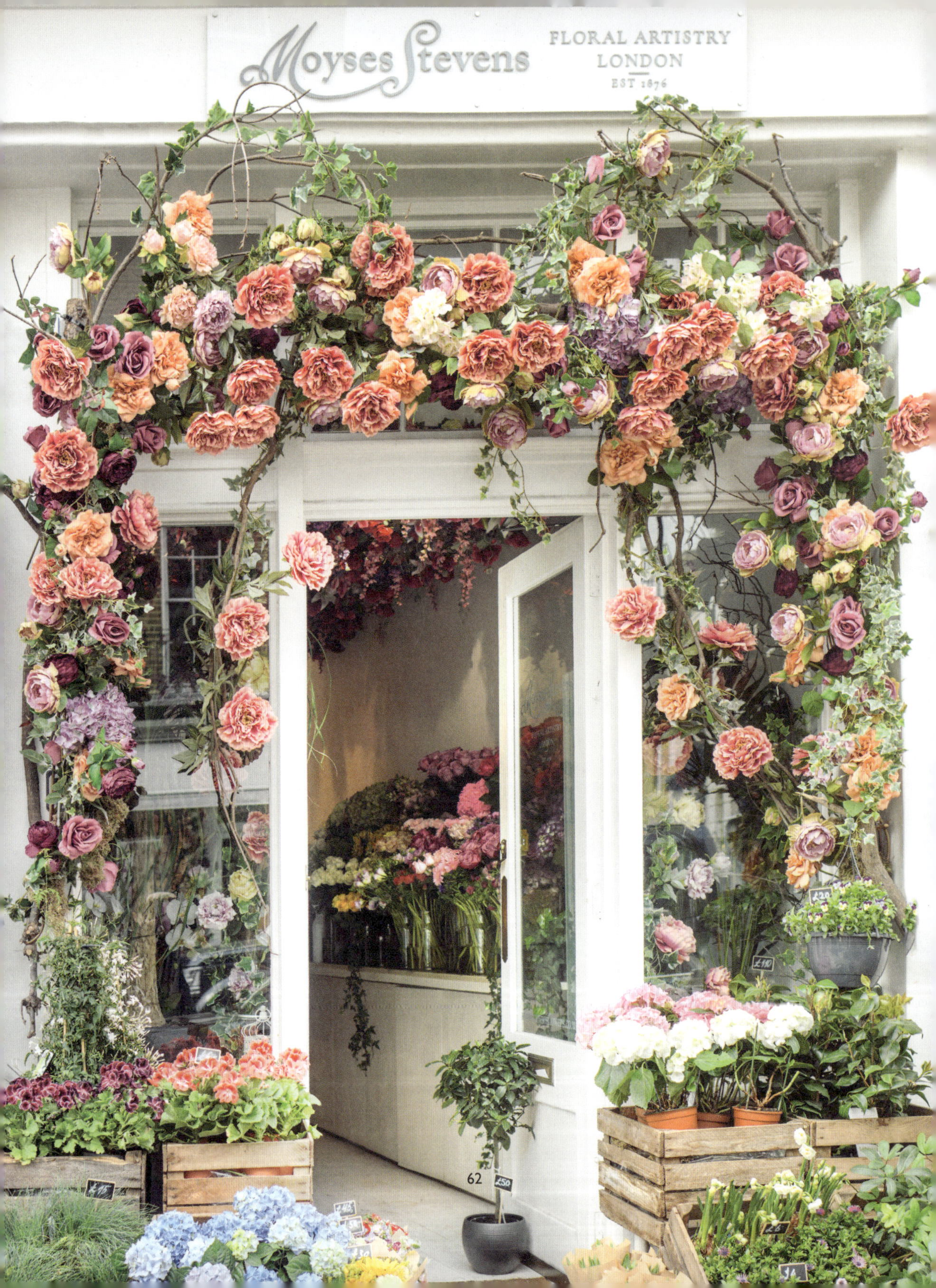

Moyses Stevens
FLORAL ARTISTRY
LONDON
EST 1876

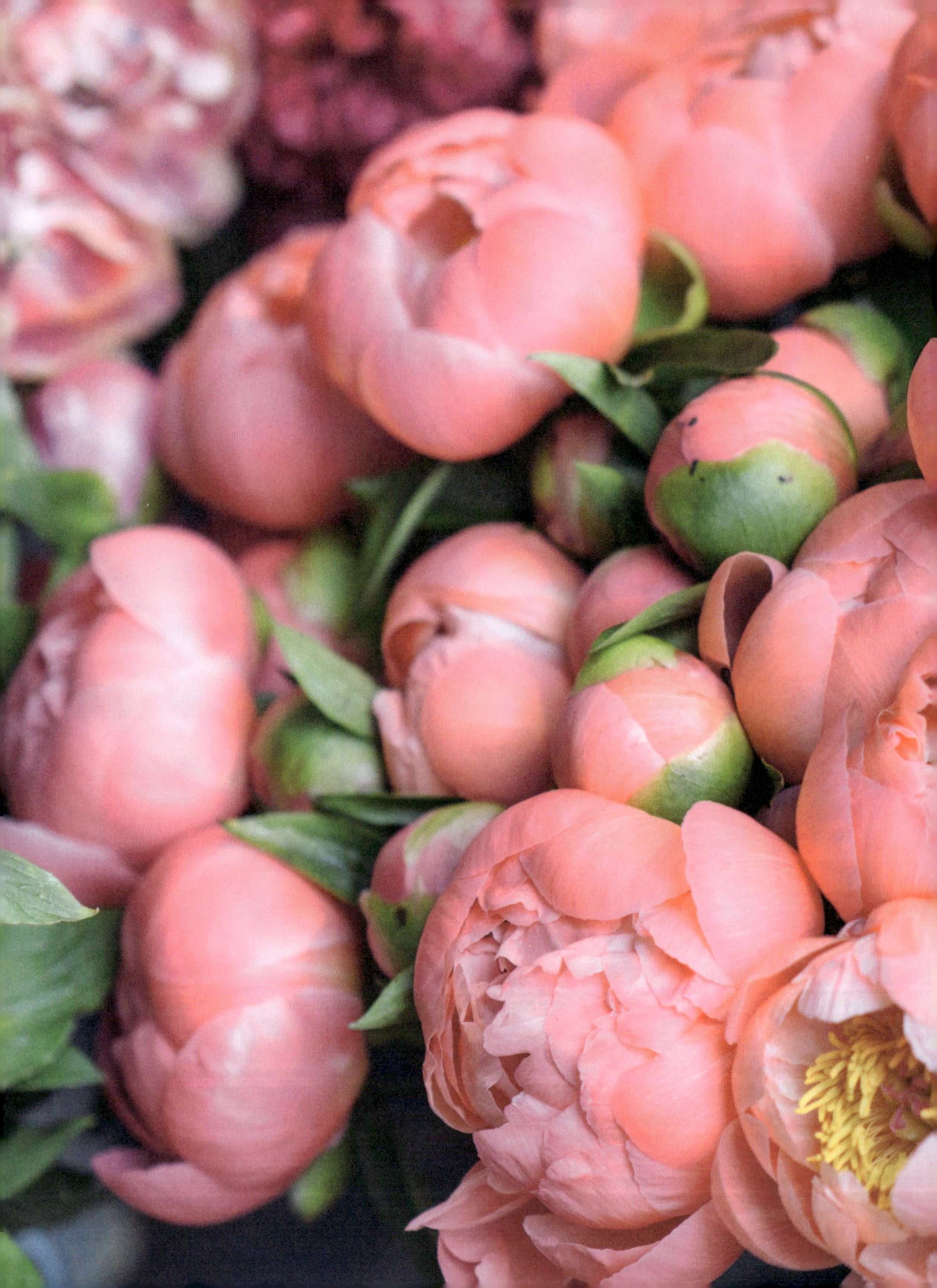

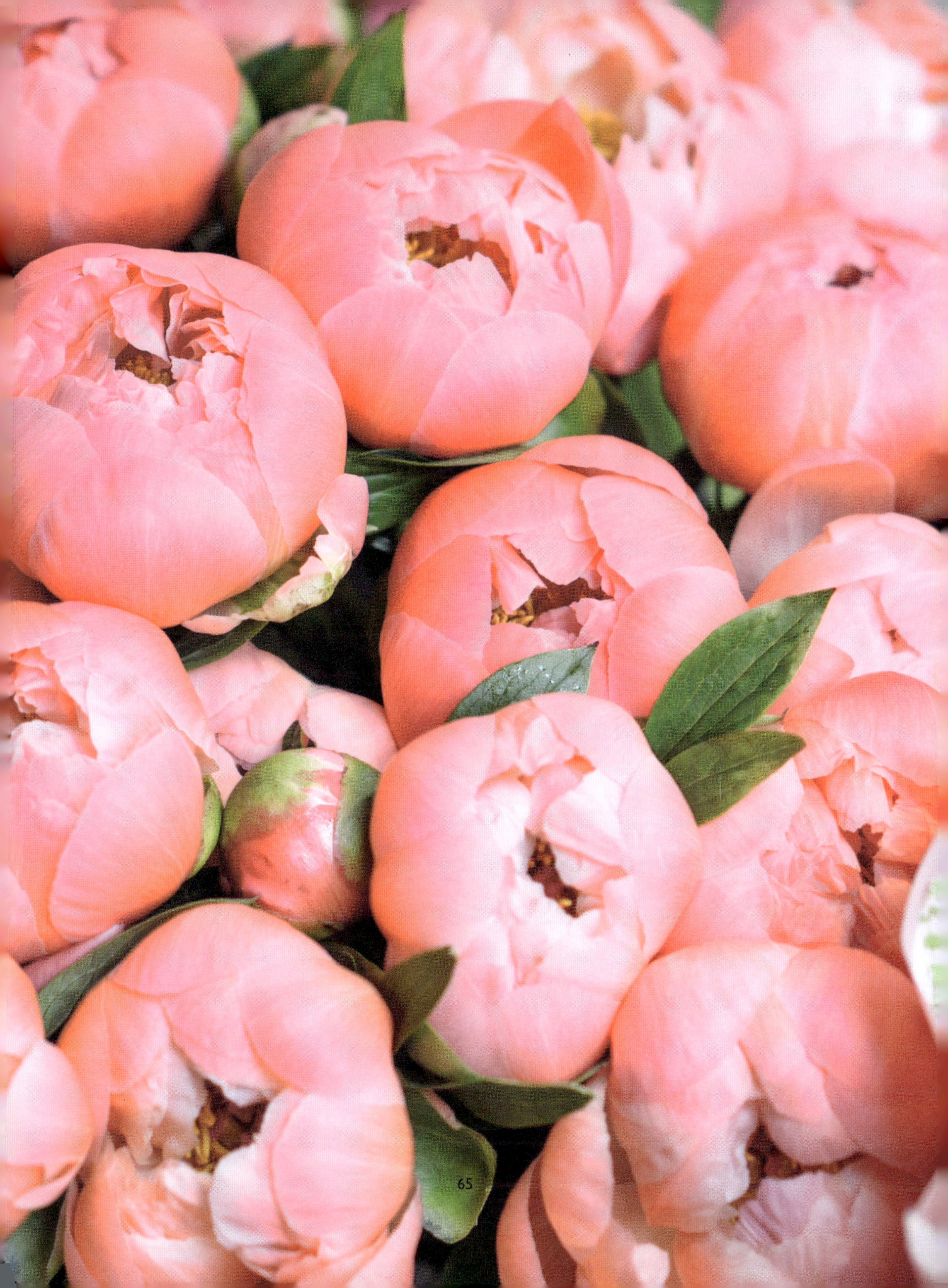

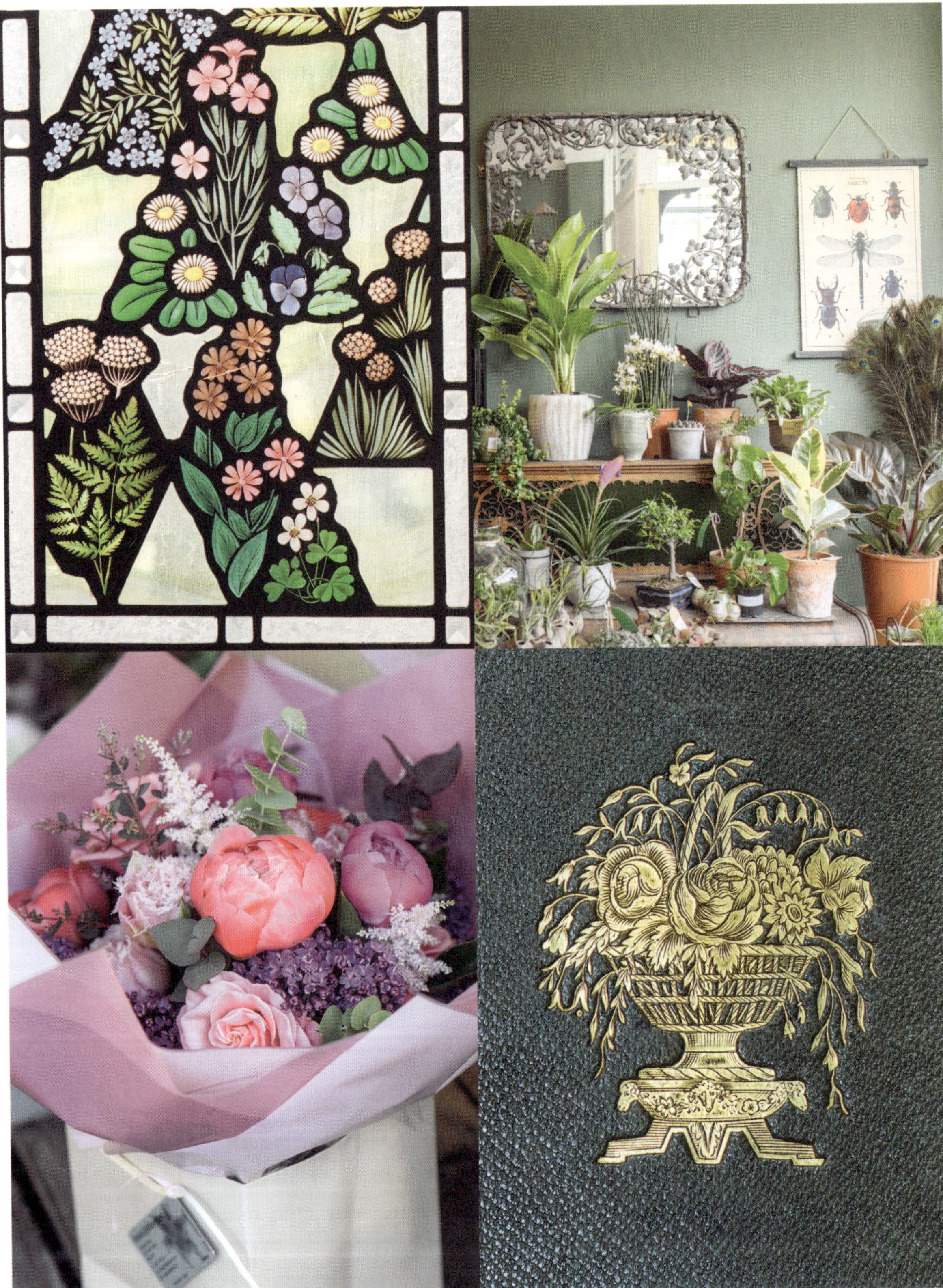

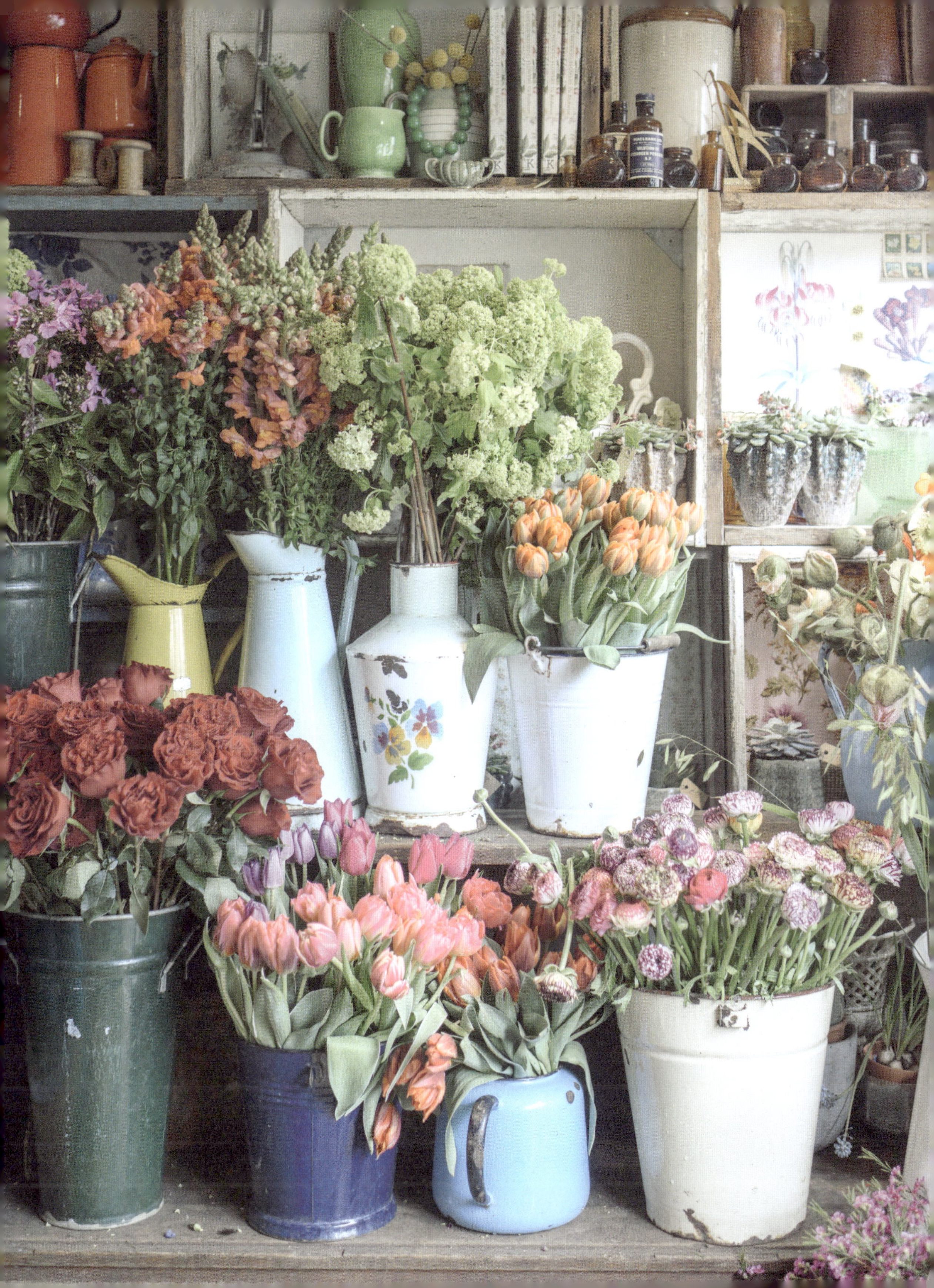

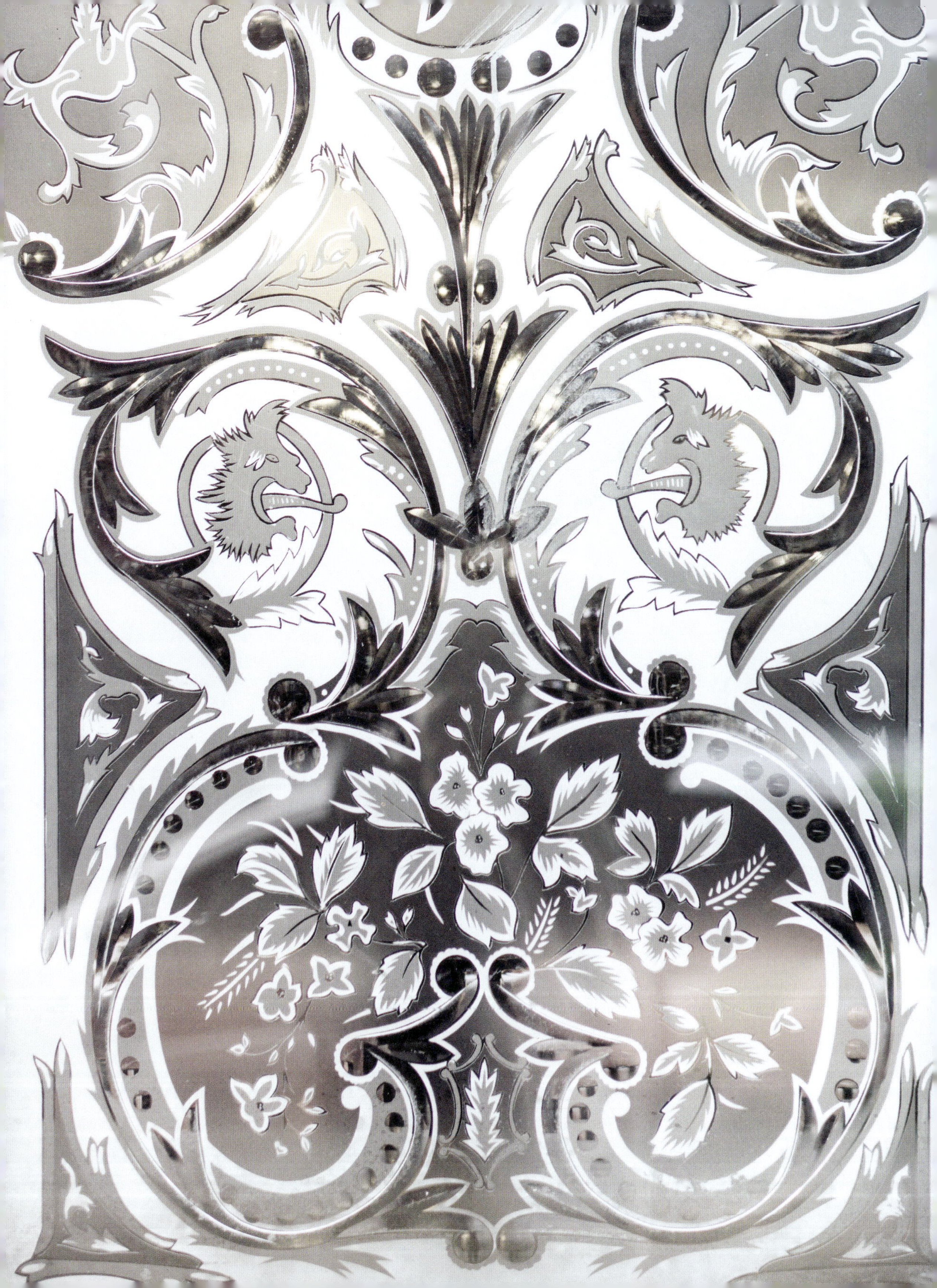

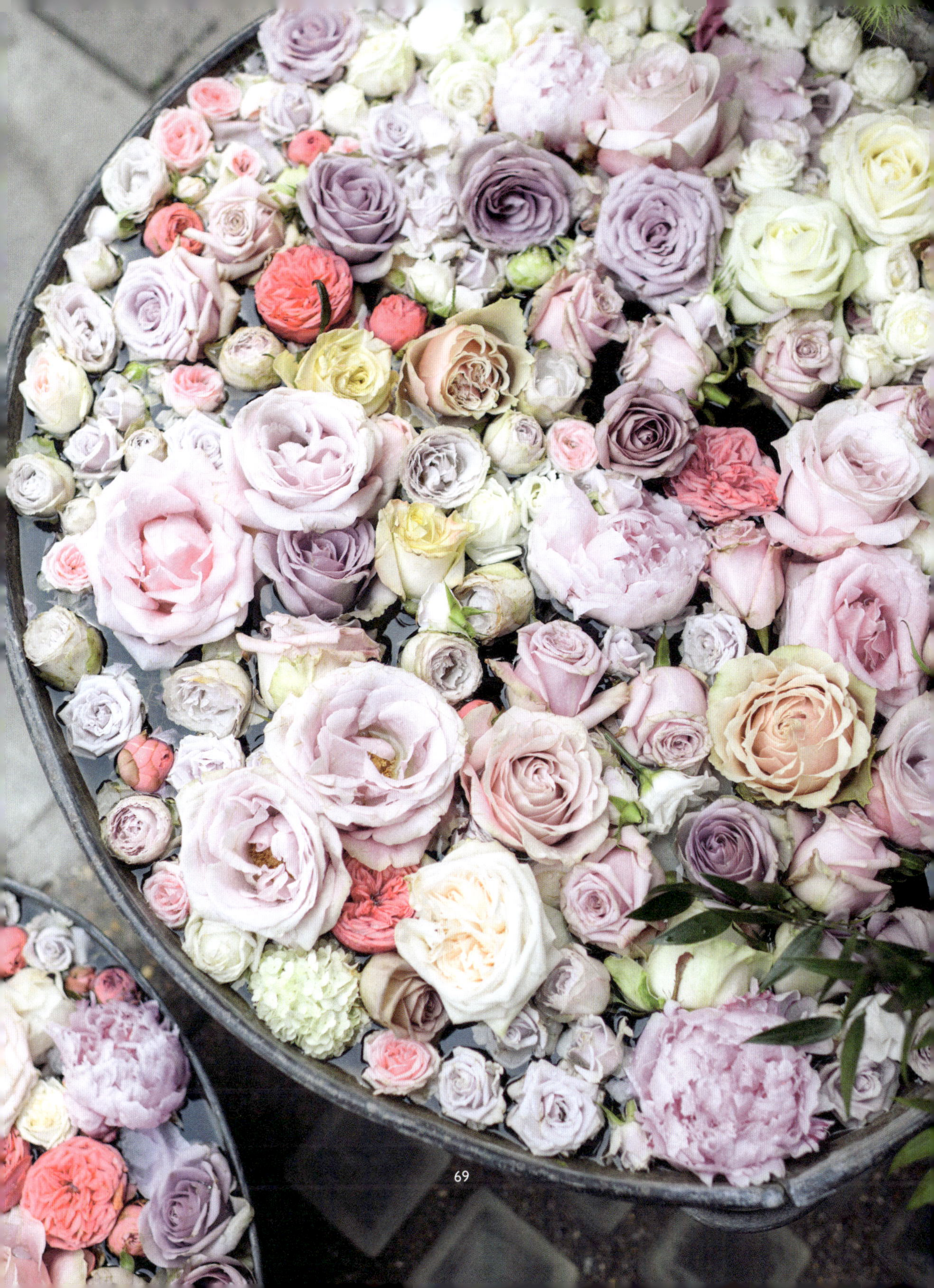

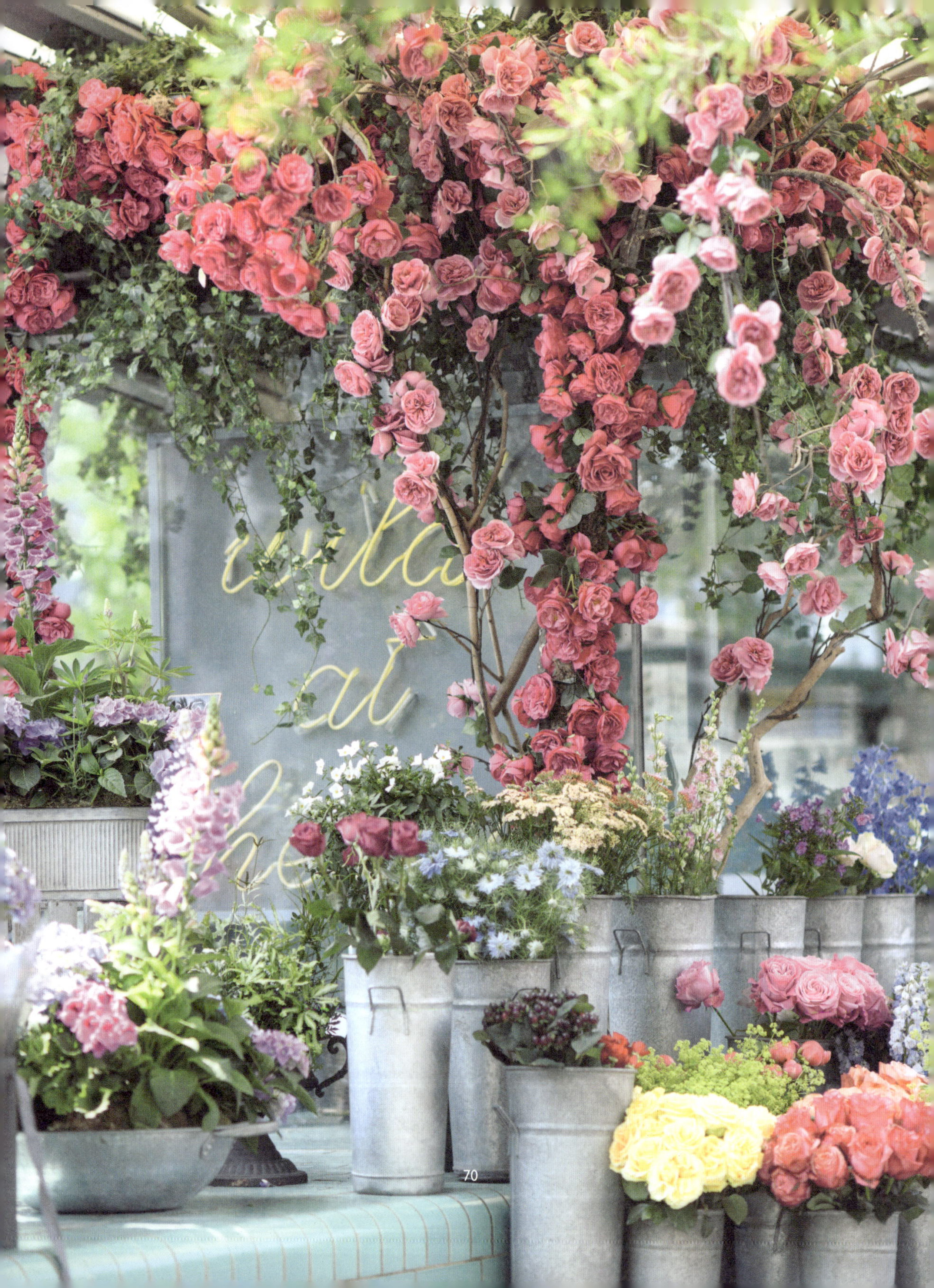

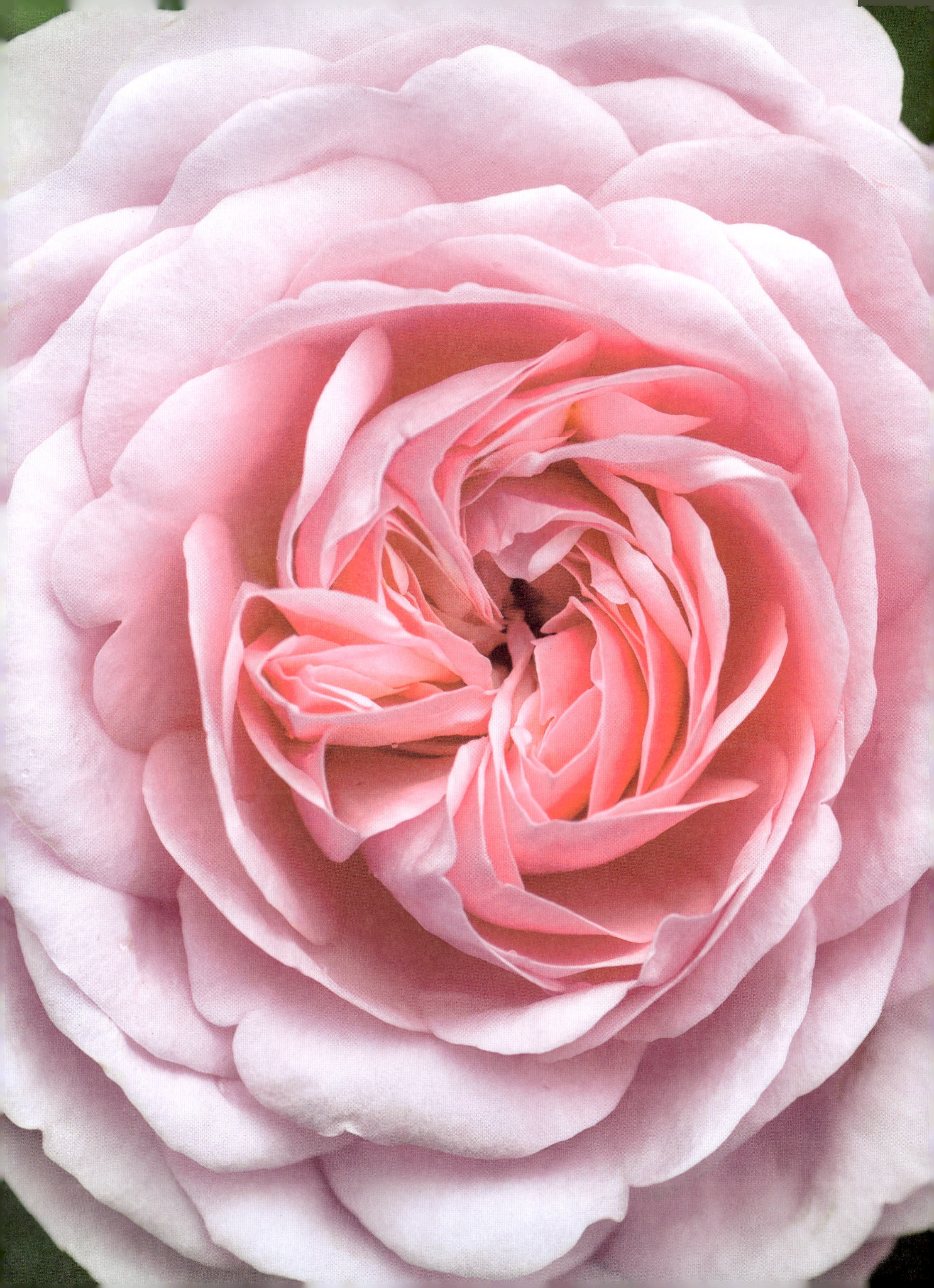

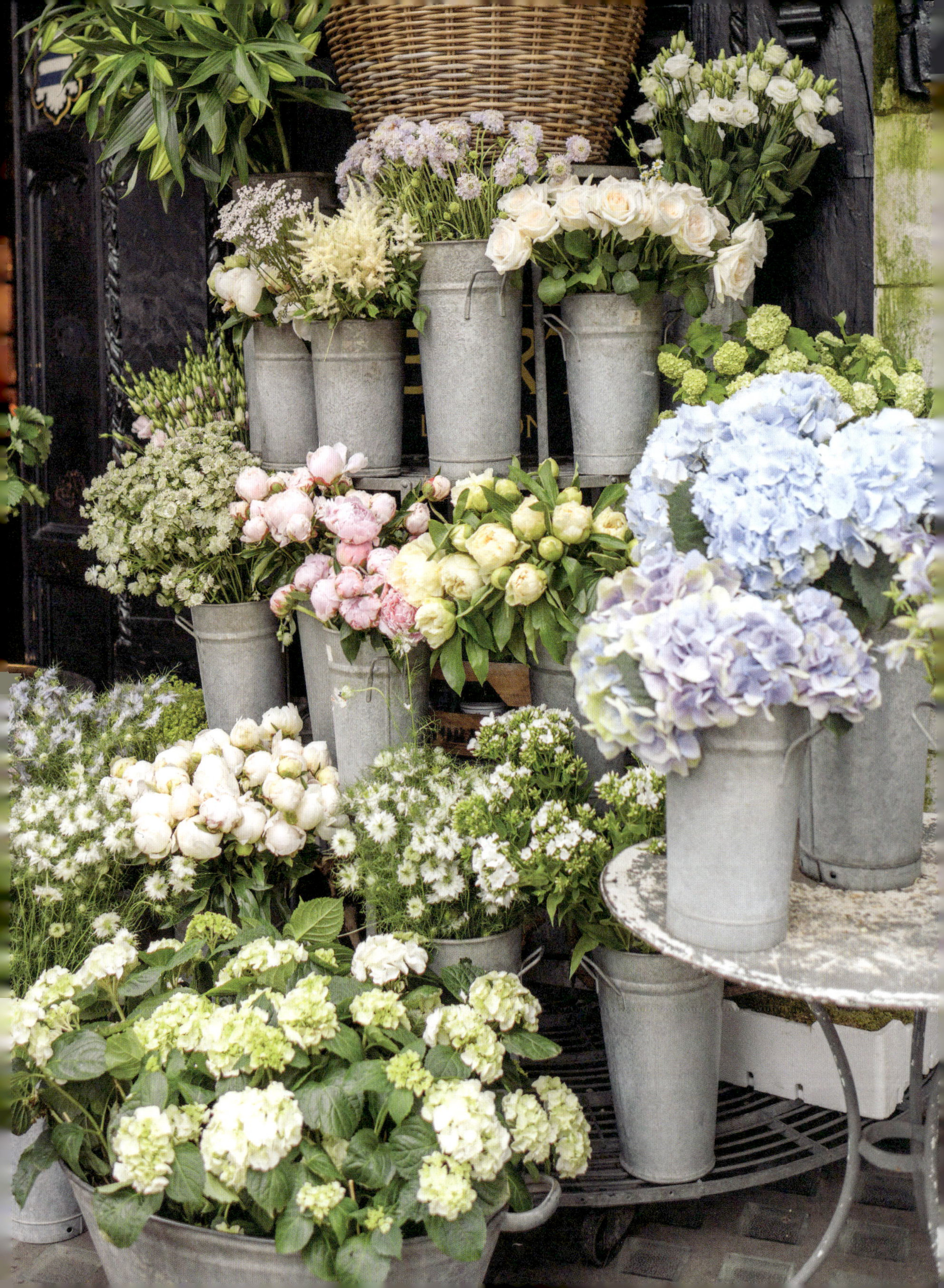

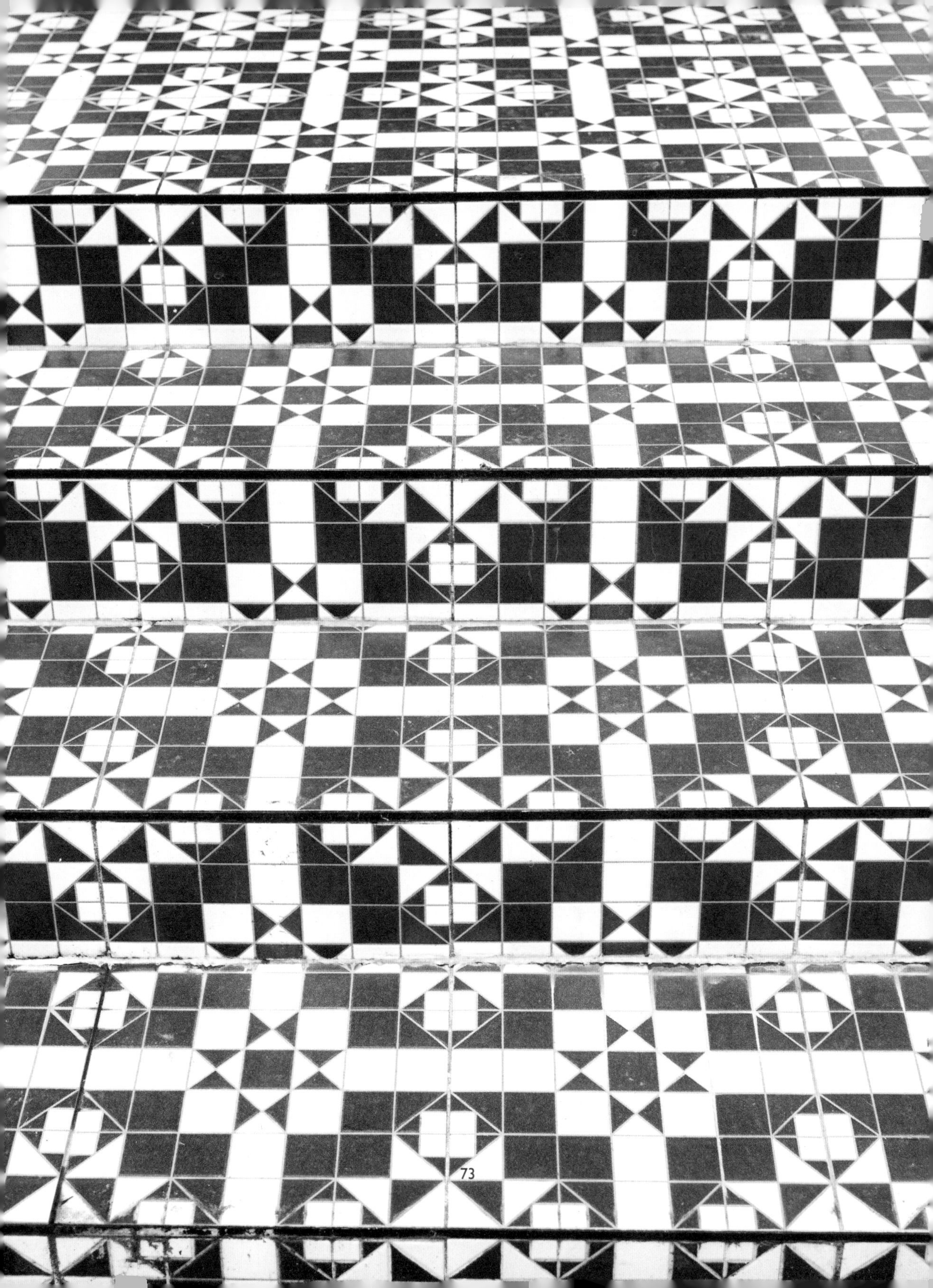

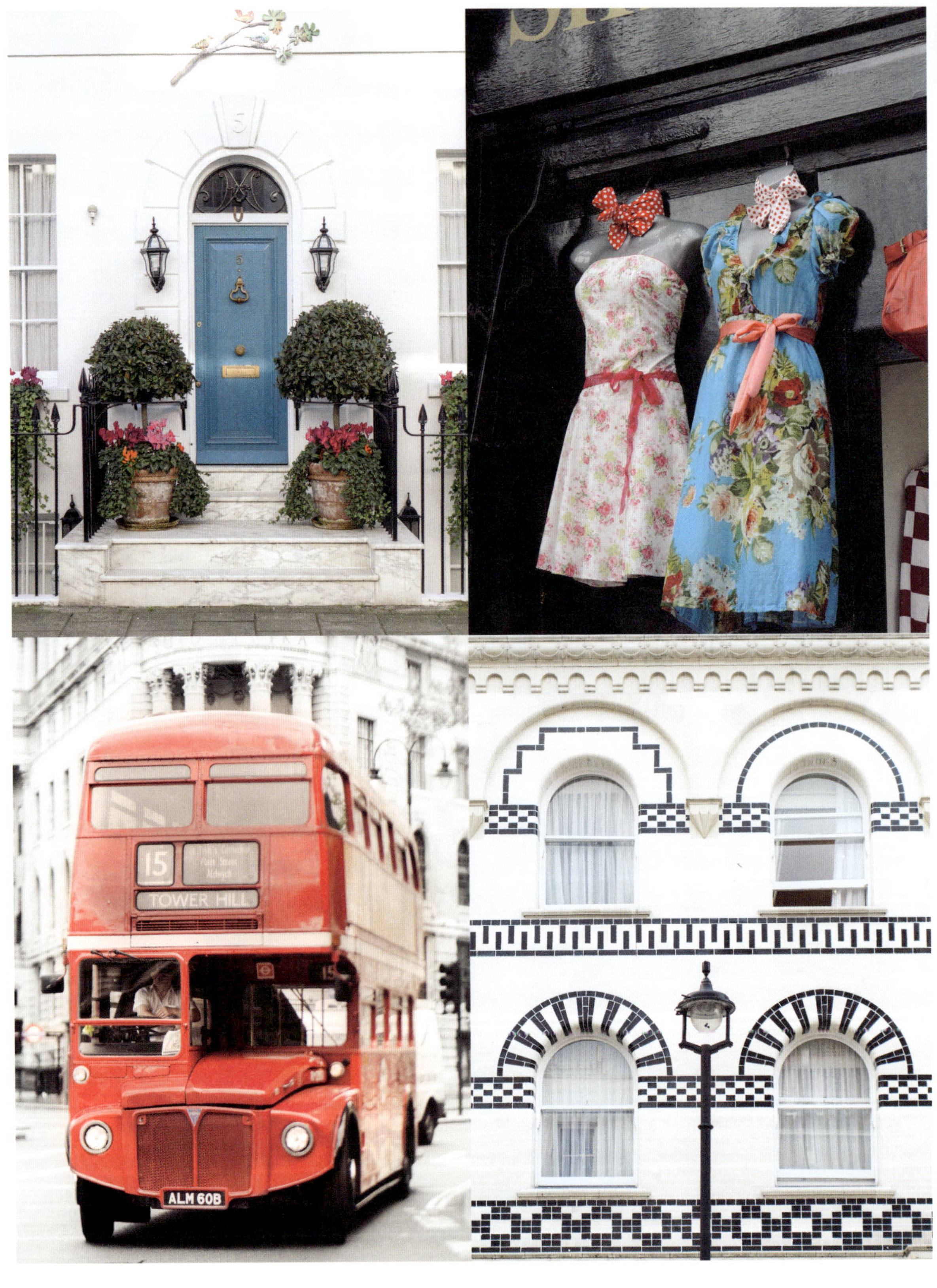
15
TOWER HILL
ALM 60B

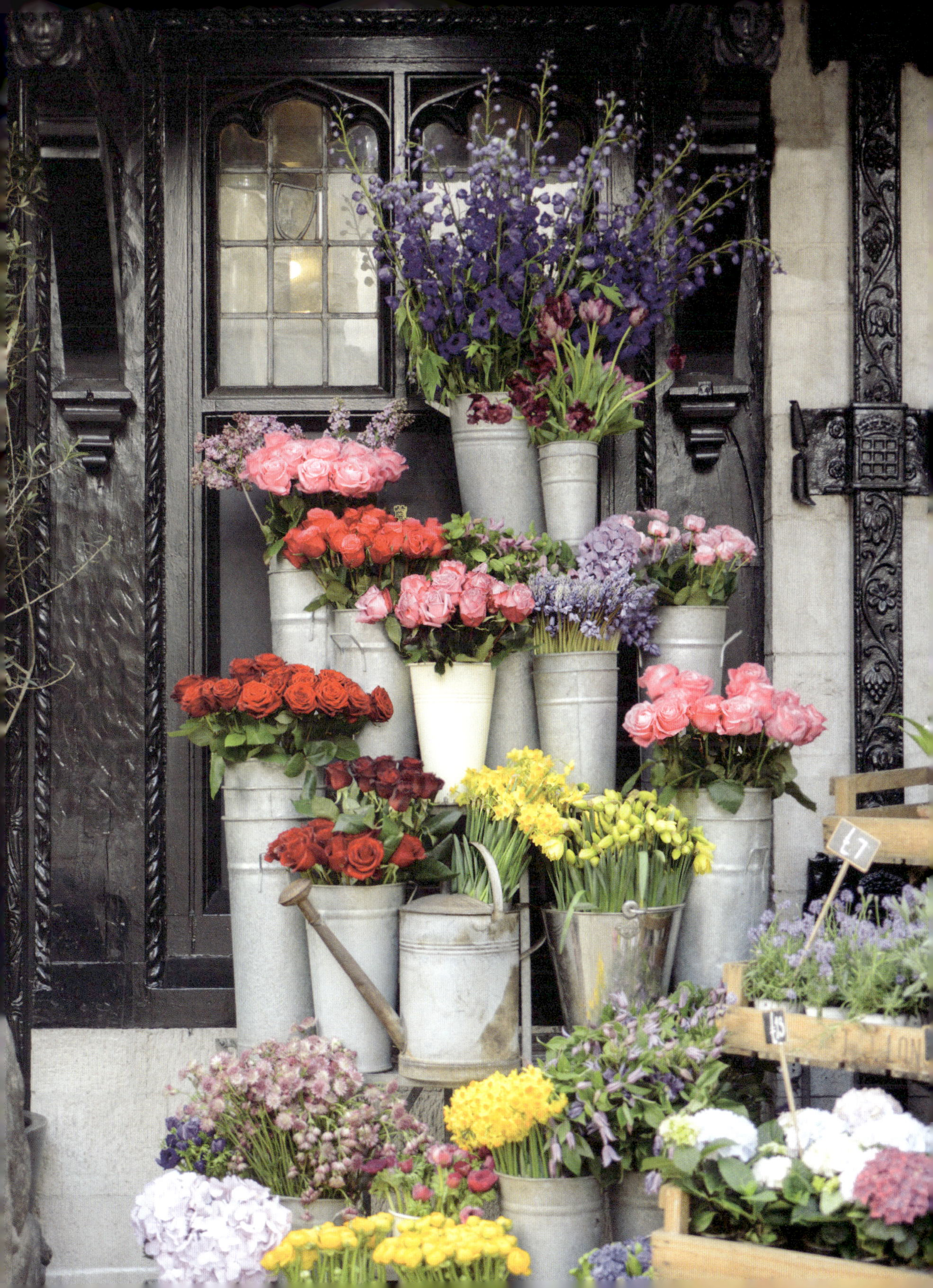

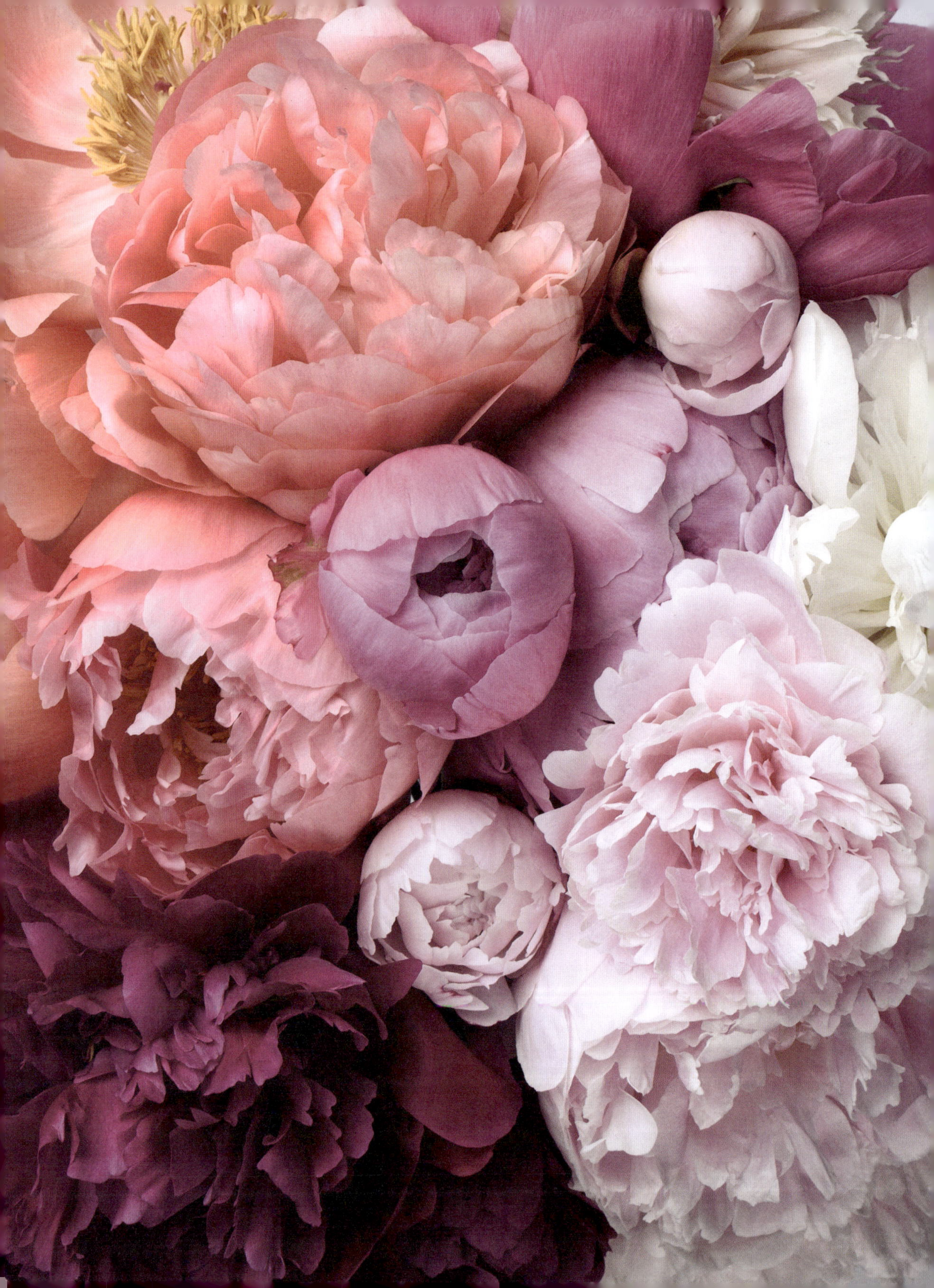

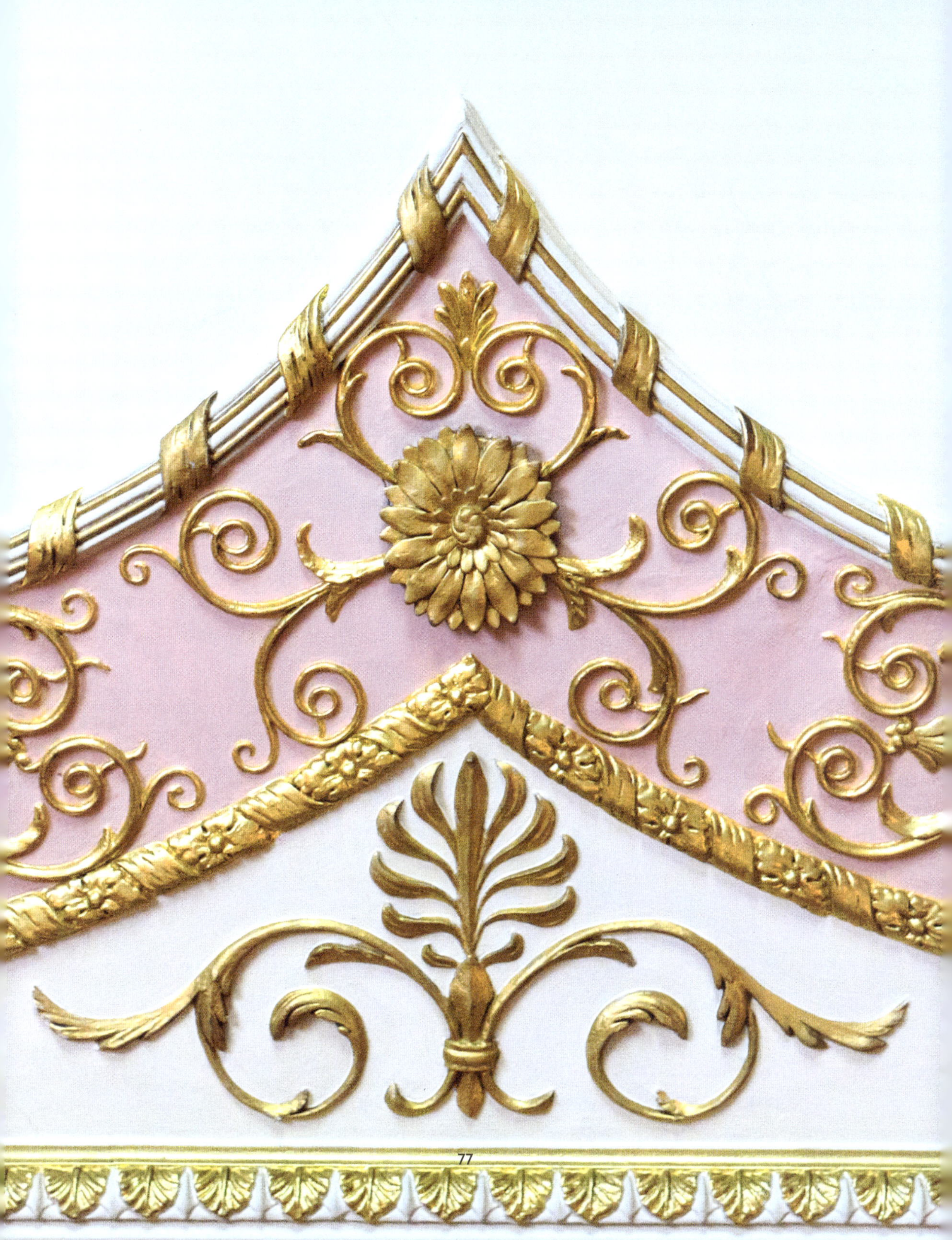

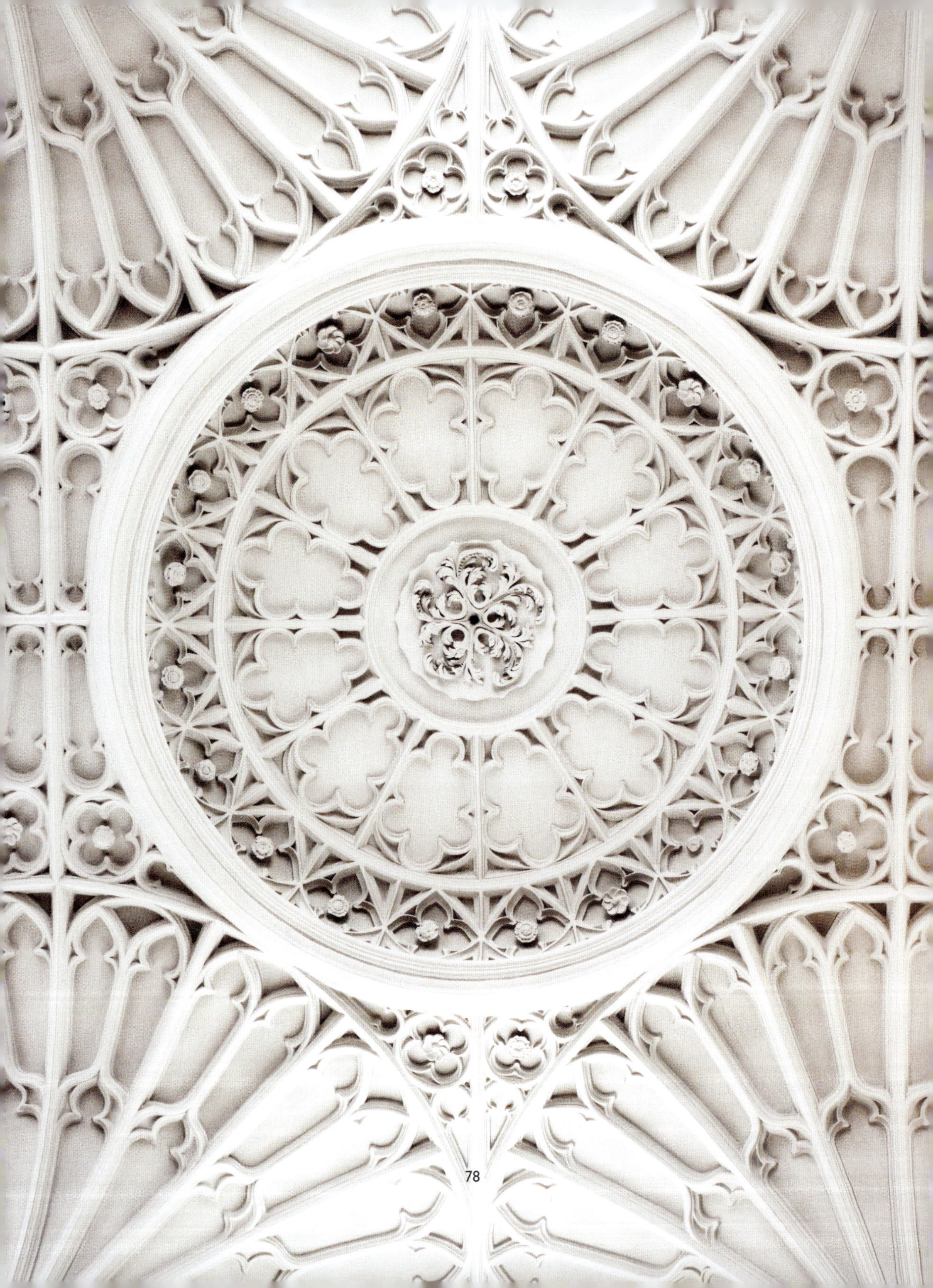

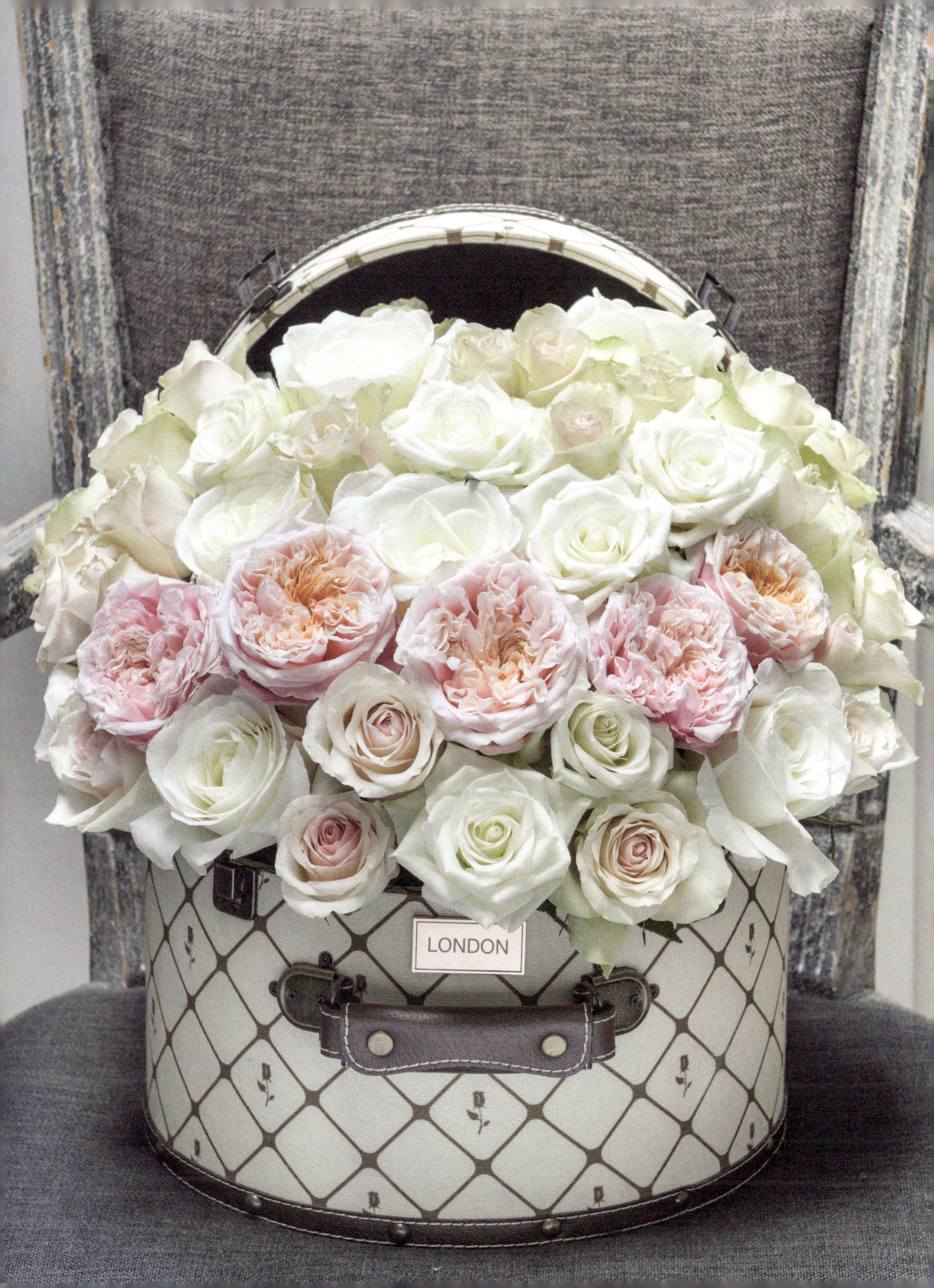
LONDON

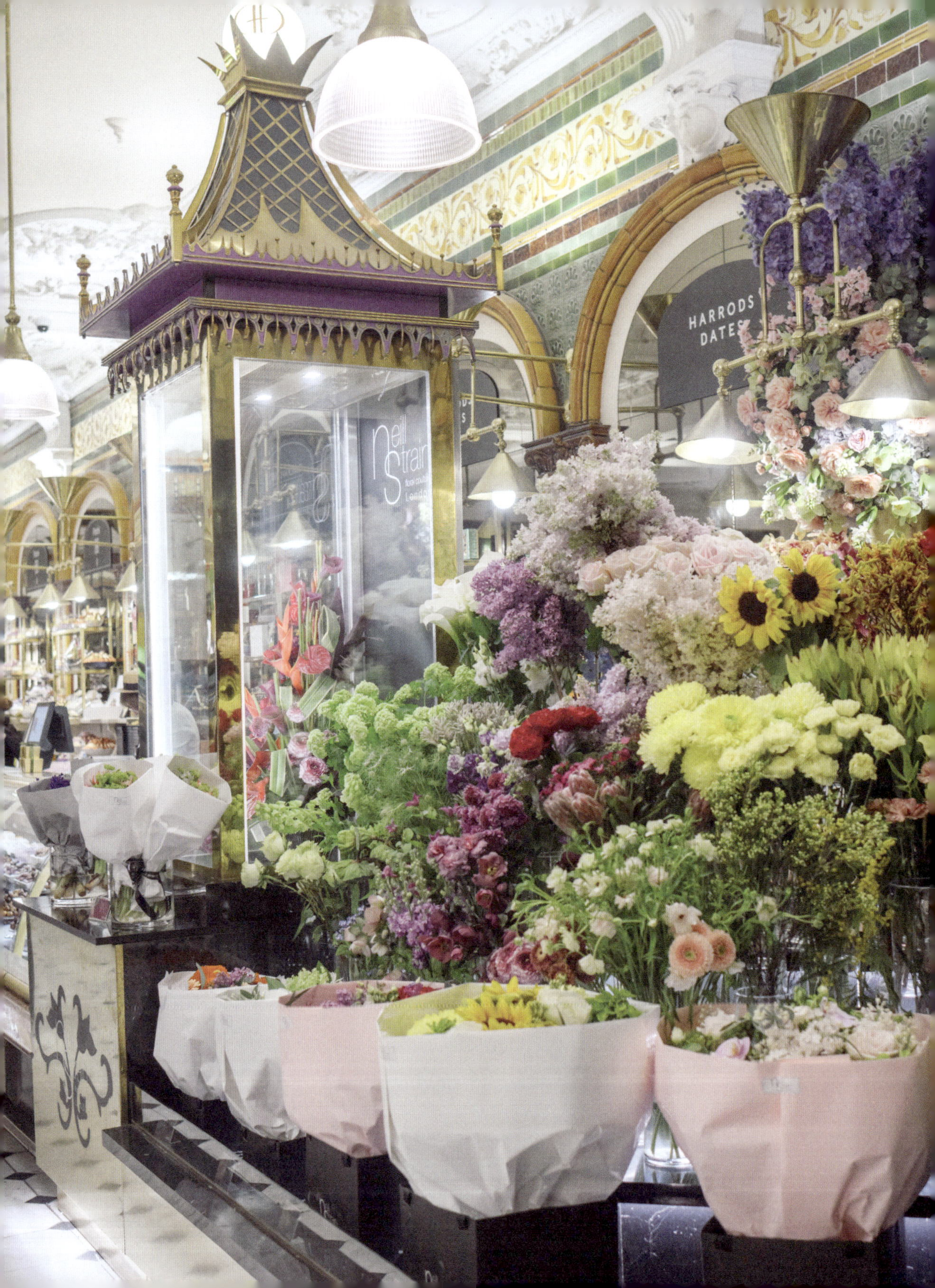
Neill Strain
HARRODS
DATES

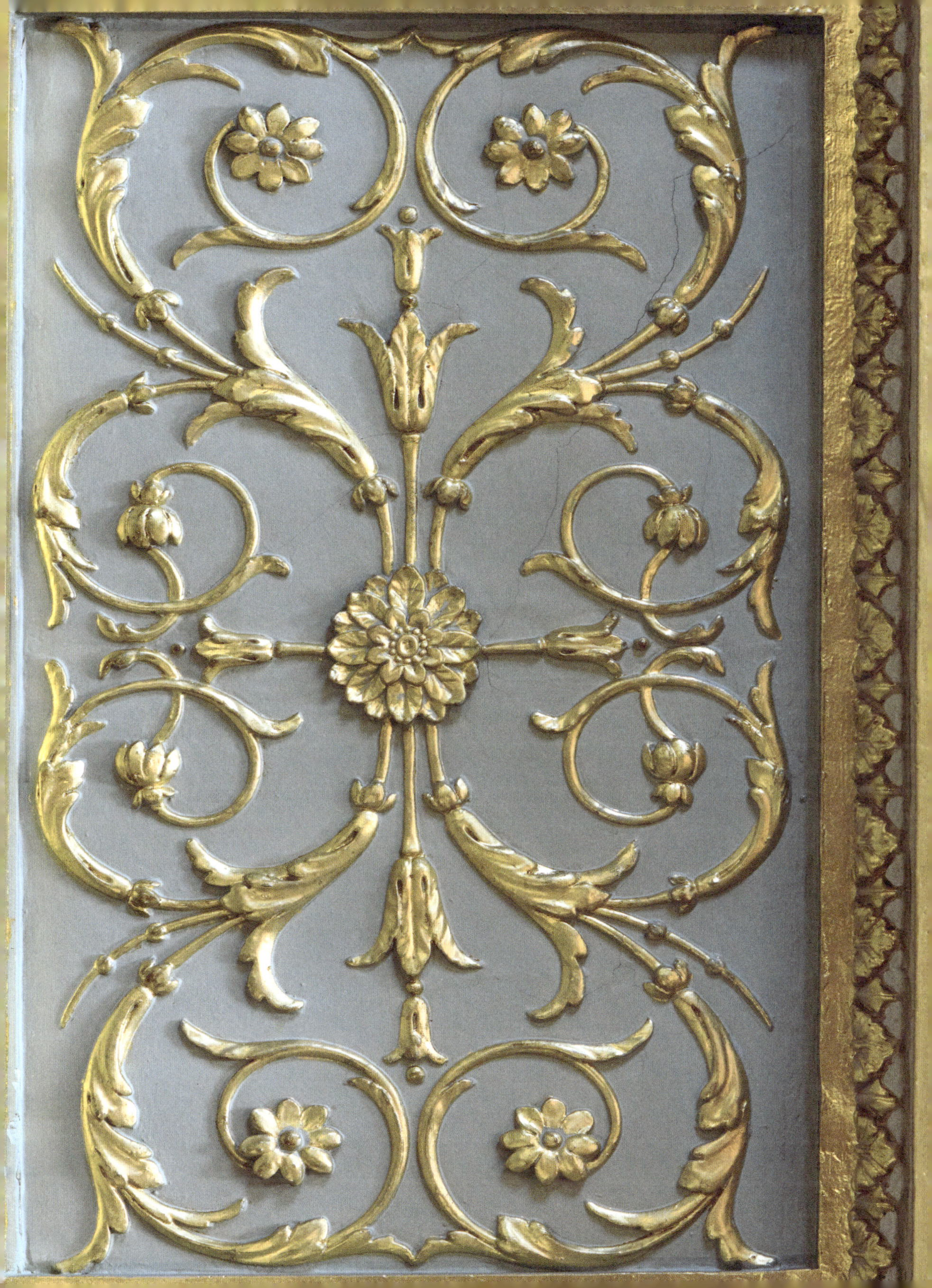

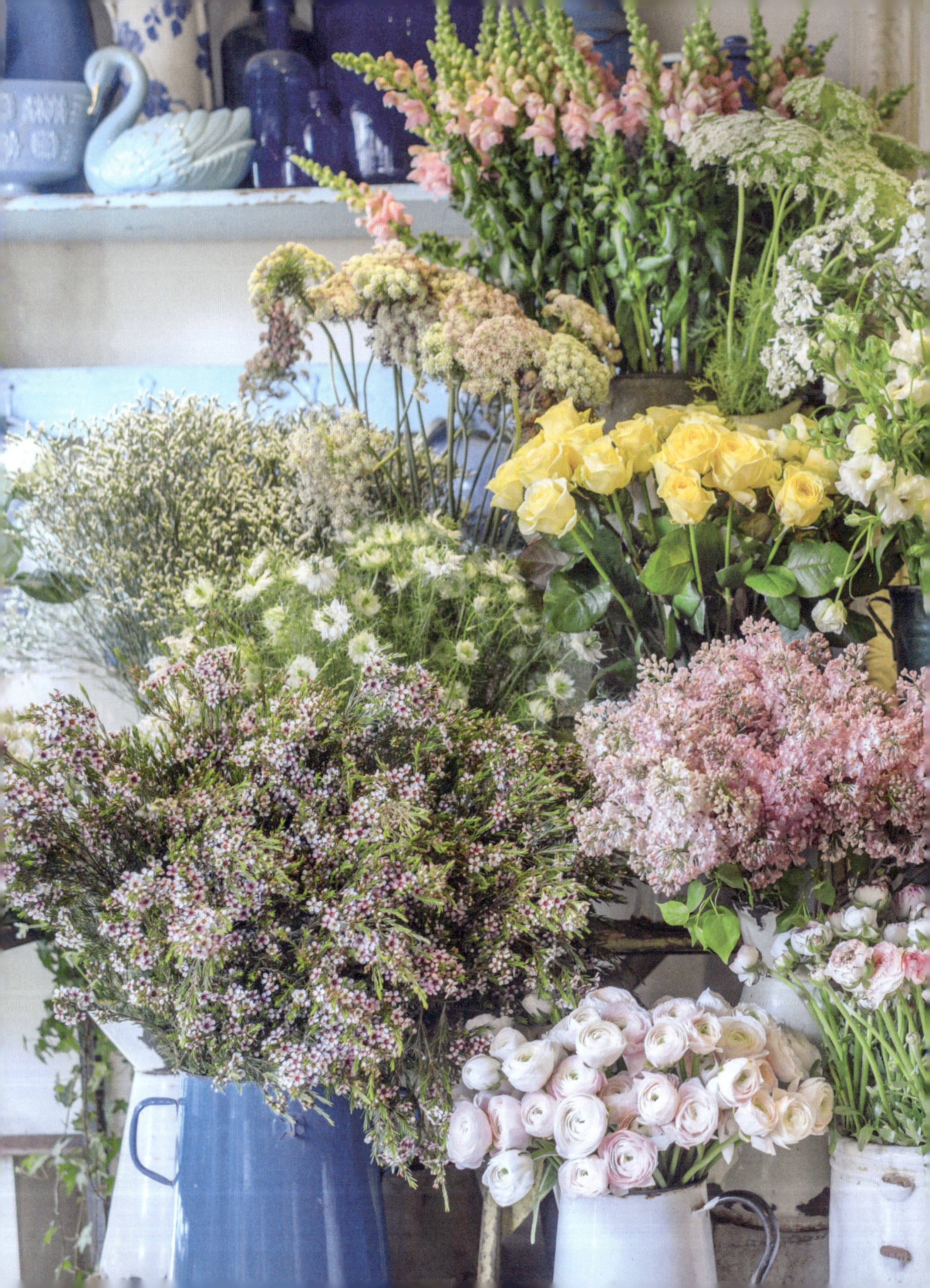

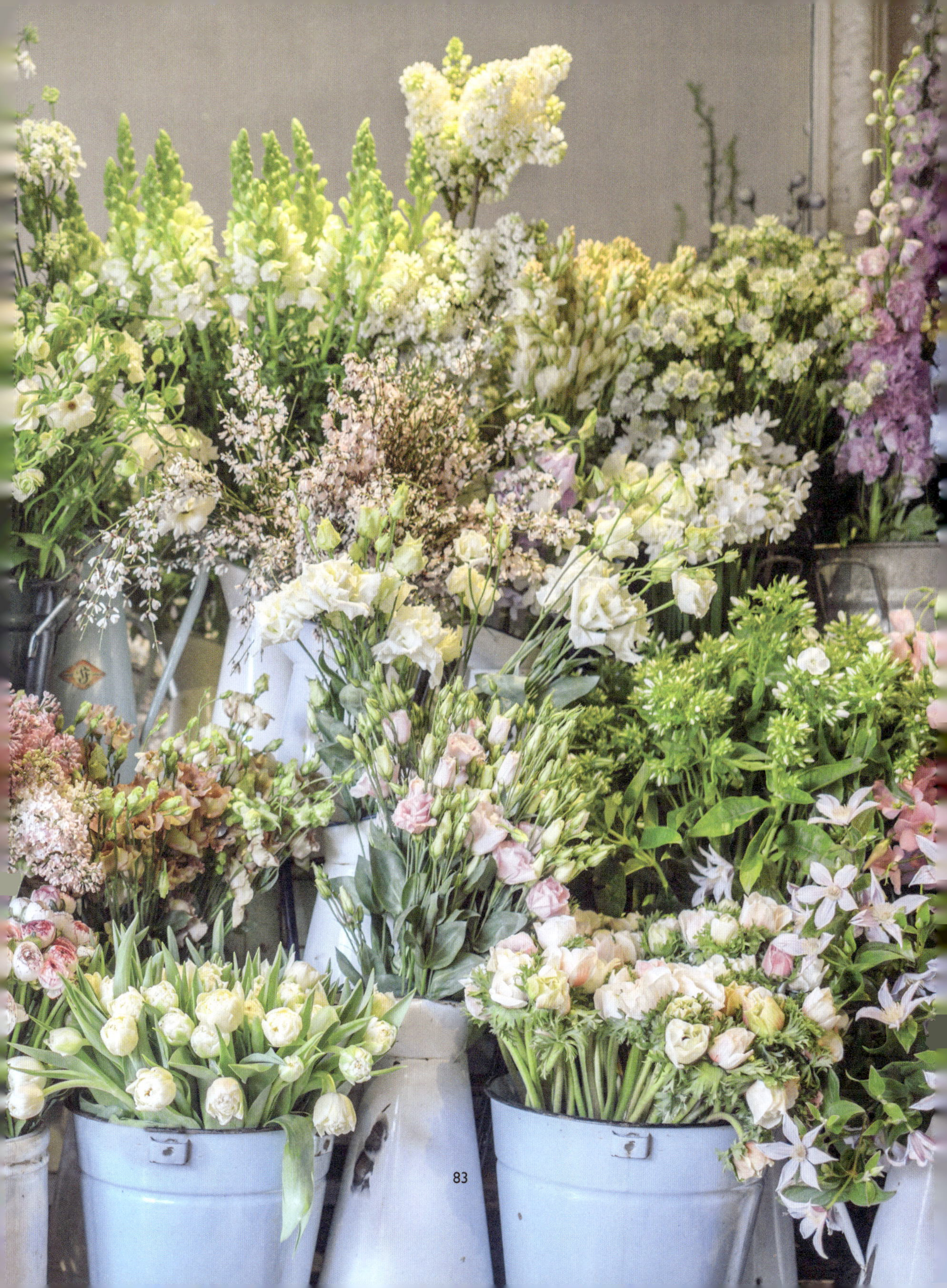

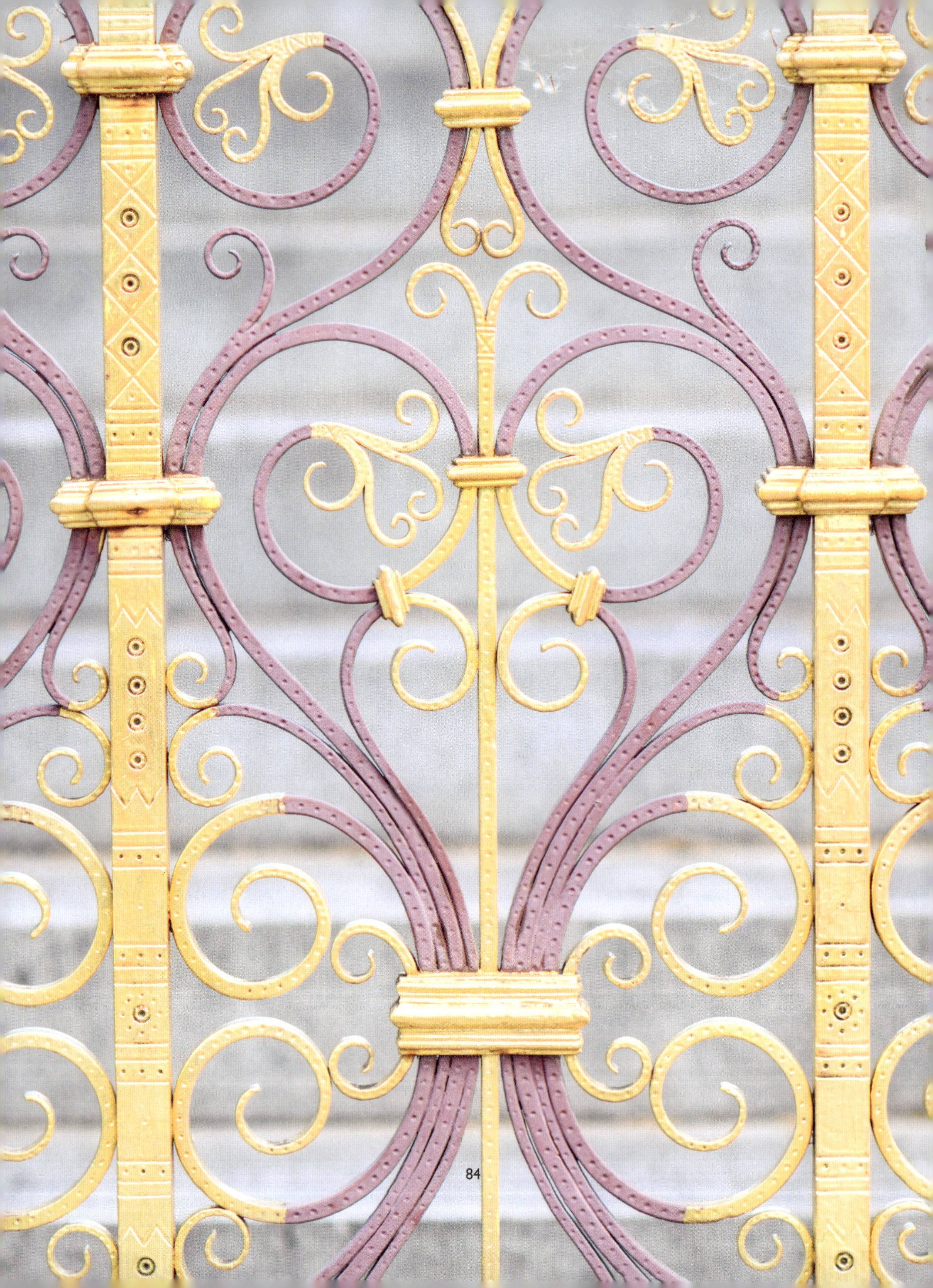

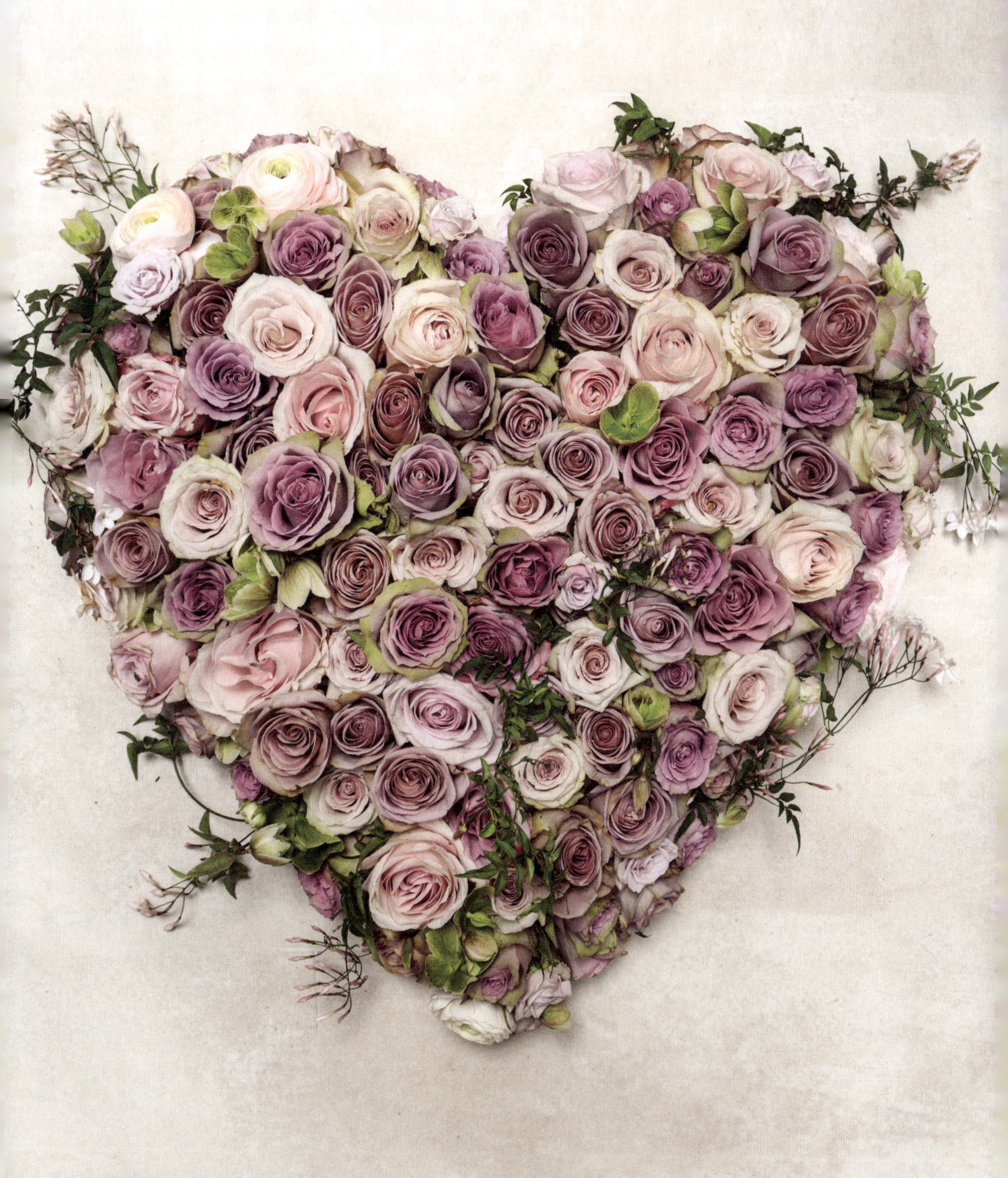

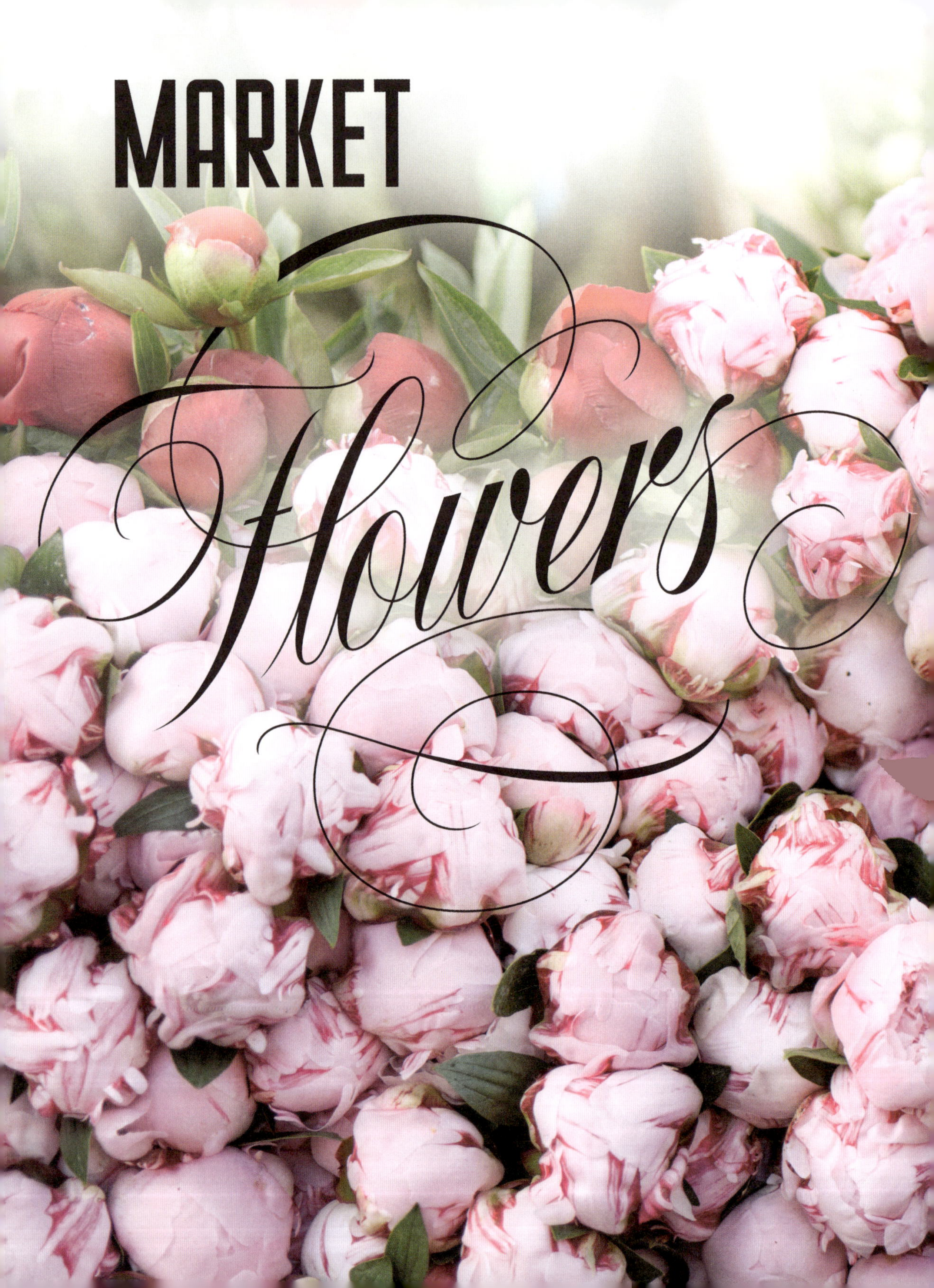
MARKET
Flowers

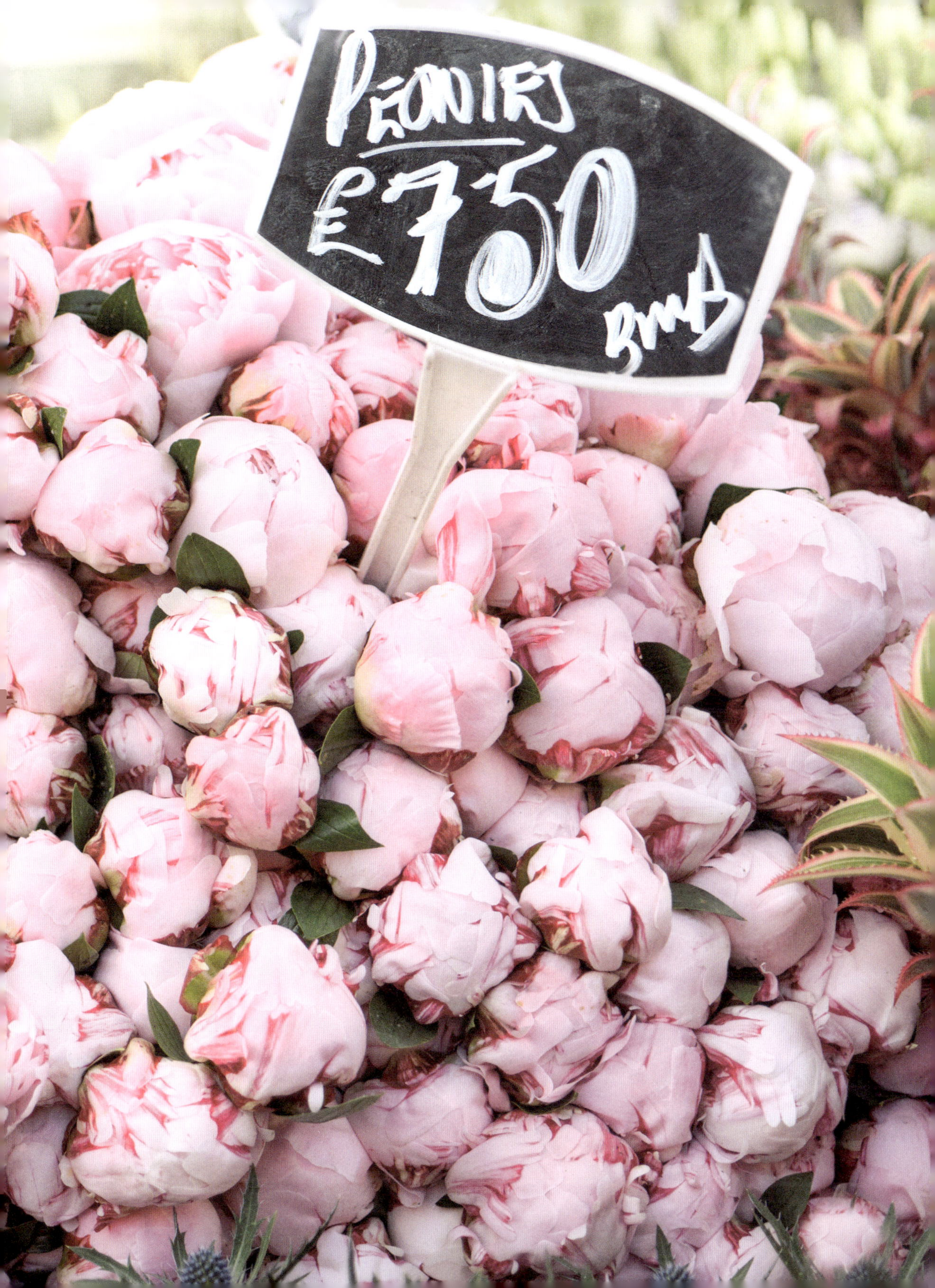

Péonies
€ 7.50
Bunch

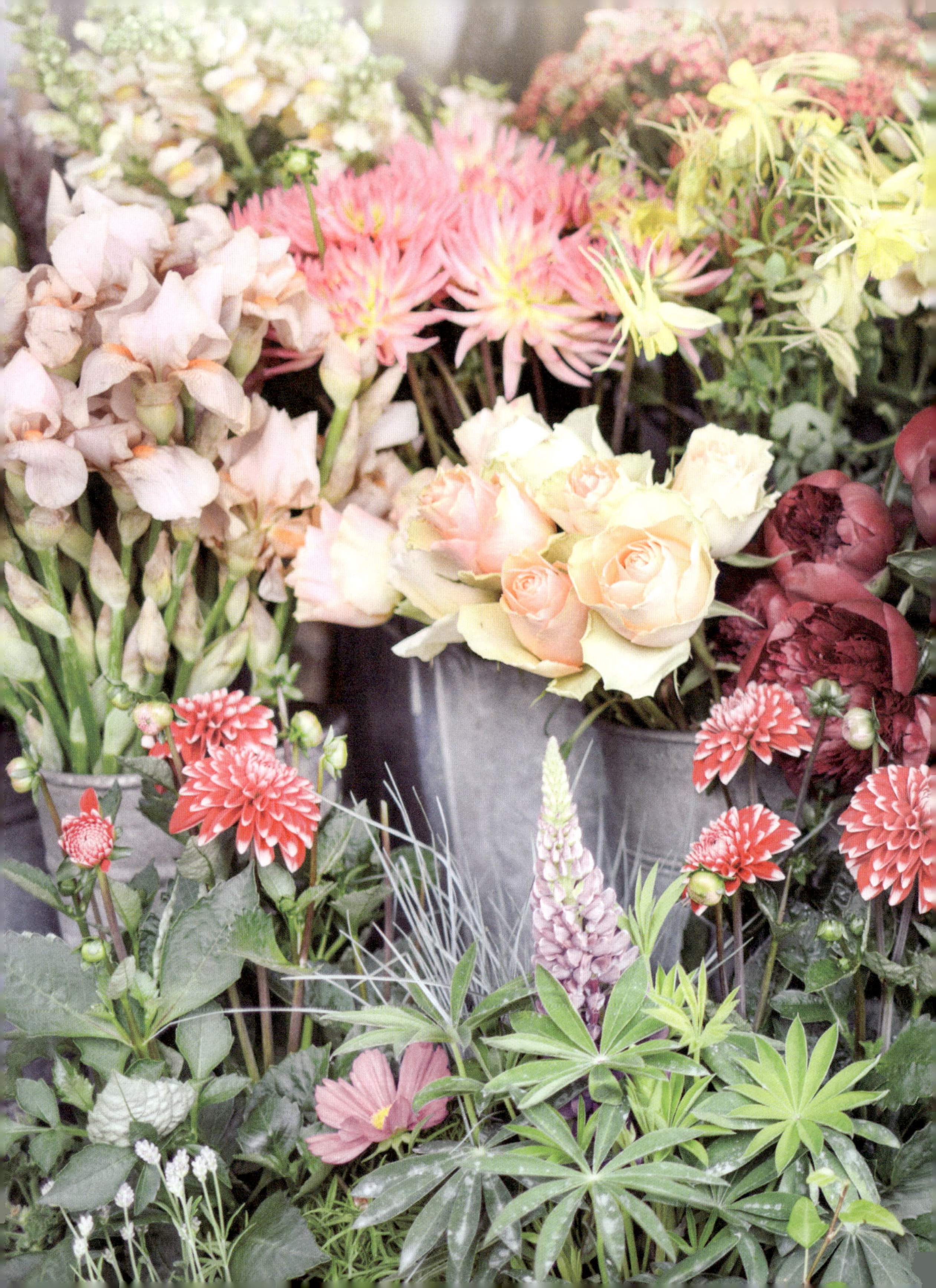

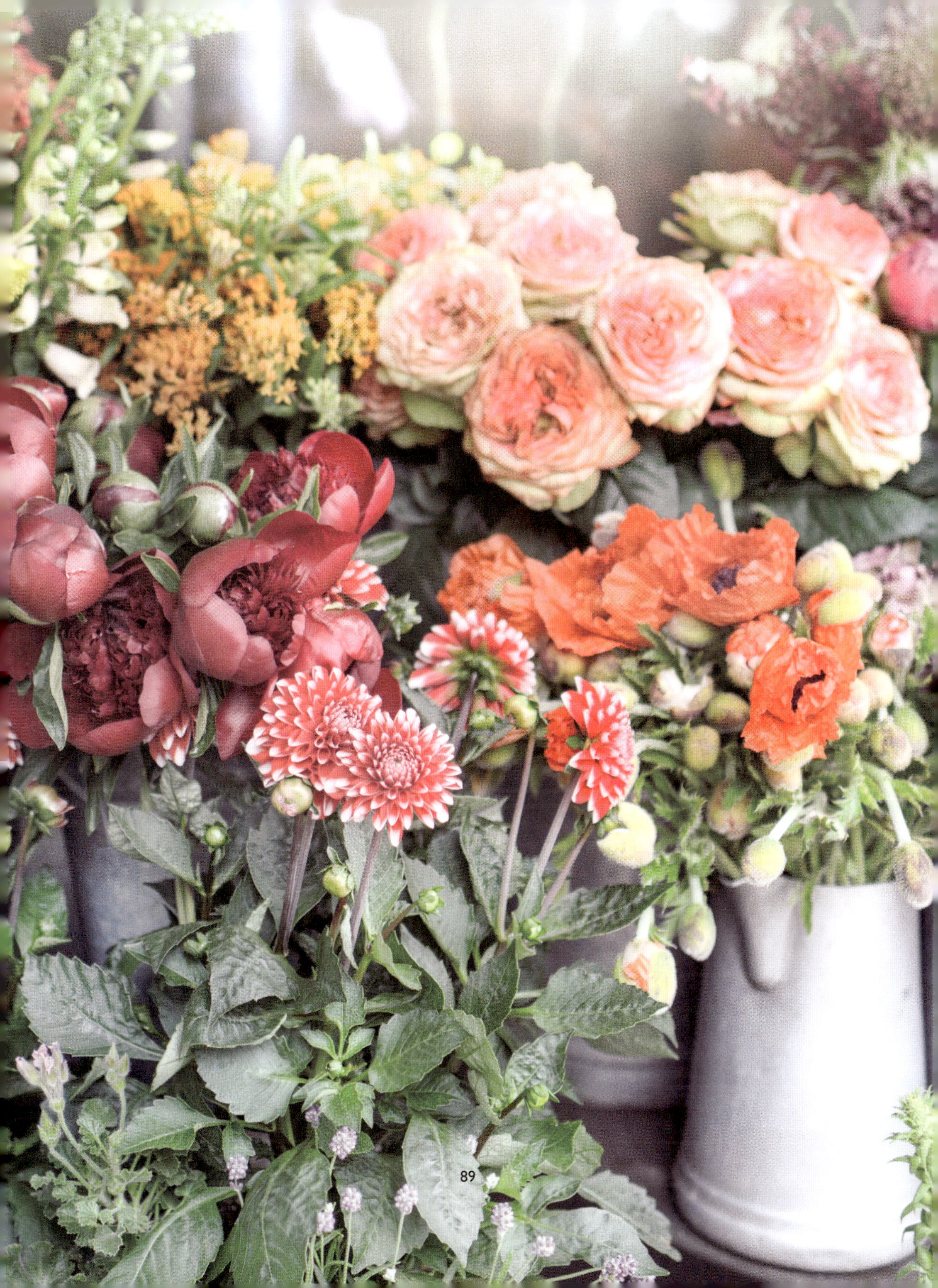

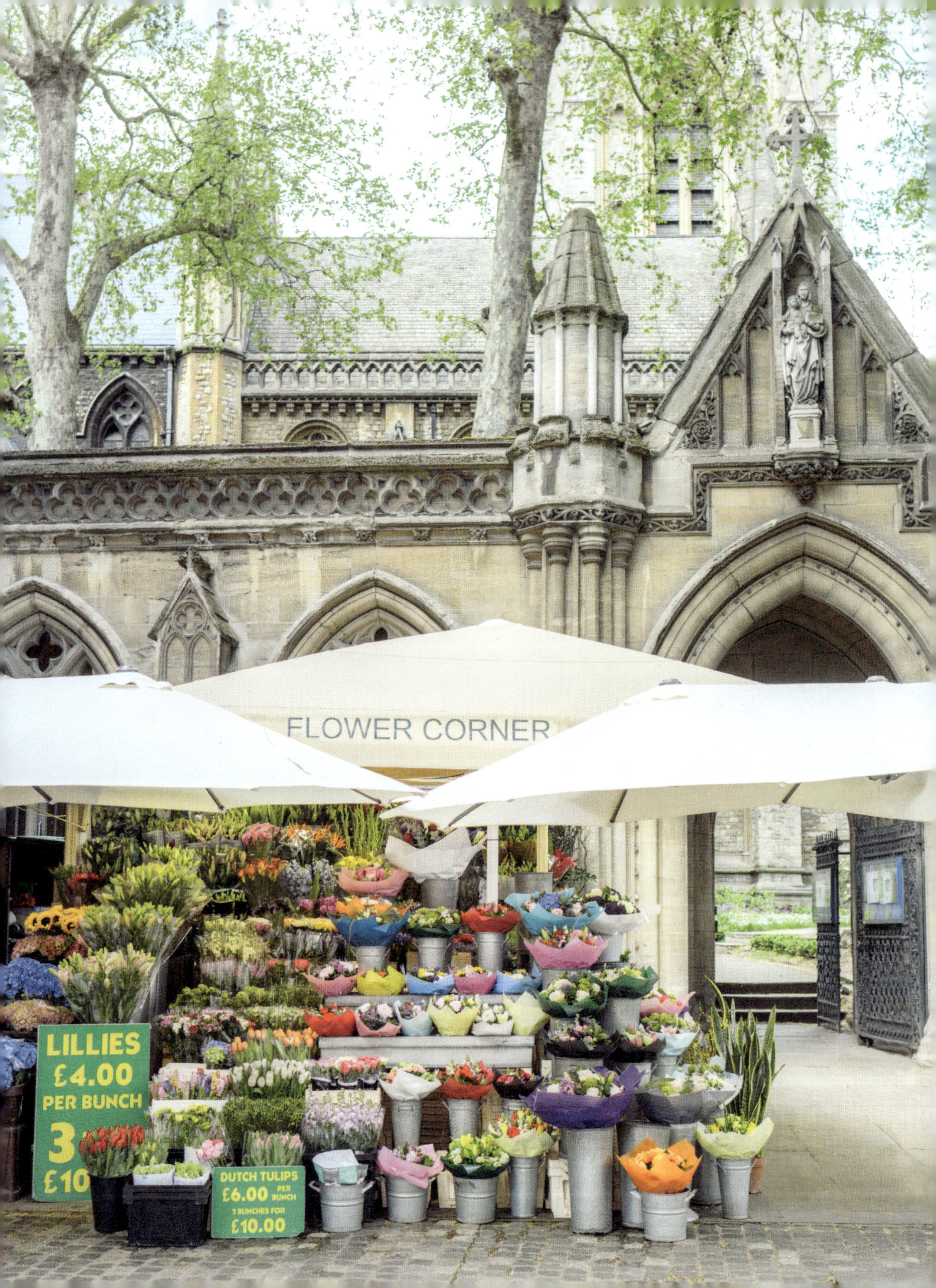

FLOWER CORNER
LILLIES
£4.00
PER BUNCH
3
£10
DUTCH TULIPS
£6.00
PER BUNCH
2 BUNCHES FOR
£10.00

Throughout London, hundreds of open-air flower stands and markets infuse the urban landscape with rejuvenating bursts of color and scent, like floral apothecaries dispensing perfumed and petaled concoctions of well-being and cheer. Flowers are nature's tonic, and these purveyors of beauty create visual elixirs on the spot, mingling fragrance, texture, and hue into bouquets, arrangements, and bundles for hurried Londoners in need of a floral restorative. No two formulas are the same— one might blend pale hyacinths with purple anemones, another, pink roses with cobalt hydrangeas, or another, flamboyant peonies with lilies. Located outside train stations, housed in vintage storefronts or local shops, flower sellers are a vital ingredient of the city's heritage.

Londoners with a small terrace or balcony create miniature gardens with the container plants available from many floral markets. Those fortunate enough to live in a charming mews house decorate the exteriors with window boxes of geraniums, potted jasmine, boxwood topiary, ferns, and small evergreens. Some dress up their lampposts with hanging baskets of sunset-hued calibrachoa, fluttery petunias, and begonias.

Stroll through Chelsea, admiring the stately brick mansions and white-columned town houses, and you'll come across two of the city's most photogenic flower sellers. The Flower Stand, at Old Church Street and Fulham Road, is a Chelsea landmark, known for more than twenty-five years for vibrant, traffic-stopping displays that cascade out onto the pavement like a rainbow waterfall. Travel a bit farther eastward on Fulham Road and you'll find Petals at Bibendum in the historic Michelin House. The building's decorative stained glass and teal art deco tile complement the luscious flowers arrayed in tin buckets reaching out to the street. Among the bountiful offerings are tissue-wrapped bouquets, flowering branches, viburnum, foliage, columbine, narcissus, orchids, snapdragons, iris, and lisianthus in season.

Another favorite, Kensington Flower Corner, located next to the sheltering trees at the intersection of Kensington High Street and Kensington Church Street, sells cut stems of everything from sunflowers to cerulean-blue hydrangeas and creates eye-catching bouquets, which are wrapped in multicolored tissue paper. And at the Embankment tube station, the Pink Pansy flower stall is a London institution that has provided fresh seasonal flowers since 1946.

A visit to the Columbia Road Flower Market in Bethnal Green is a cherished Sunday tradition. Londoners and visitors alike flock to the lively atmosphere, reasonable prices, and entertaining vendors. Approaching the street, one is struck by the redolent scents of that particular season's blooms—hyacinth and narcissus in spring, roses and peonies in June, lilies and lavender in midsummer. Fat bunches of ranunculus and tulips in pastel and primary colors share the scene with cheery potted pansies, fluffy hydrangeas, and prickly succulents. Jovial sellers chant the day's floral and plant bargains, most only a "fiver." Flanked by art galleries, bakeries, vintage clothing stores, antiques shops, pubs, and cafes, the market provides a cornucopia of sensory delights.

Proudly selling flowers since 1670, the New Covent Garden Market is the city's premiere wholesale outlet and custodian of generations of flower knowledge, where tours can be scheduled for interested visitors. The market also sponsors British Flowers Week, which is held annually in June and celebrates the abundant variety of British-grown seasonal flowers and foliage through installations and design competitions.

Floral Angels, a charity whose patron is the Duchess of Cornwall, also makes its home at the market. The volunteer "angels" restyle donated floral arrangements from weddings, events, and florists into beautiful bouquets for delivery to hospitals and elder homes, where they brighten spirits and speed recovery through the positive energy and joy of flowers.

Ephemeral and fleeting, a bundle of cut blooms nonetheless has the enduring power to elevate an everyday experience to a memorable occasion. And London offers more opportunities to indulge in this pleasure than possibly any city in the world.

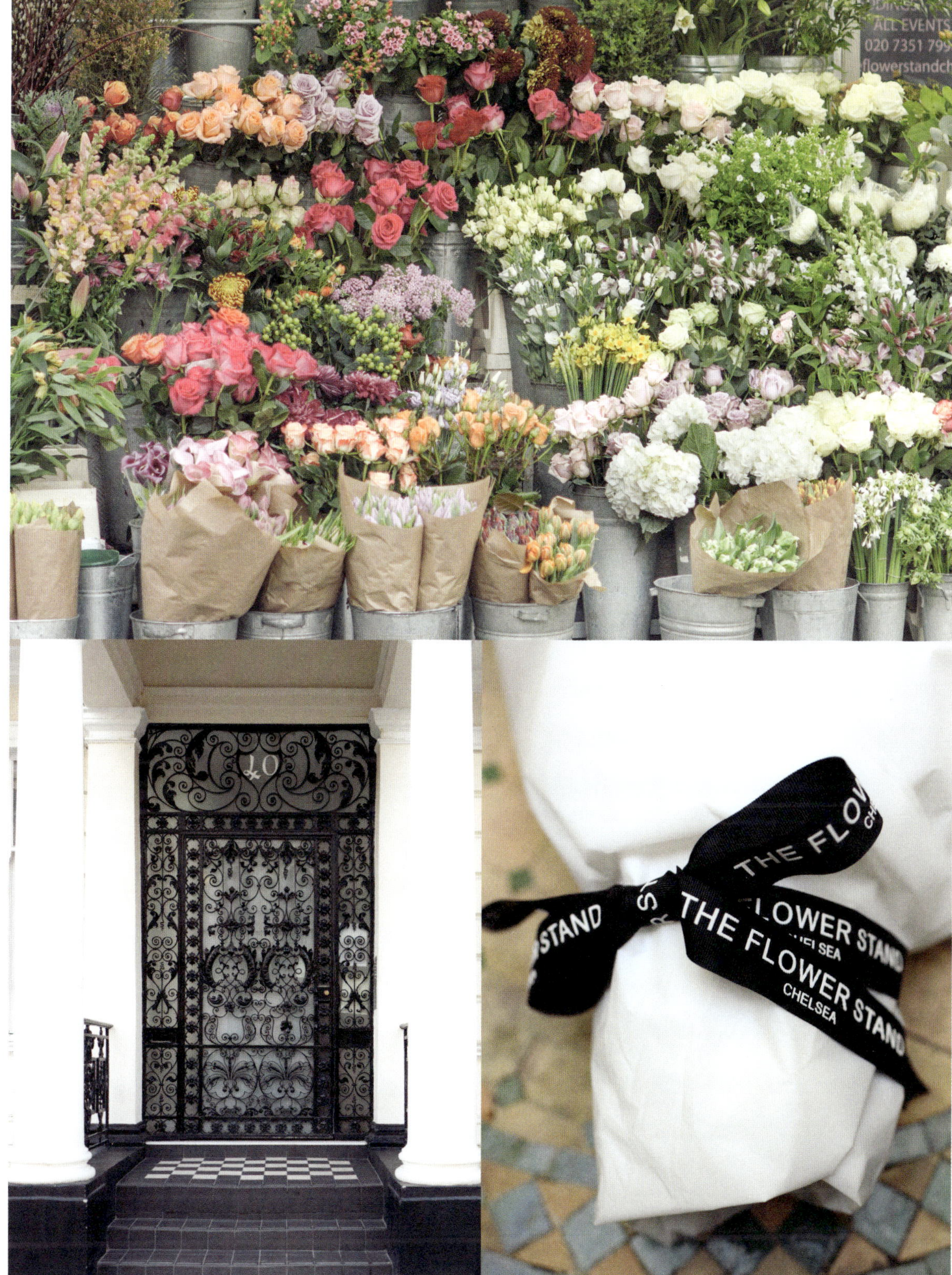
ALL EVENTS
020 7351 799
flowerstandch
THE FLOWER STAND
CHELSEA

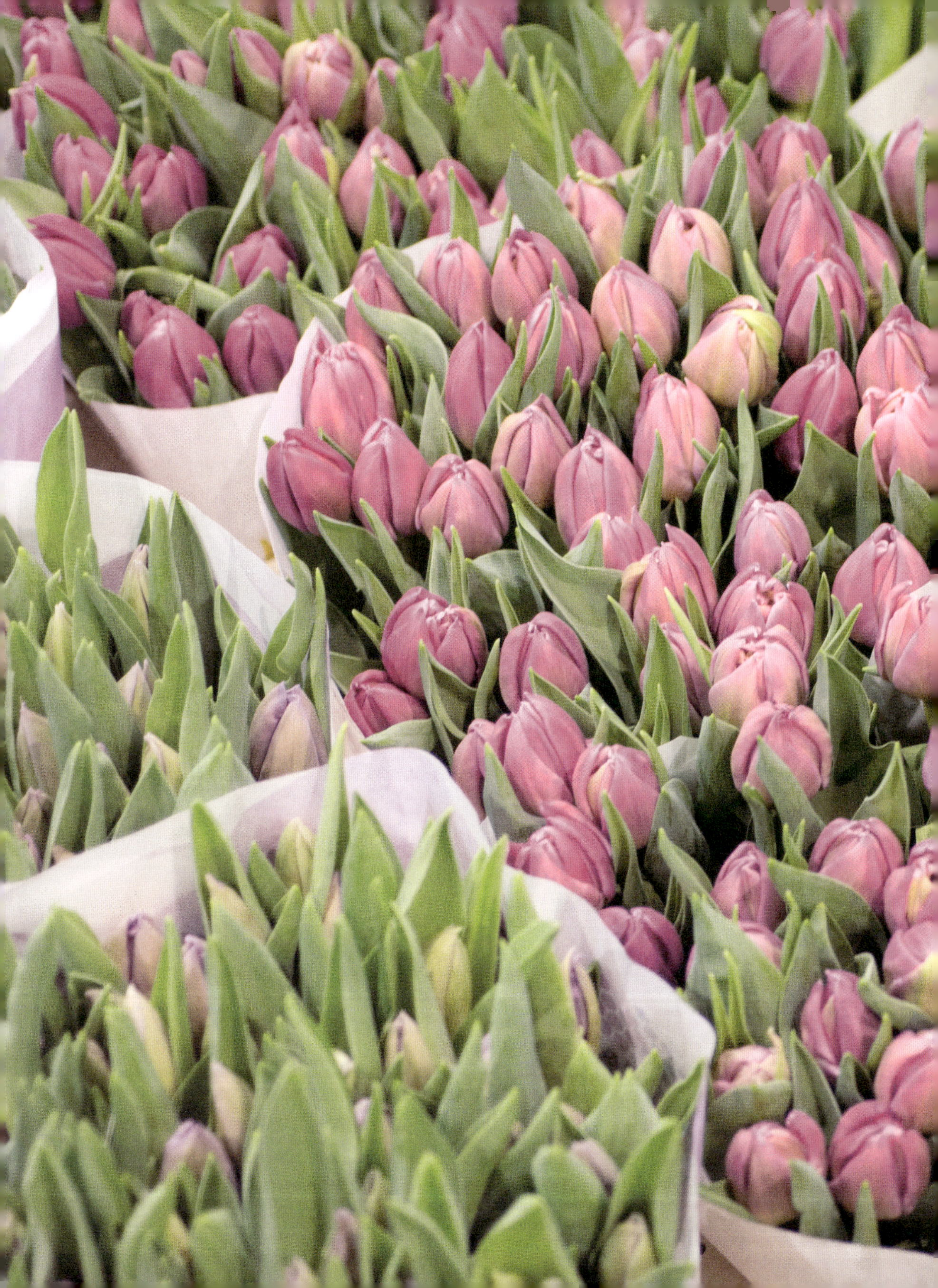

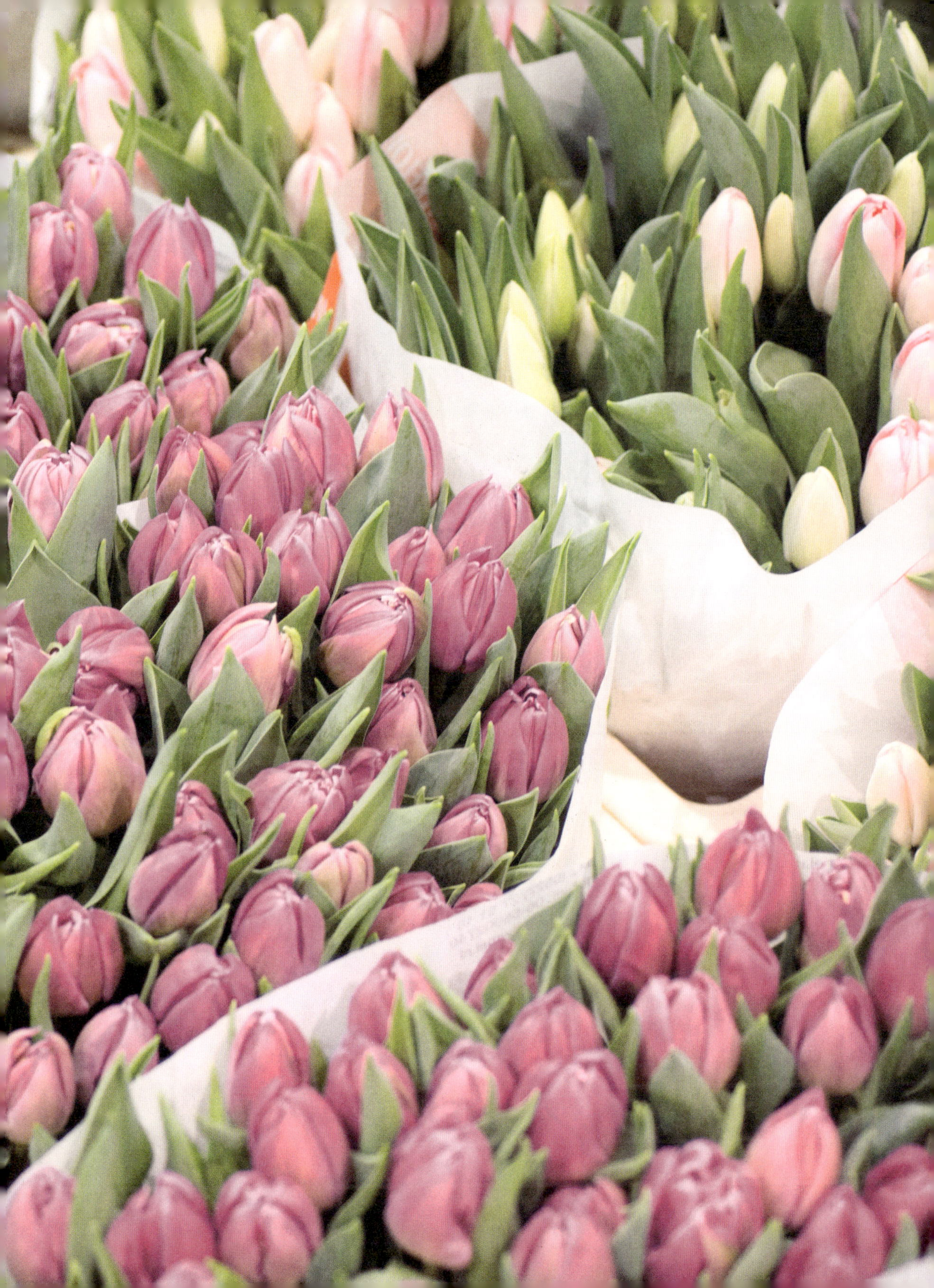

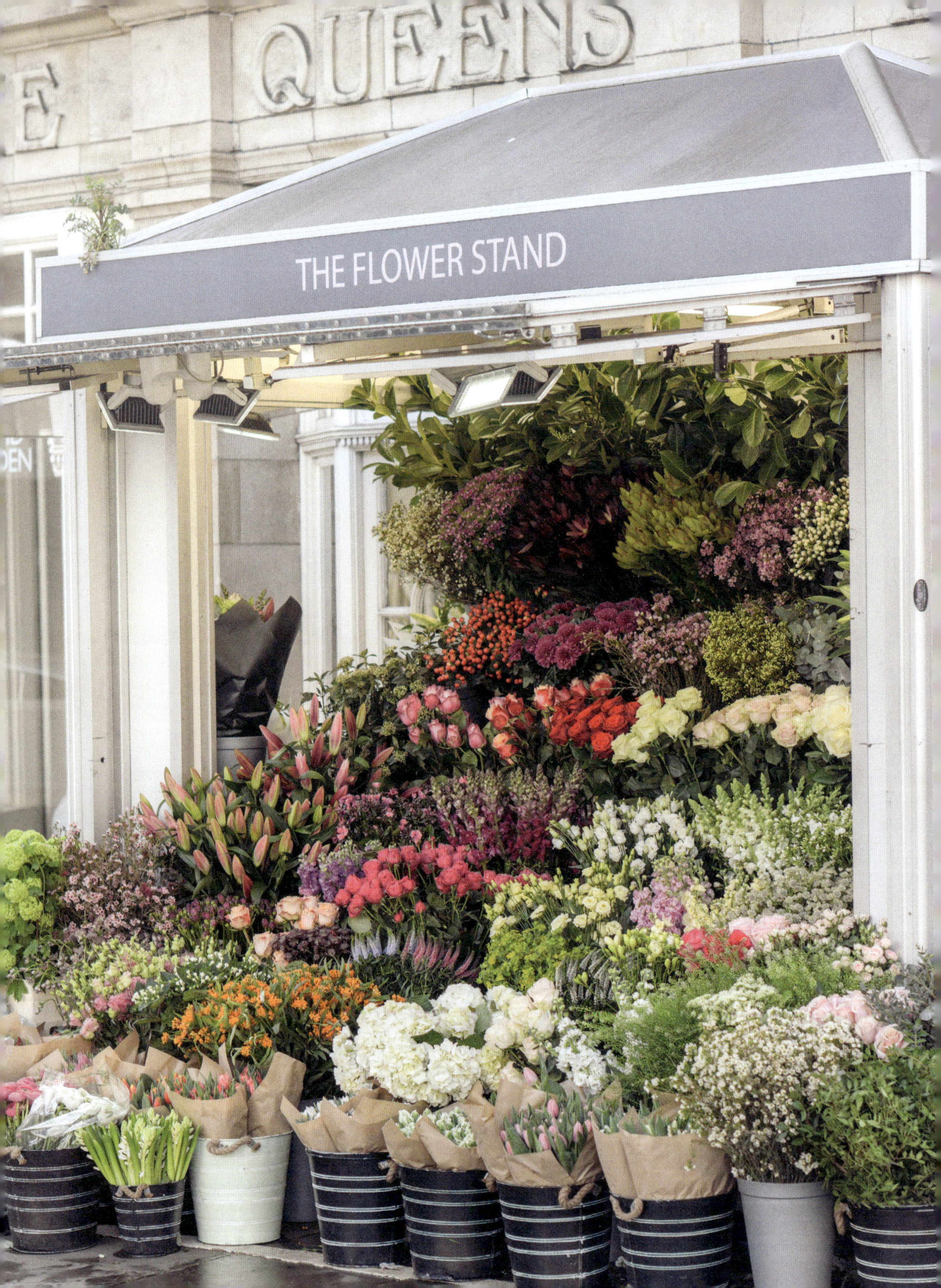
QUEENS
THE FLOWER STAND

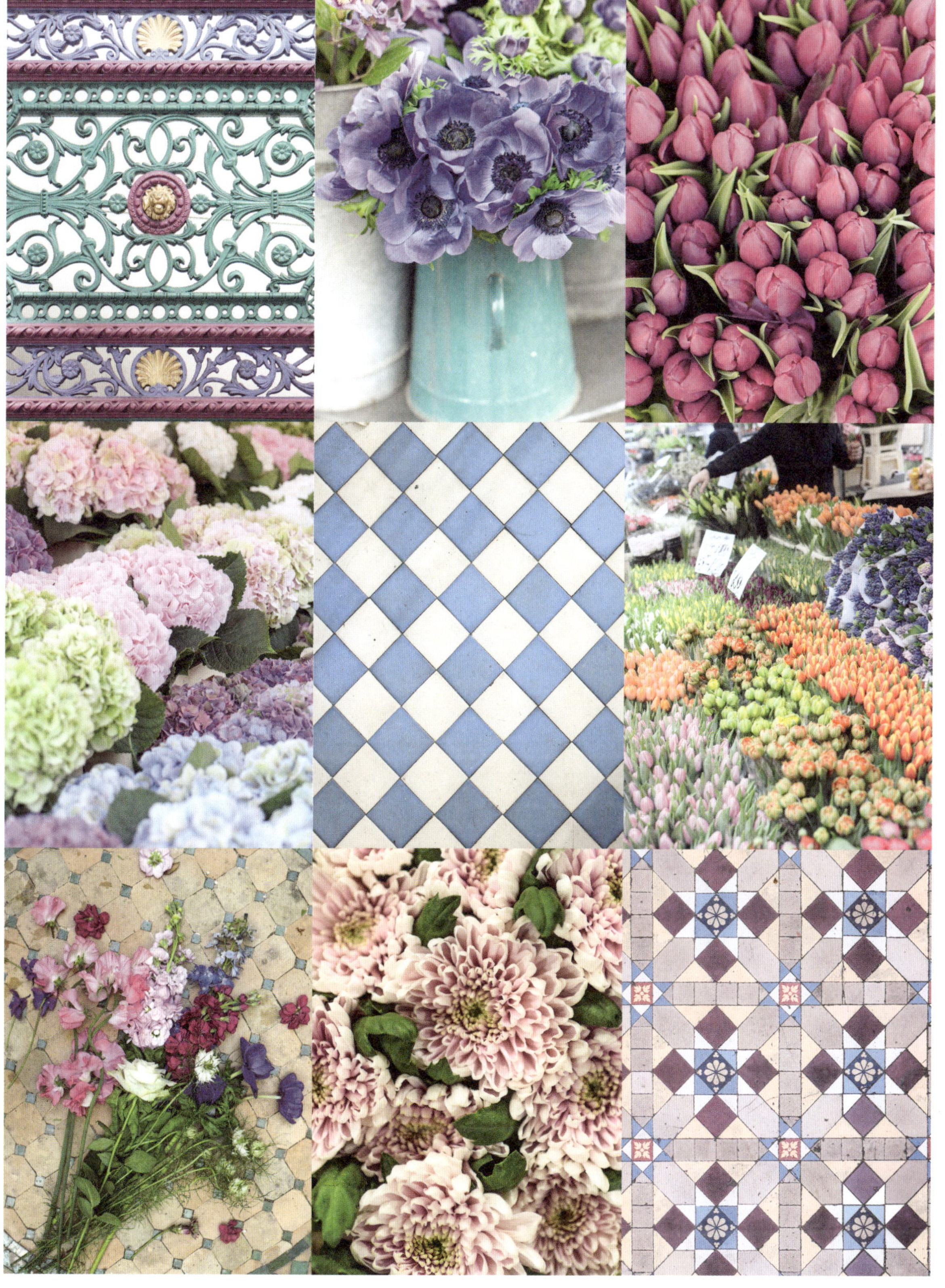

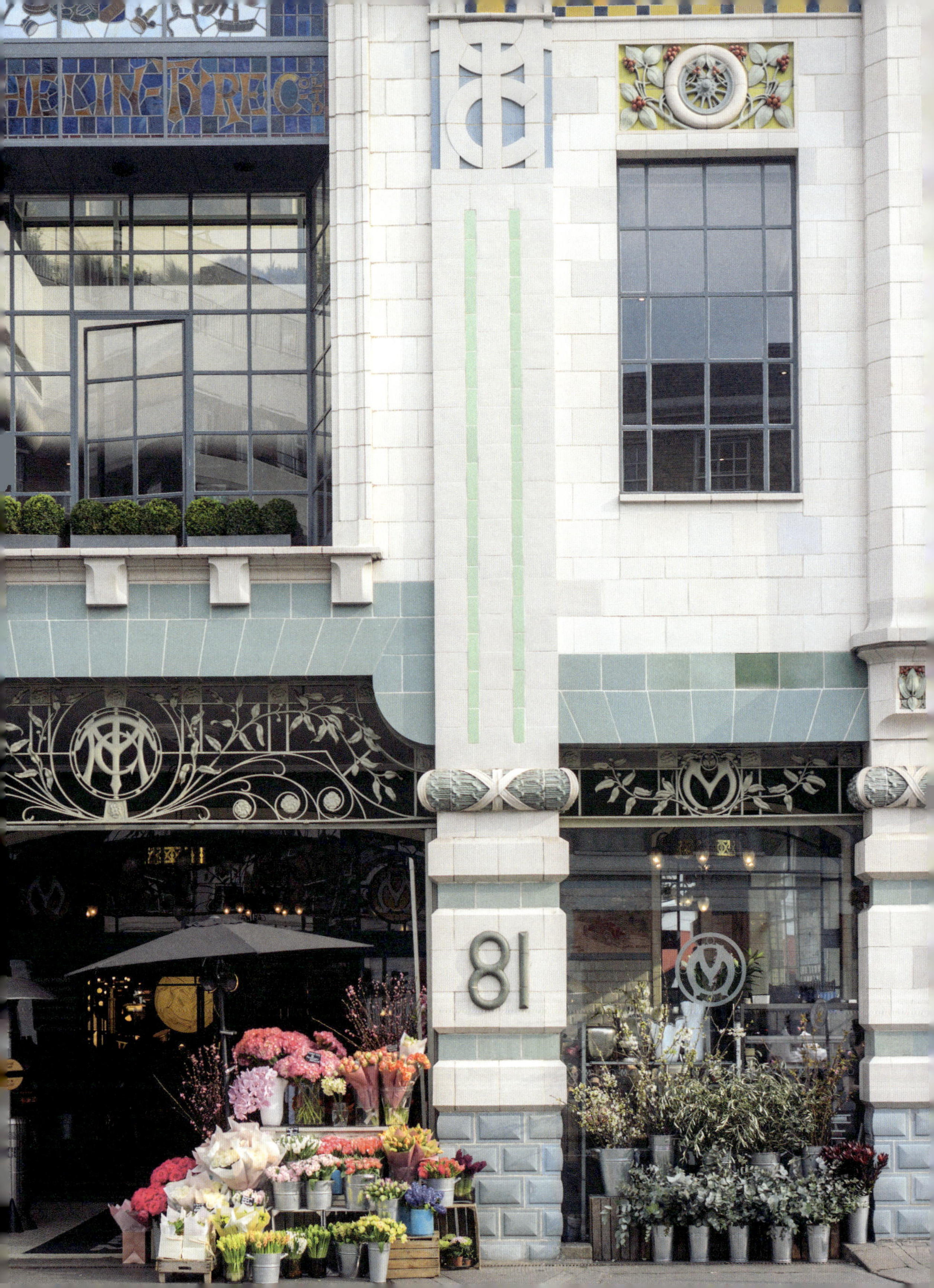

HELIN TYRE Cº
81

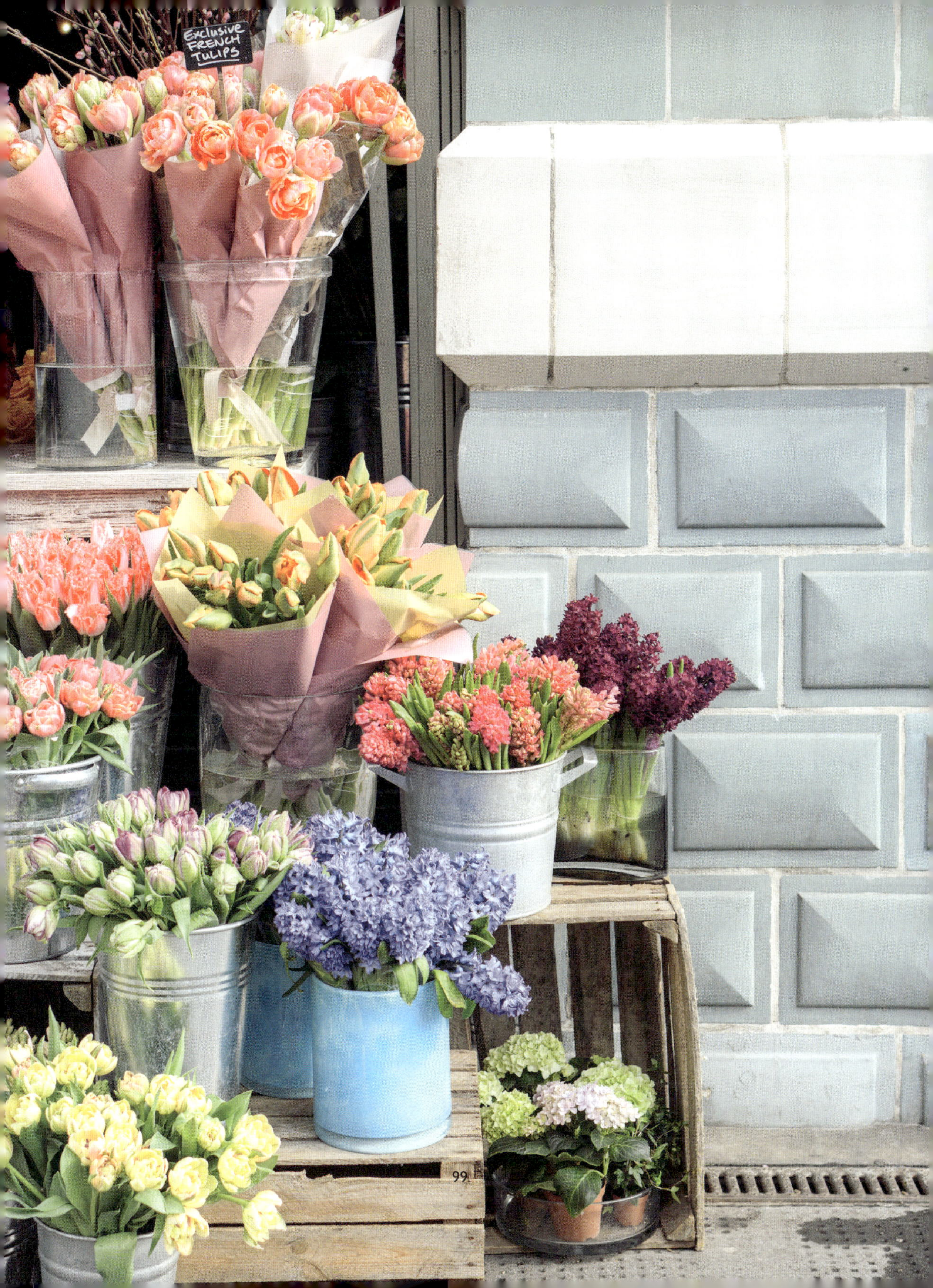
Exclusive
FRENCH
TULIPS

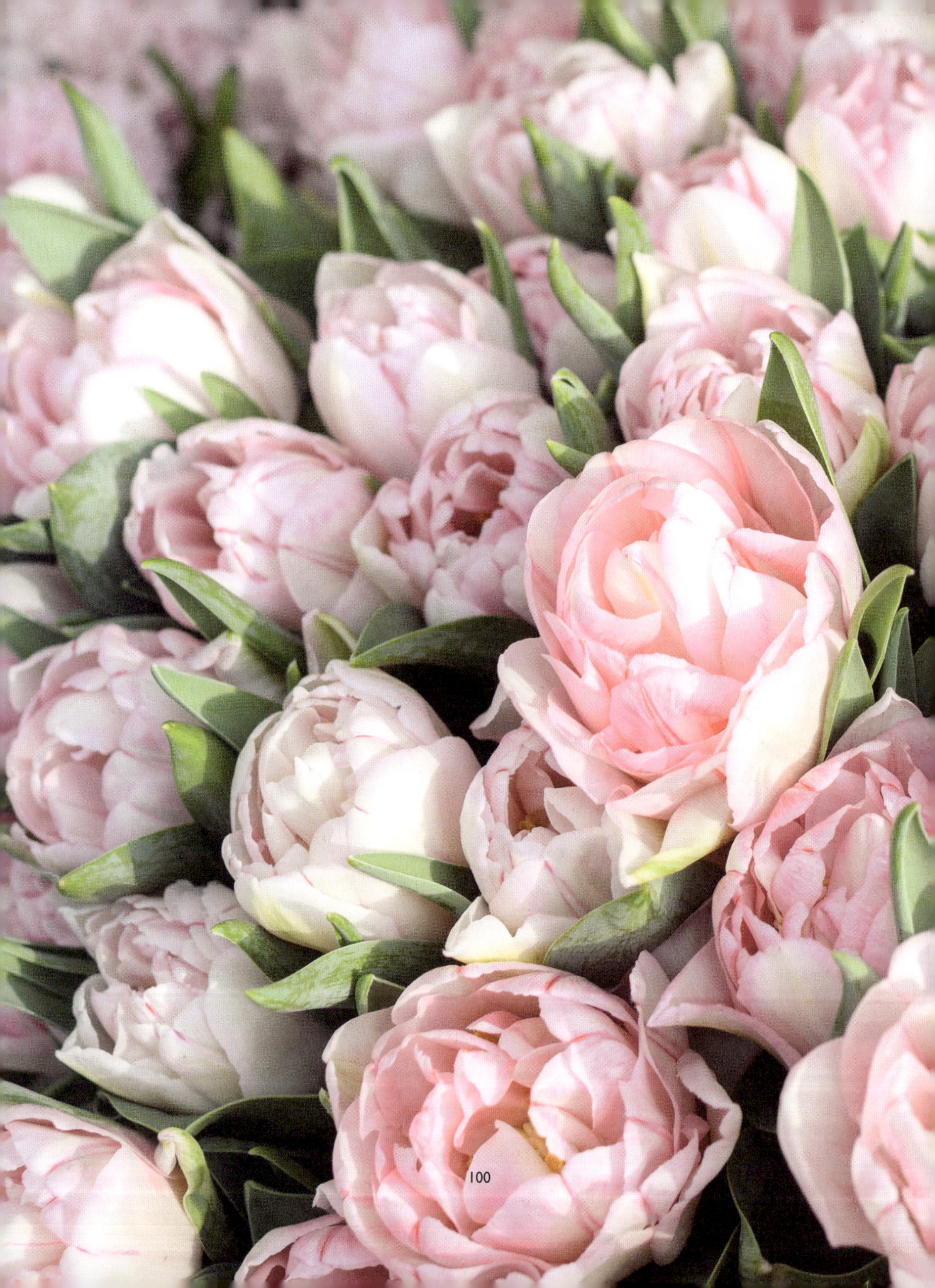

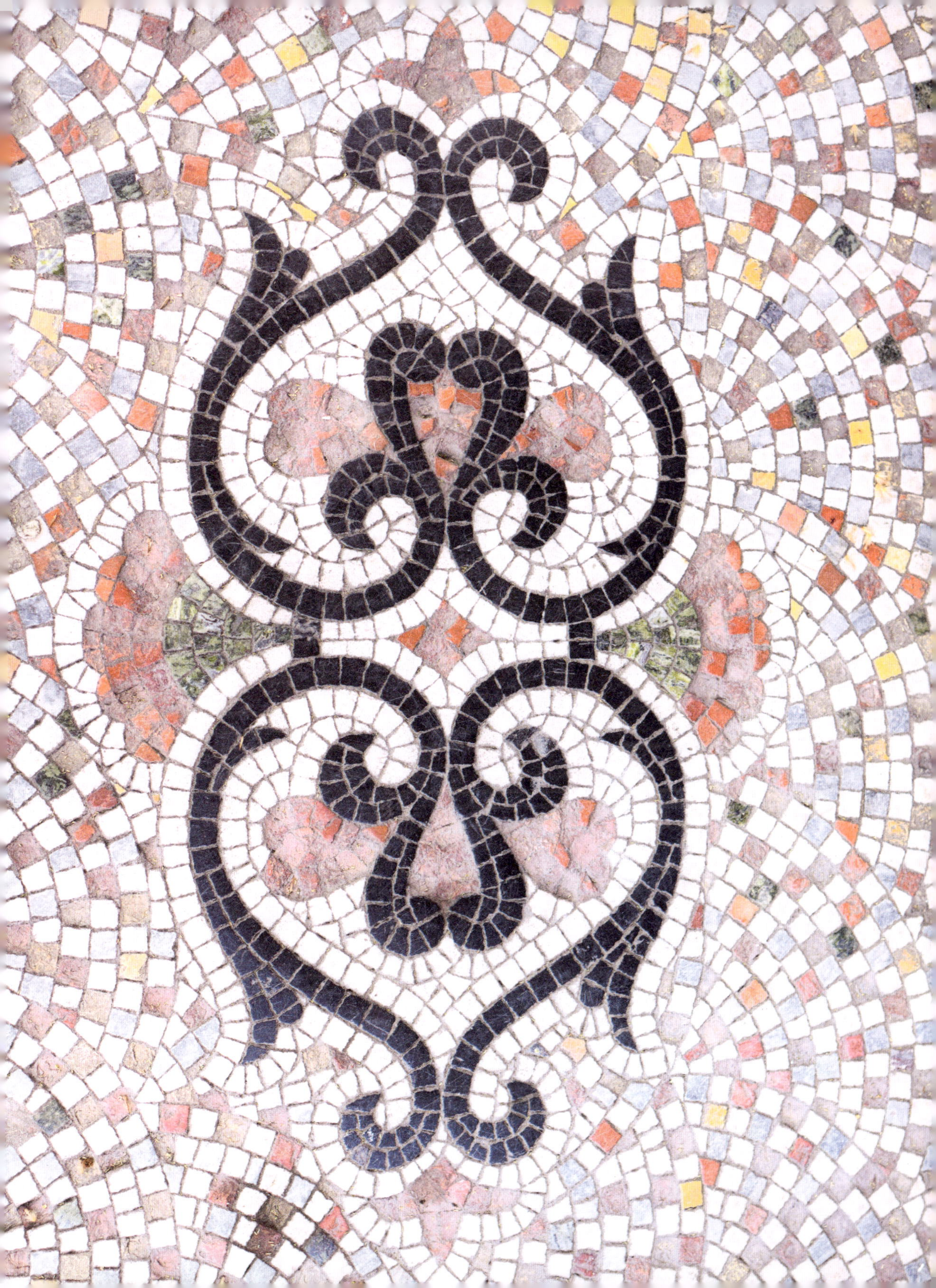

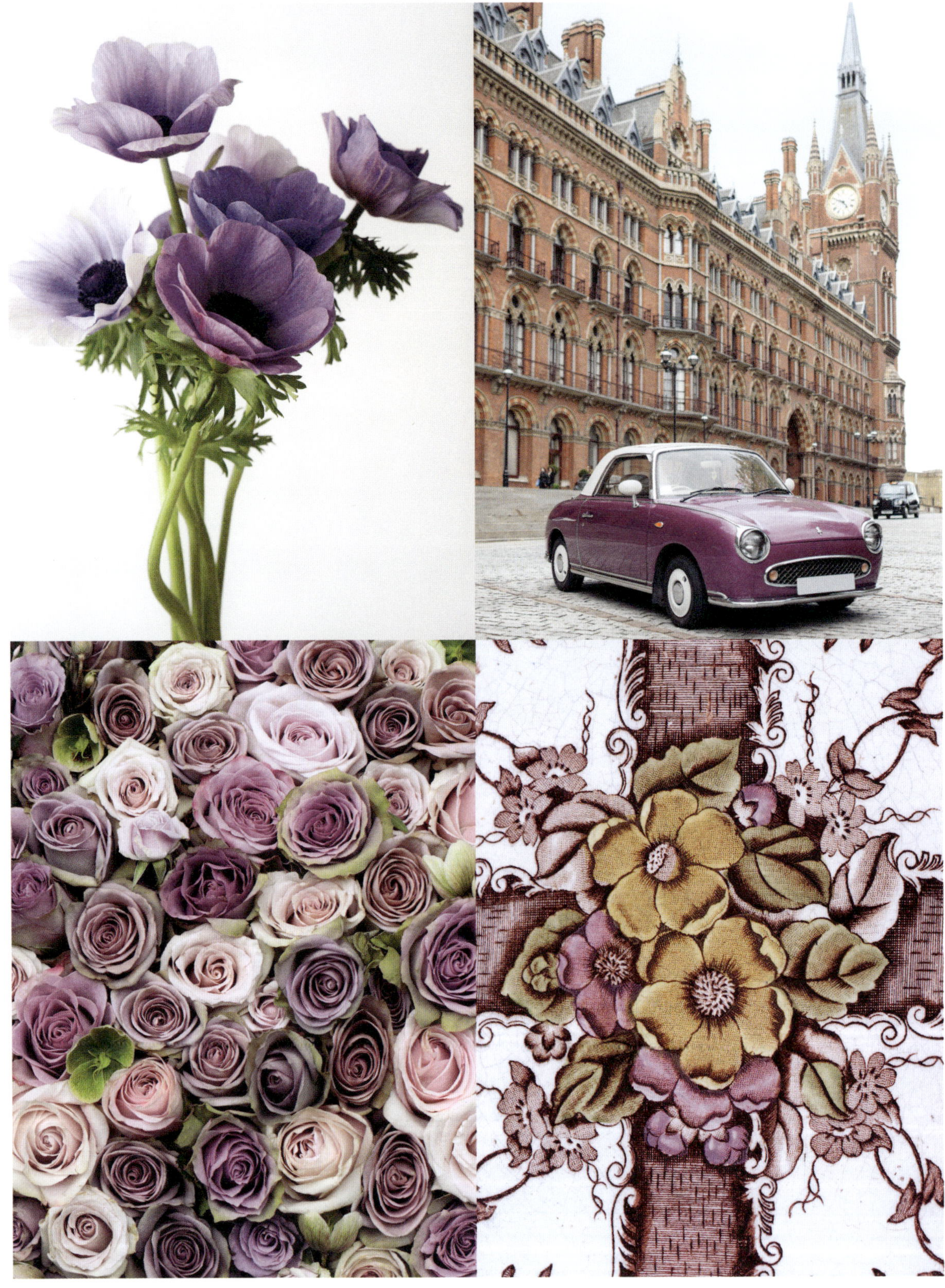

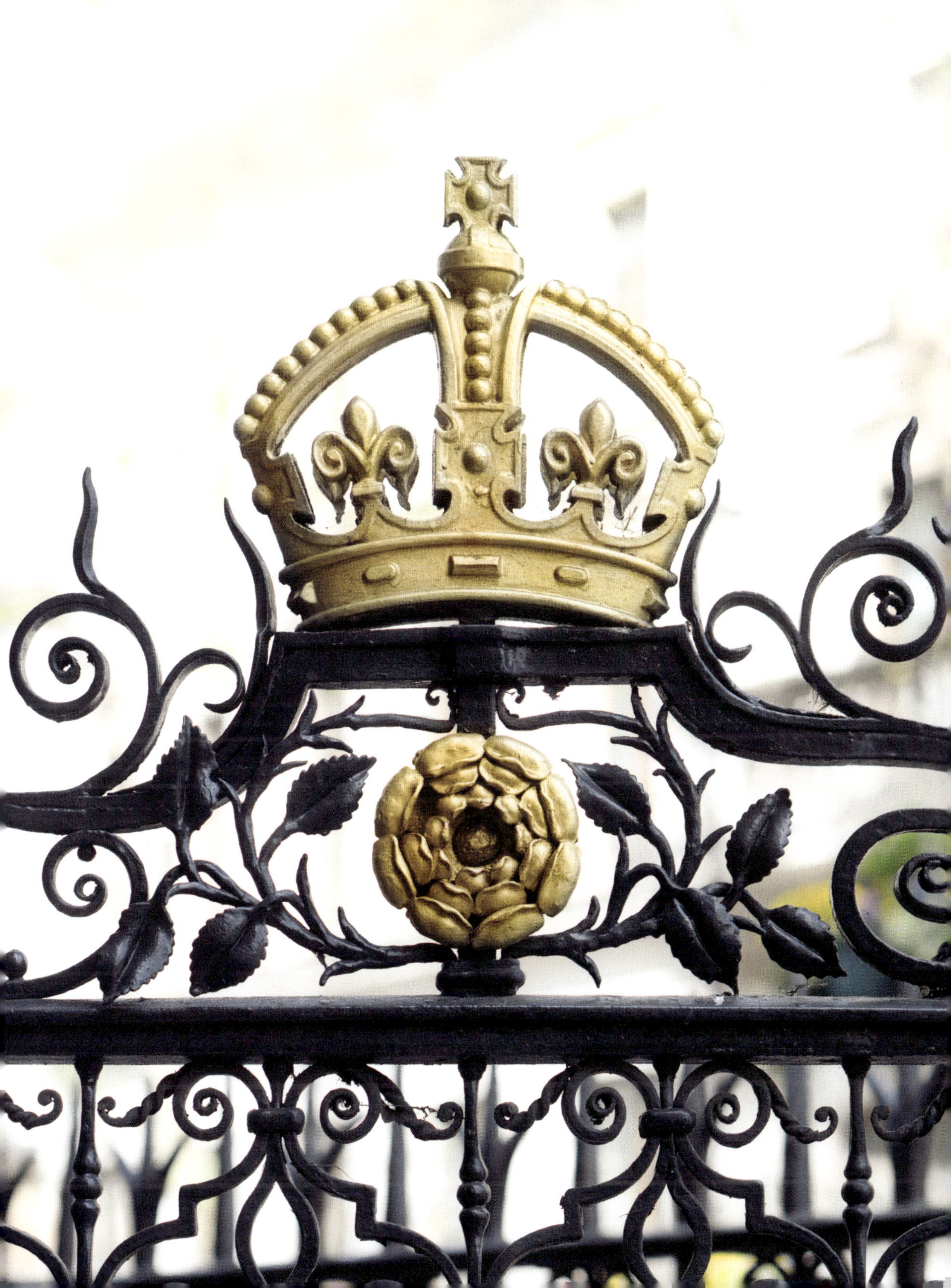

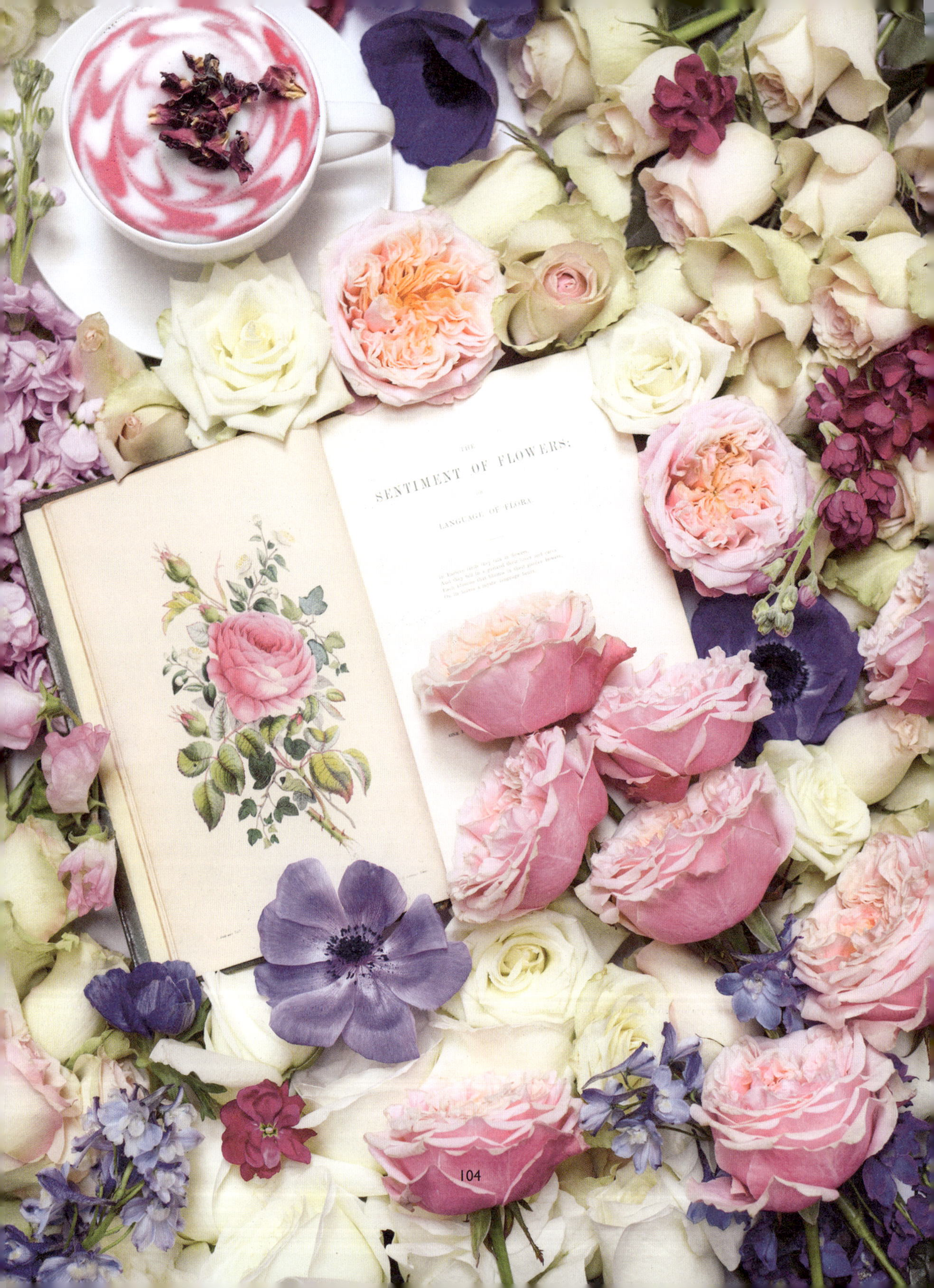
THE
SENTIMENT OF FLOWERS:
OR
LANGUAGE OF FLORA.

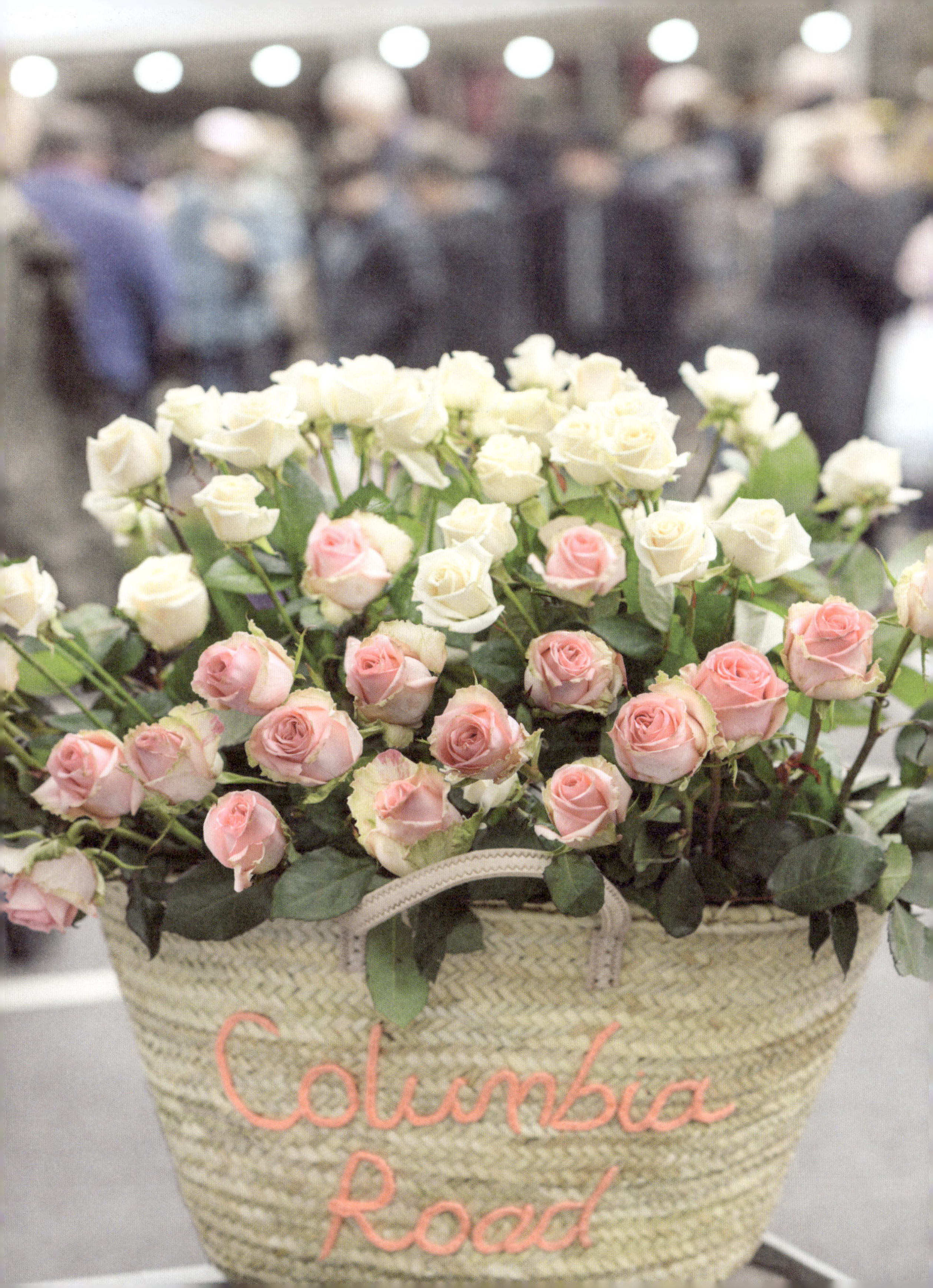

Columbia
Road

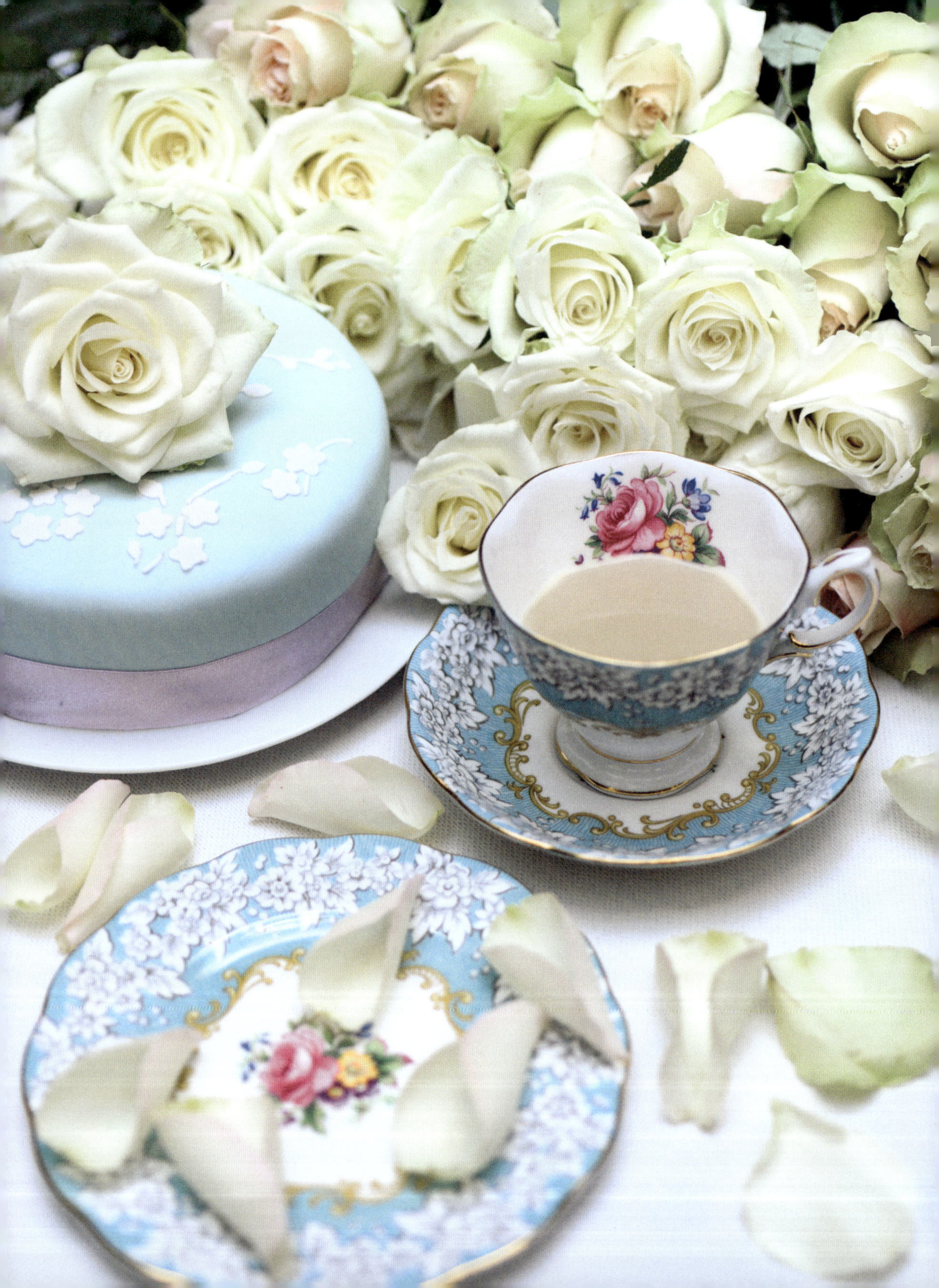

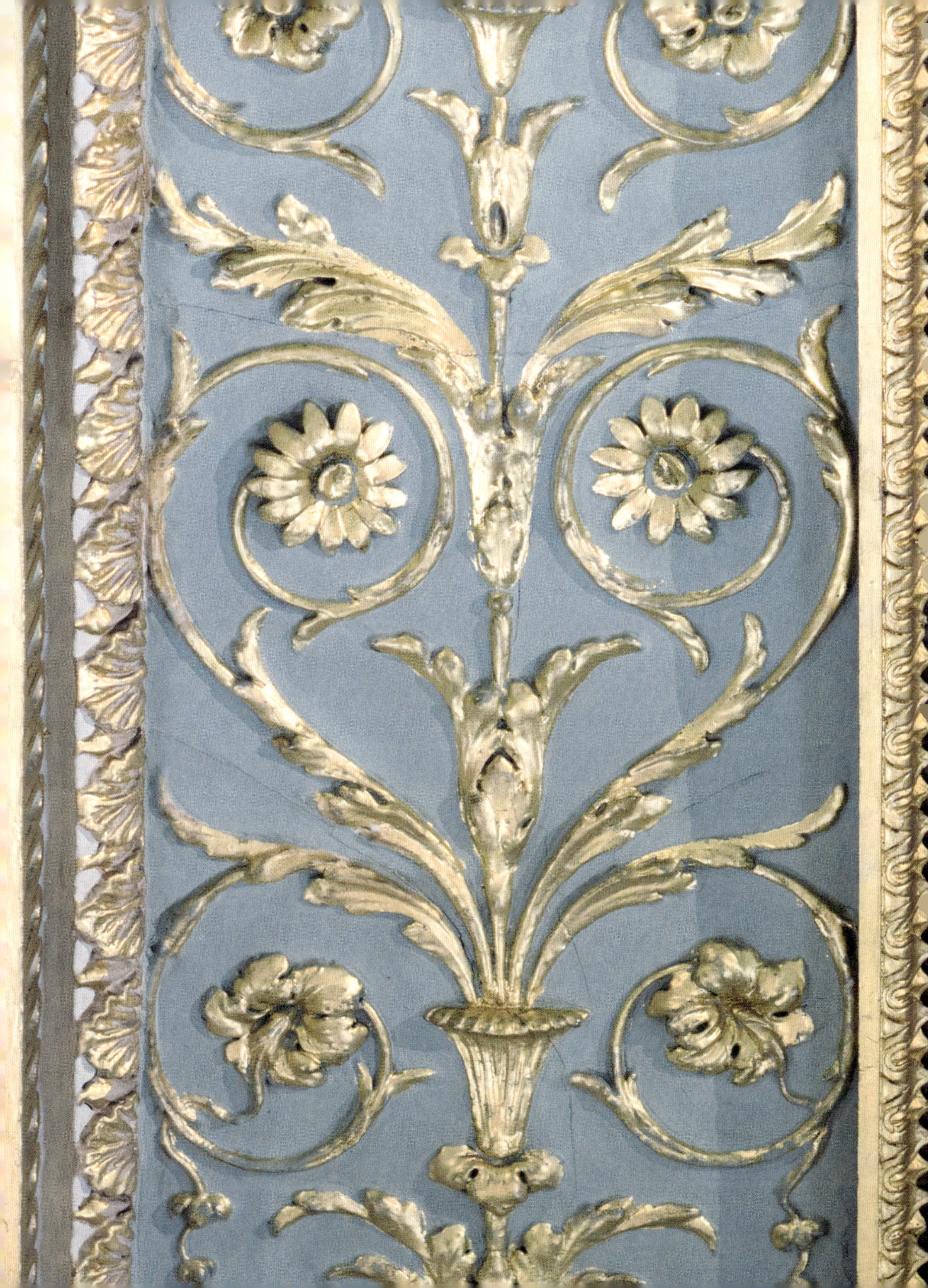

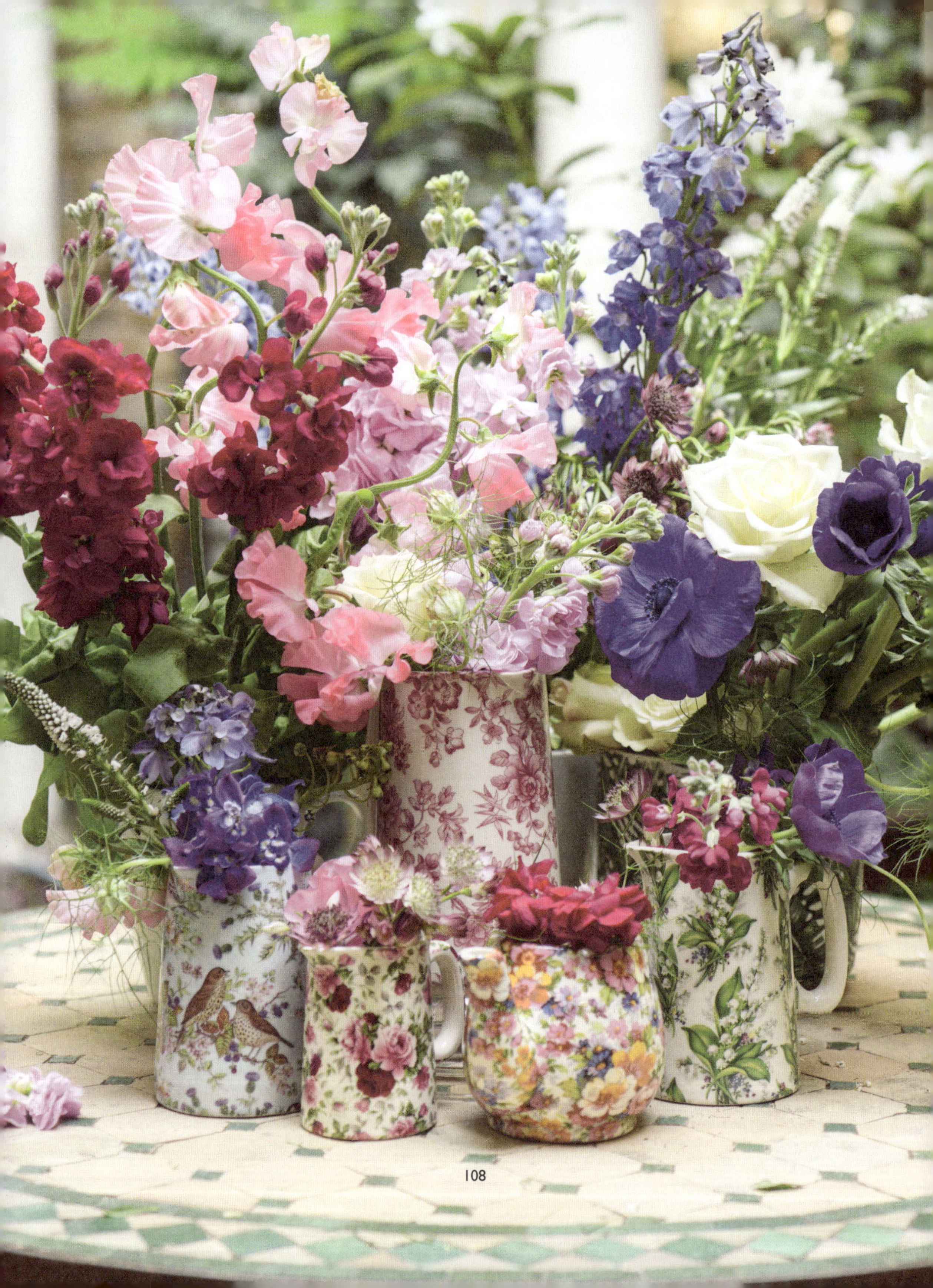

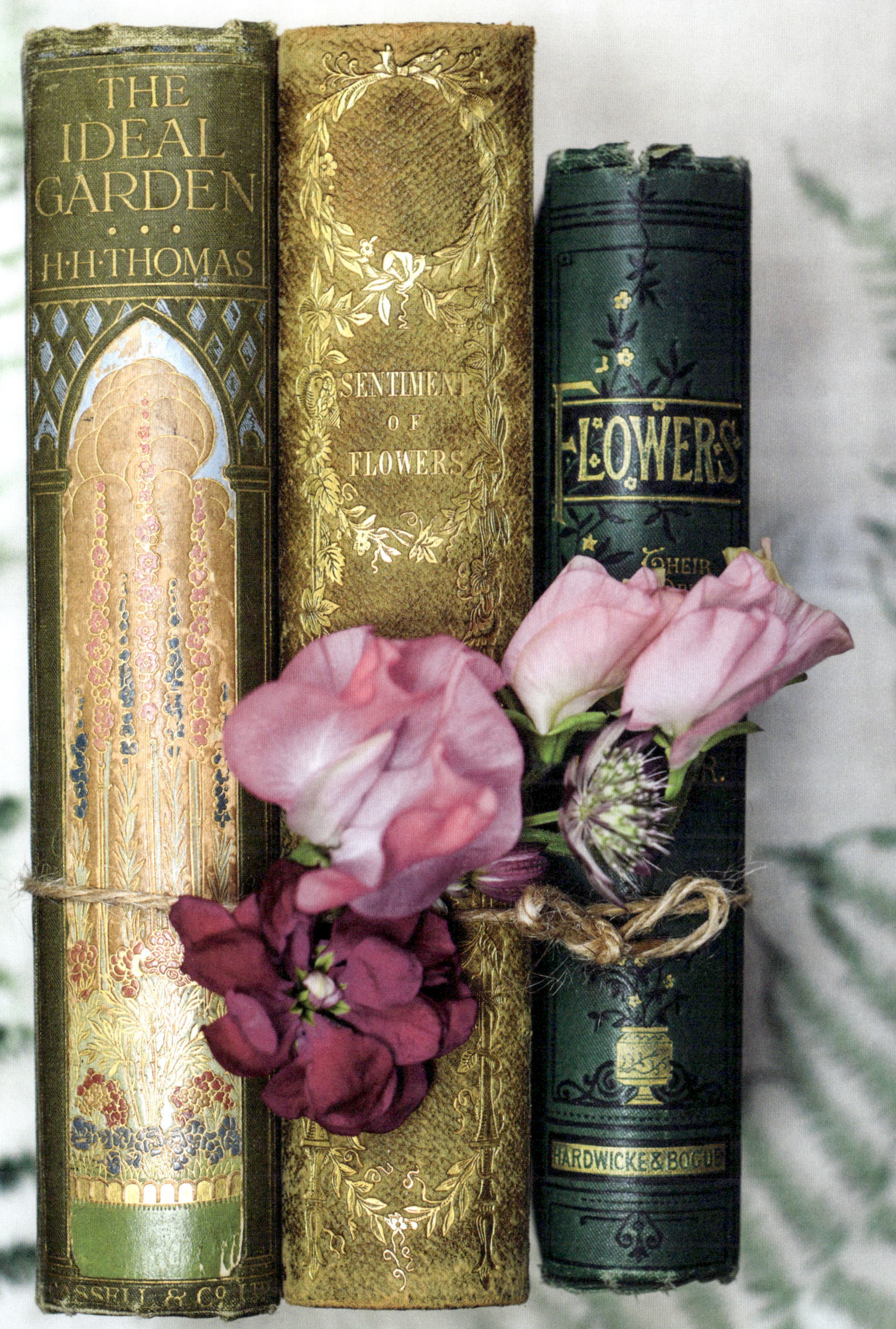

THE IDEAL GARDEN
H·H·THOMAS
SENTIMENT OF FLOWERS
FLOWERS
HARDWICKE & BOGUE

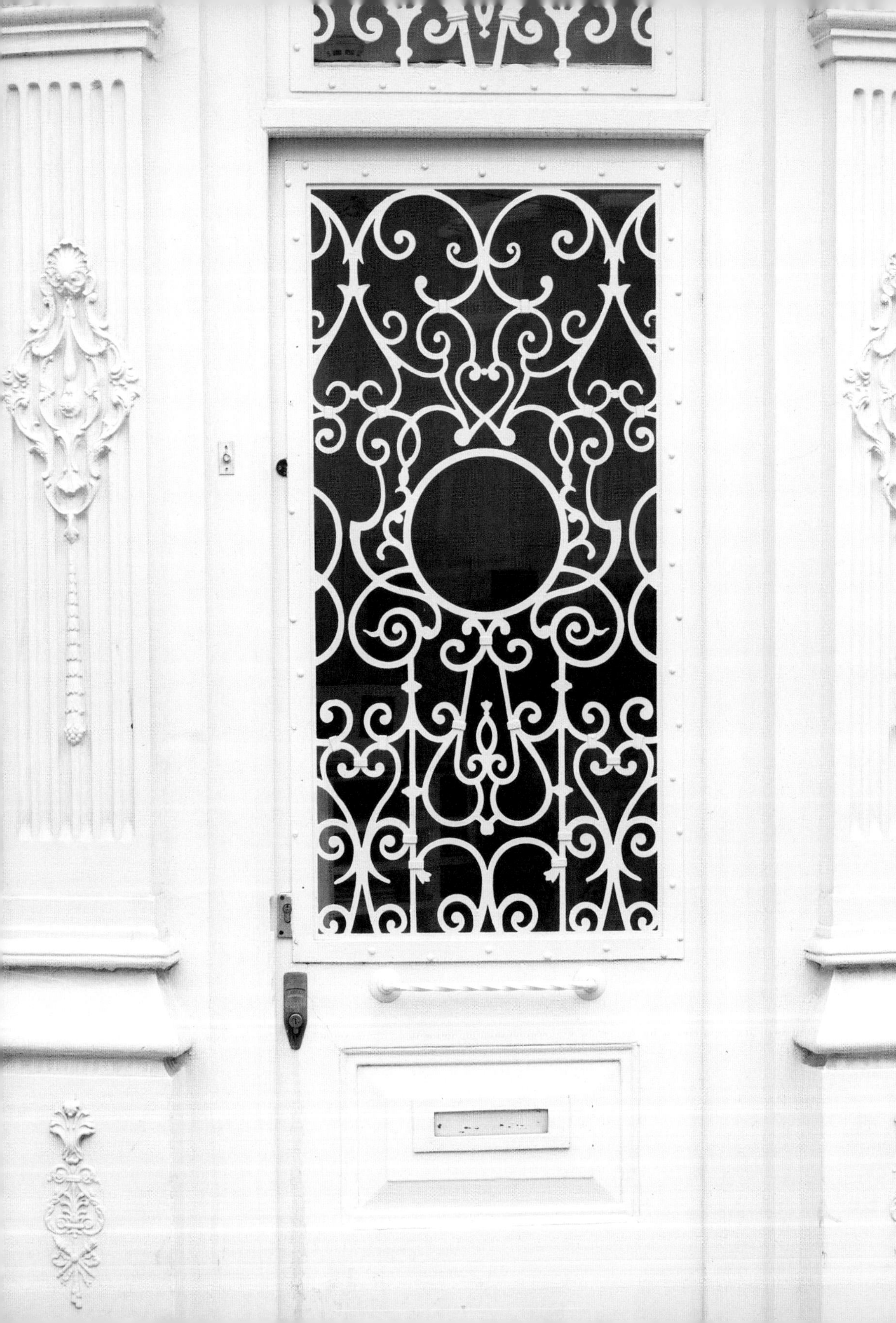

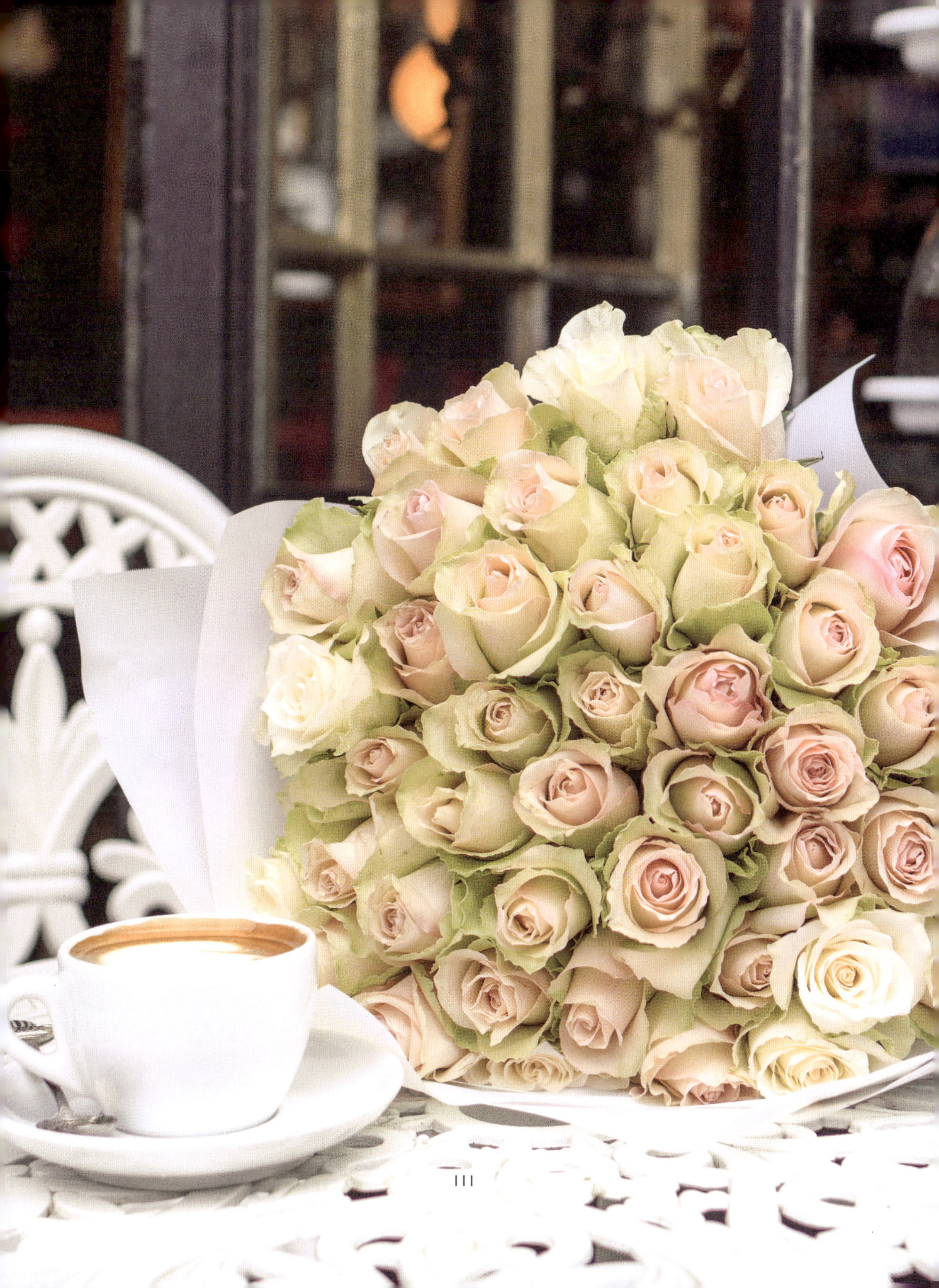

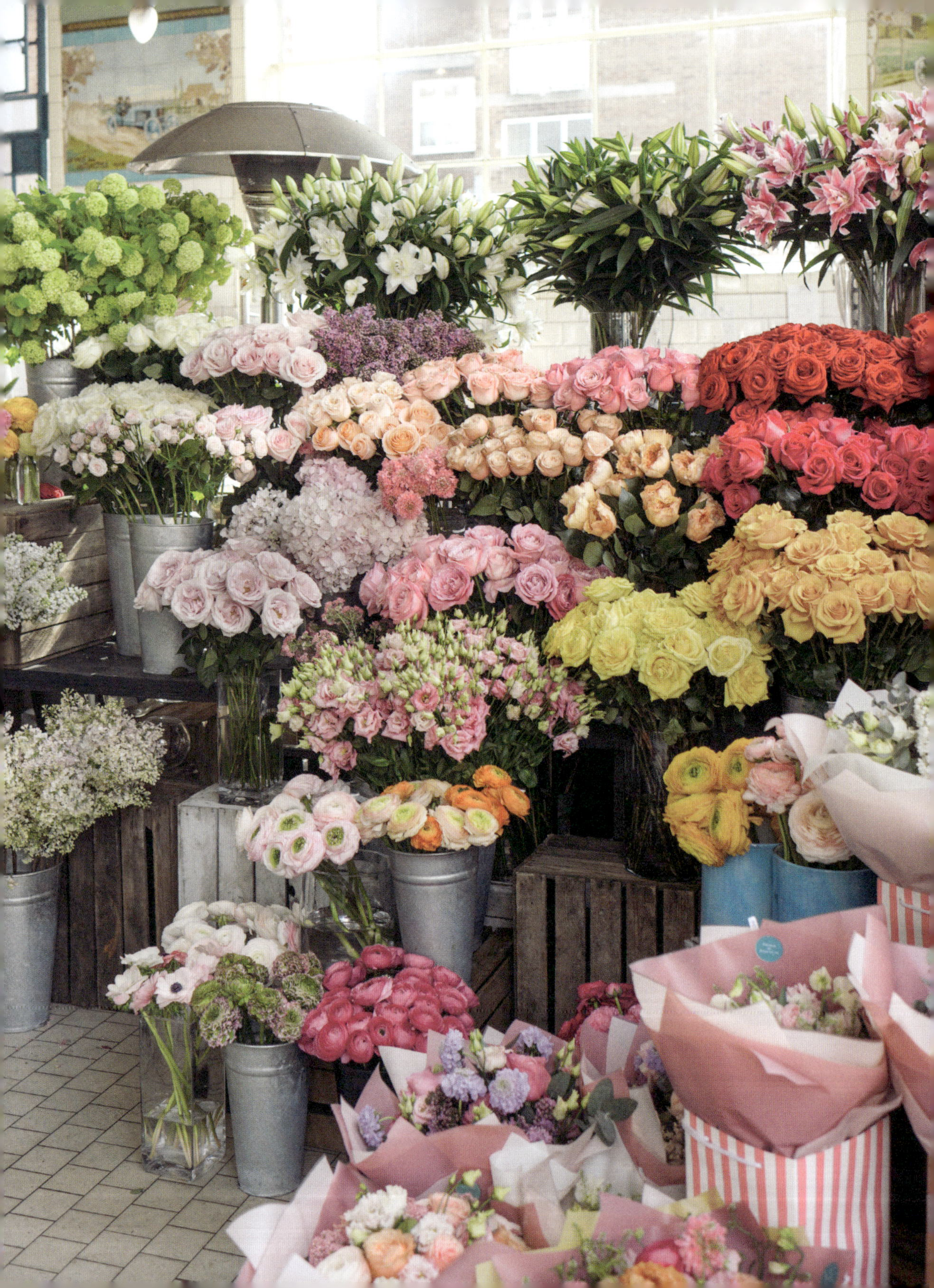

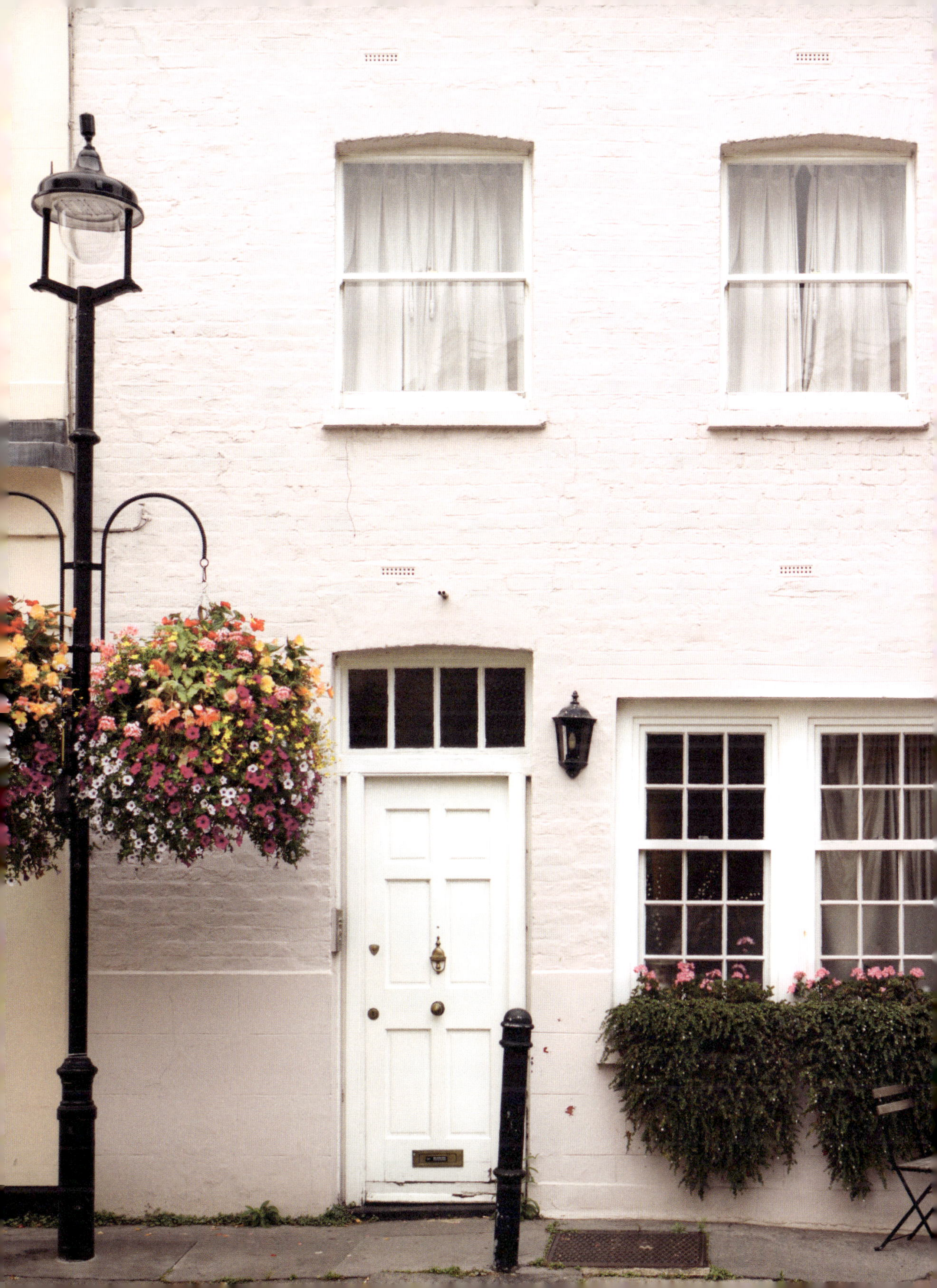

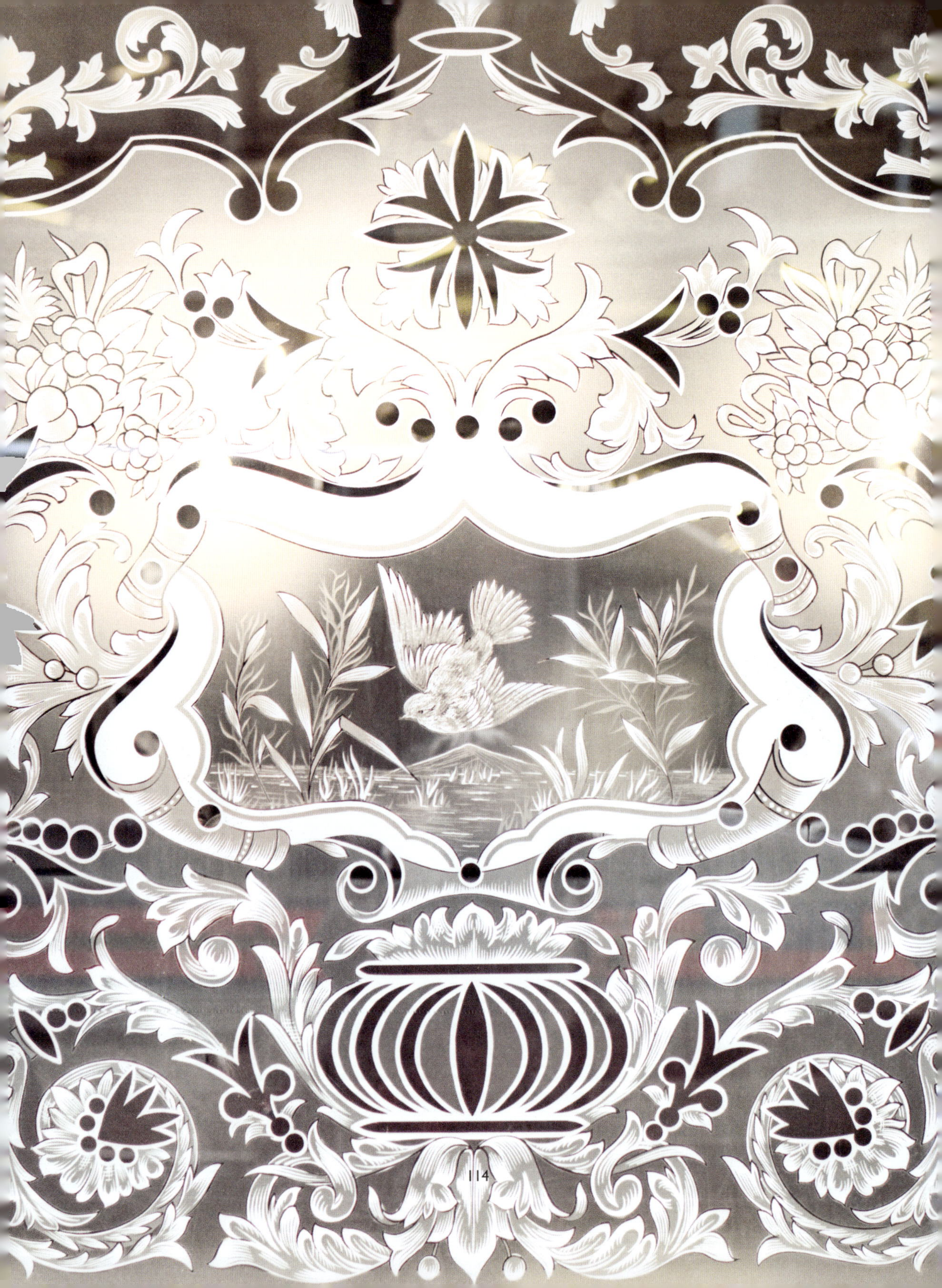

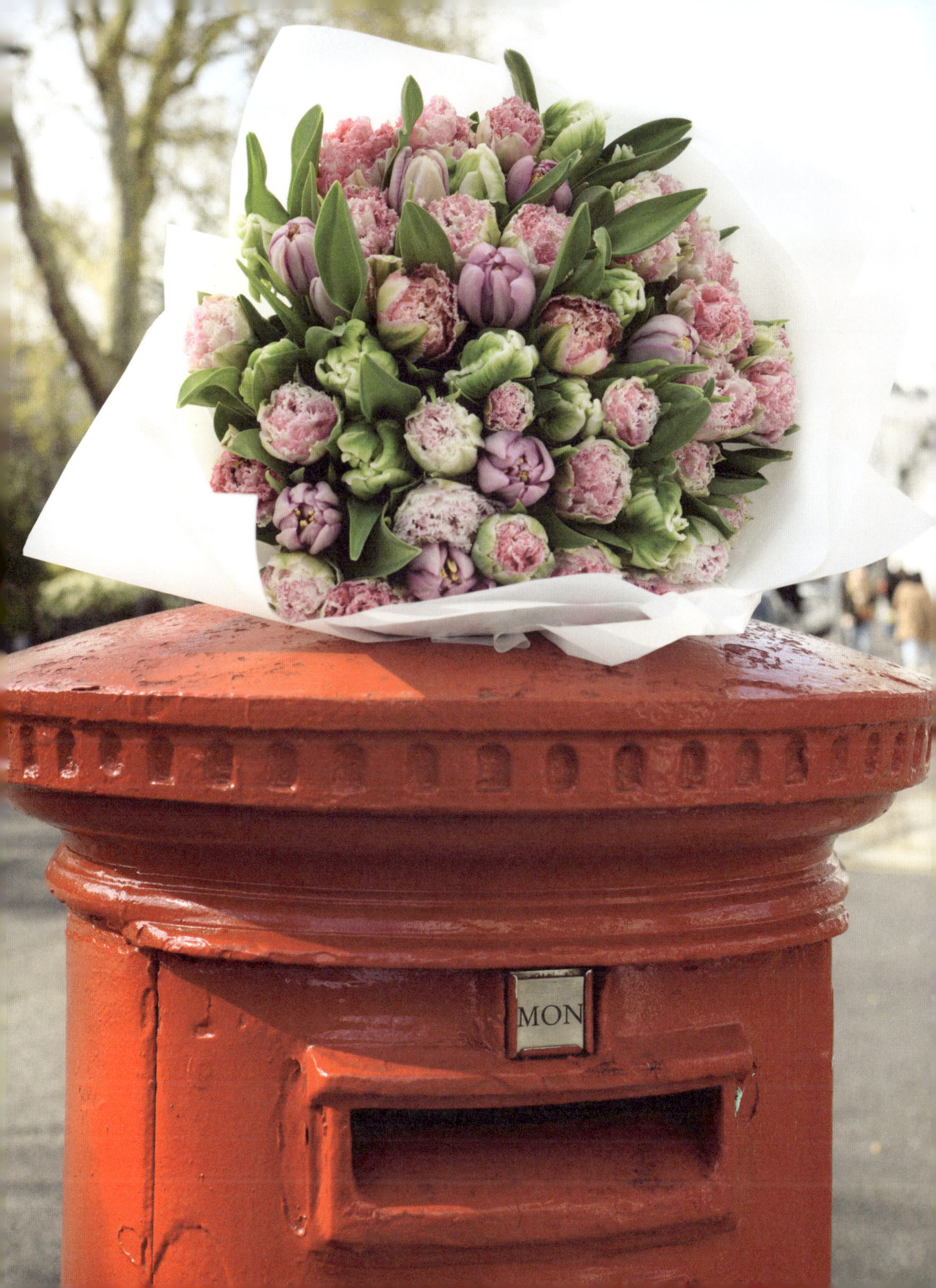
MON

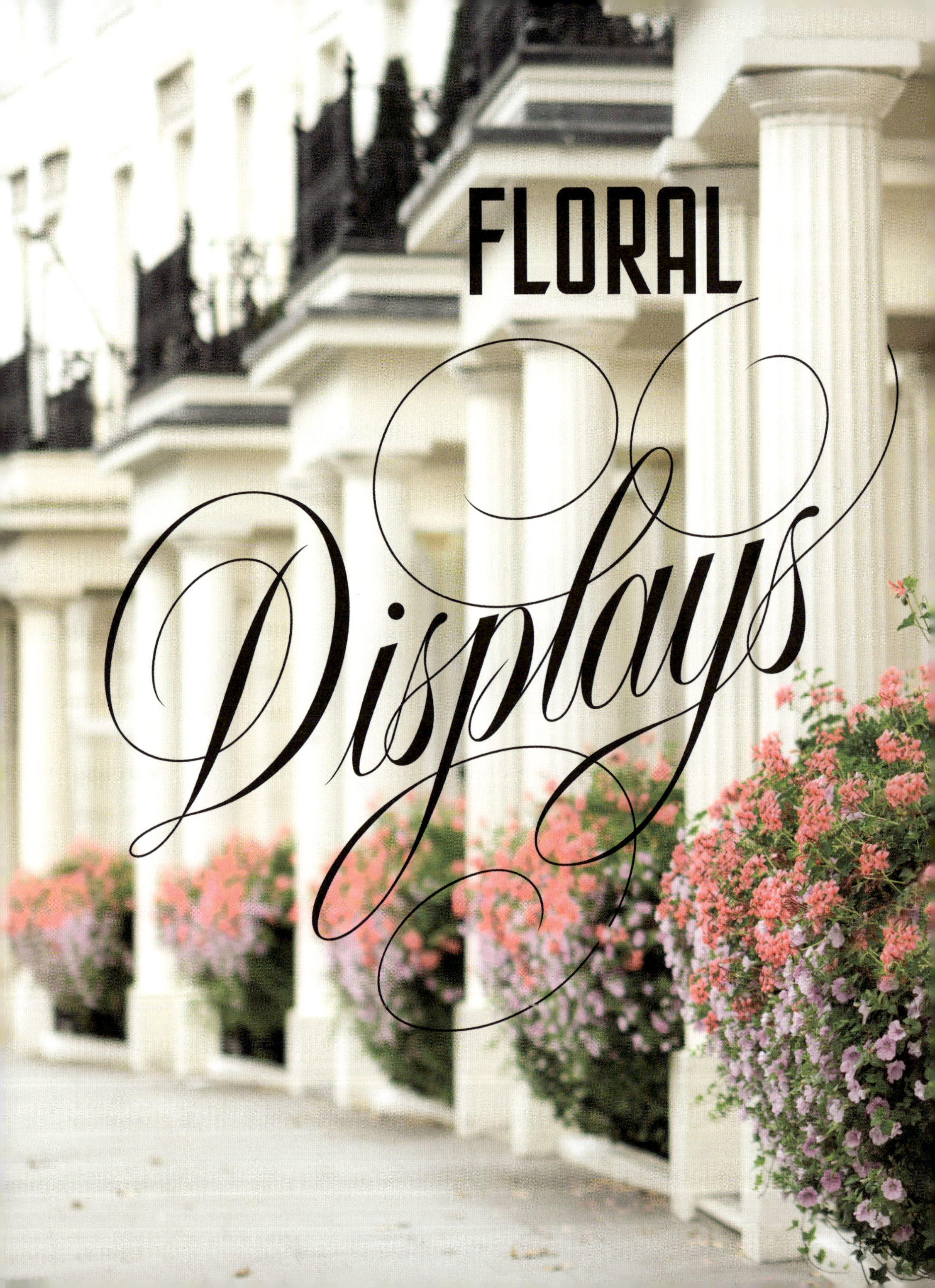

FLORAL
Displays

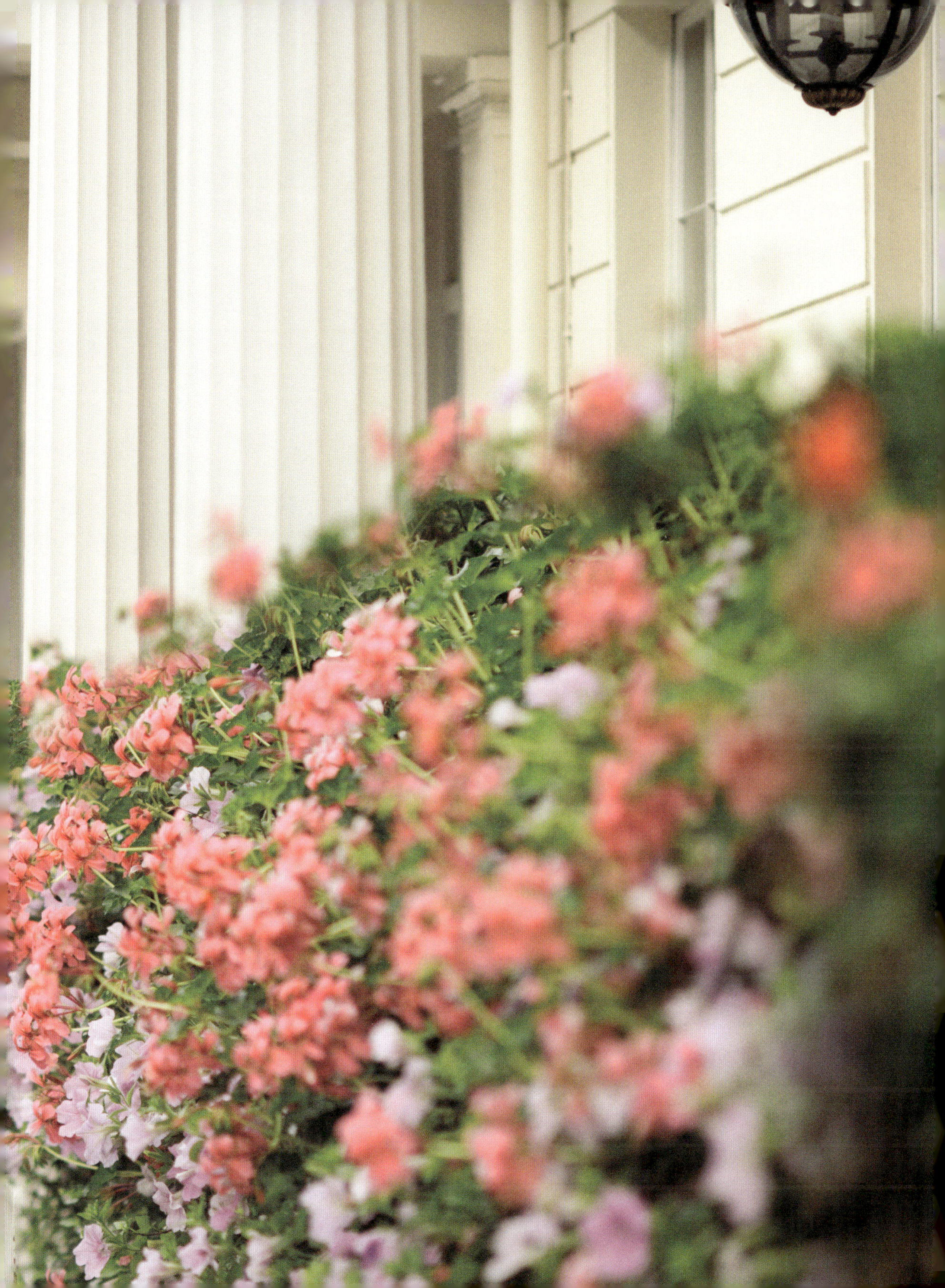

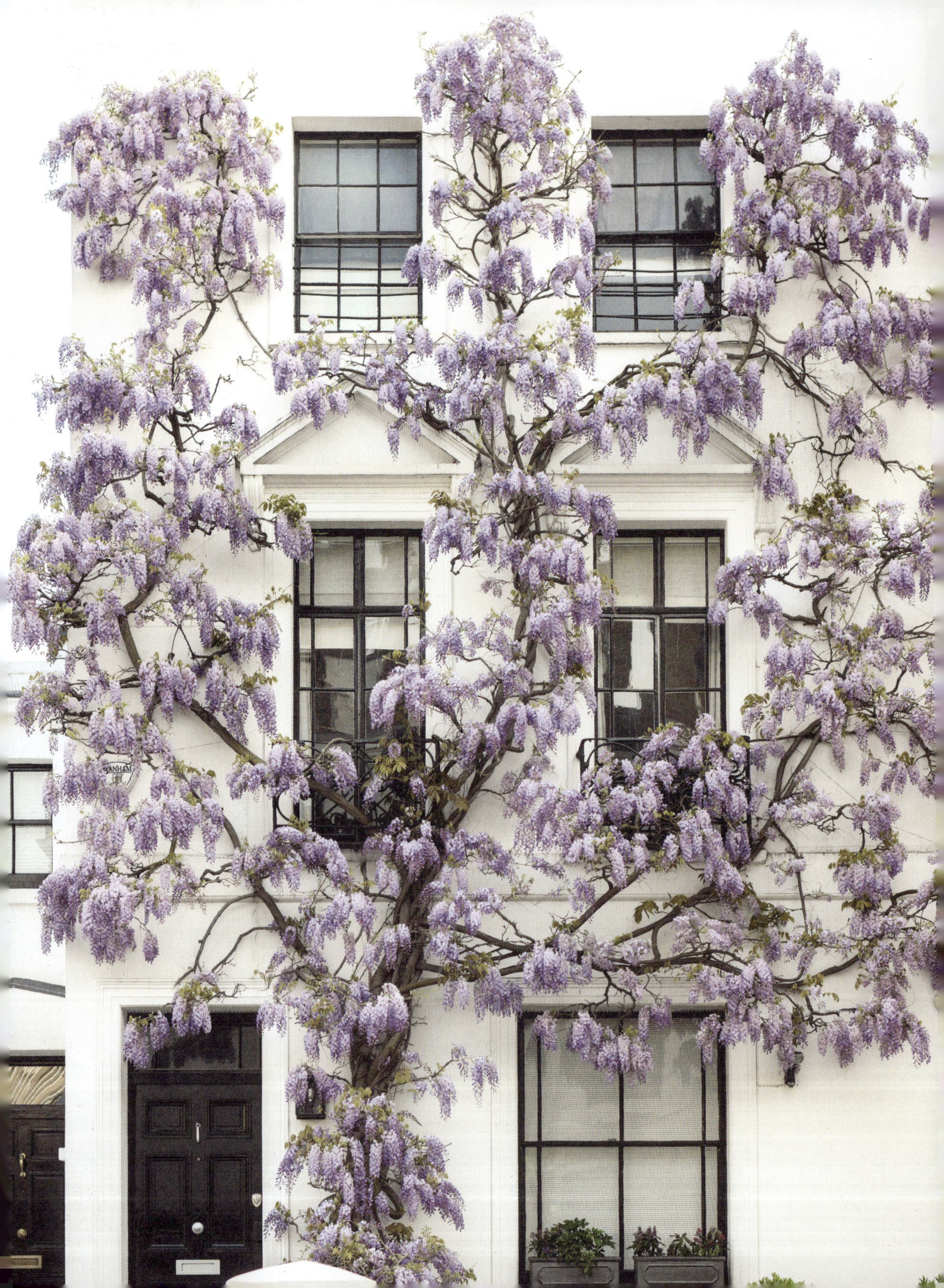

Spend even a short time in London and you'll be delighted and awed by the enthusiasm with which its residents adorn their homes and businesses with flowery embellishments. This devotion to beautifying their spaces is an extension of the English passion for gardening and innate understanding of the positive effect of flowers.

Most common are the gaily colored window boxes of fresh geraniums and other annuals that brighten up thousands of private and public facades from April to November. Columned crescent streets and hidden mews are all canvases for an artistic flourish of hanging plants.

Carefully tended and cherished heirloom wisteria vines, some more than a hundred years old, festoon notable homes and burst into prominence in late April, painting the city in cascades of purple. Many of these houses bear blue plaques that honor the illustrious men and women who once lived or worked in them.

The renowned Chelsea Flower Show, presented by the Royal Horticultural Society on the grounds of the Royal Hospital Chelsea, is the premiere gardening exhibition in Britain, and possibly the world. Held annually in the third week of May, it showcases the best in garden and floral design by the top nurseries and designers throughout the country, who vie for the coveted Gold Medal awards. The fantastic and unforgettable presentations take months to prepare and are planned years in advance. During Chelsea, the weather is traditionally summery, the champagne is flowing, and visitors experience a marvelous day out filled with floral magnificence.

The offshoot neighborhood festivals—Chelsea in Bloom, Belgravia in Bloom, and Mayfair in Bloom—occur concurrently and are outdoor floral art shows transforming the streets with eye-catching displays. The designs, judged by an expert panel, are based on an annually changing theme, which is interpreted and rendered by each entrant entirely in fresh flowers. Expect to see wild animals, flower-filled cars and chairs, soaring arches, flower walls, undersea creatures, and giant hearts generating a playful and joyous mood for all to enjoy.

The exteriors of many pubs astound with jaw-dropping panoramas of hanging flower baskets, greenery, and vertically growing plants. The best-known and most extravagant are at the Churchill Arms on Kensington Church Street. As you walk down the street, your gaze is arrested by the sight, and your mind attempts to grasp the logistics involved in executing such an astonishing display. Nearly as impressive are the red and white geraniums that scale the facade of the Masons Arms on Devonshire Street in Fitzrovia. Most neighborhood pubs join in the game with window boxes and baskets for patrons to appreciate throughout the summer months.

Trendy pastel-painted cafes and tea shops, lavished with garlands of artificial blooms, are magnets for residents and visitors alike who relish the photogenic environment as much as the designer cakes and pastries on the menu. Among the favorites are the Peggy Porschen locations: candy-pink tea parlors in the fashionable neighborhoods of Belgravia and Chelsea that command attention, draw constant crowds, and even slow the hectic city traffic.

Many restaurants change their floral garments seasonally with dramatic effect, turning an ordinary entrance into a beckoning fantasy world. The illusion is often carried through to the interiors, where ceilings appear as flowery skies or the walls become a flower-laden forest.

At the highest end of the scale, opulent gala events at five-star hotels, such as the Savoy or the Lanesborough, present ballrooms filled with tens of thousands of fresh roses, orchids, and hydrangeas, dazzling guests with unbelievable opulence.

Londoners understand, perhaps more than any other city dwellers, that no better attention-getter or mood lifter exists than the exquisite beauty of an abundance of joyfully placed flowers.

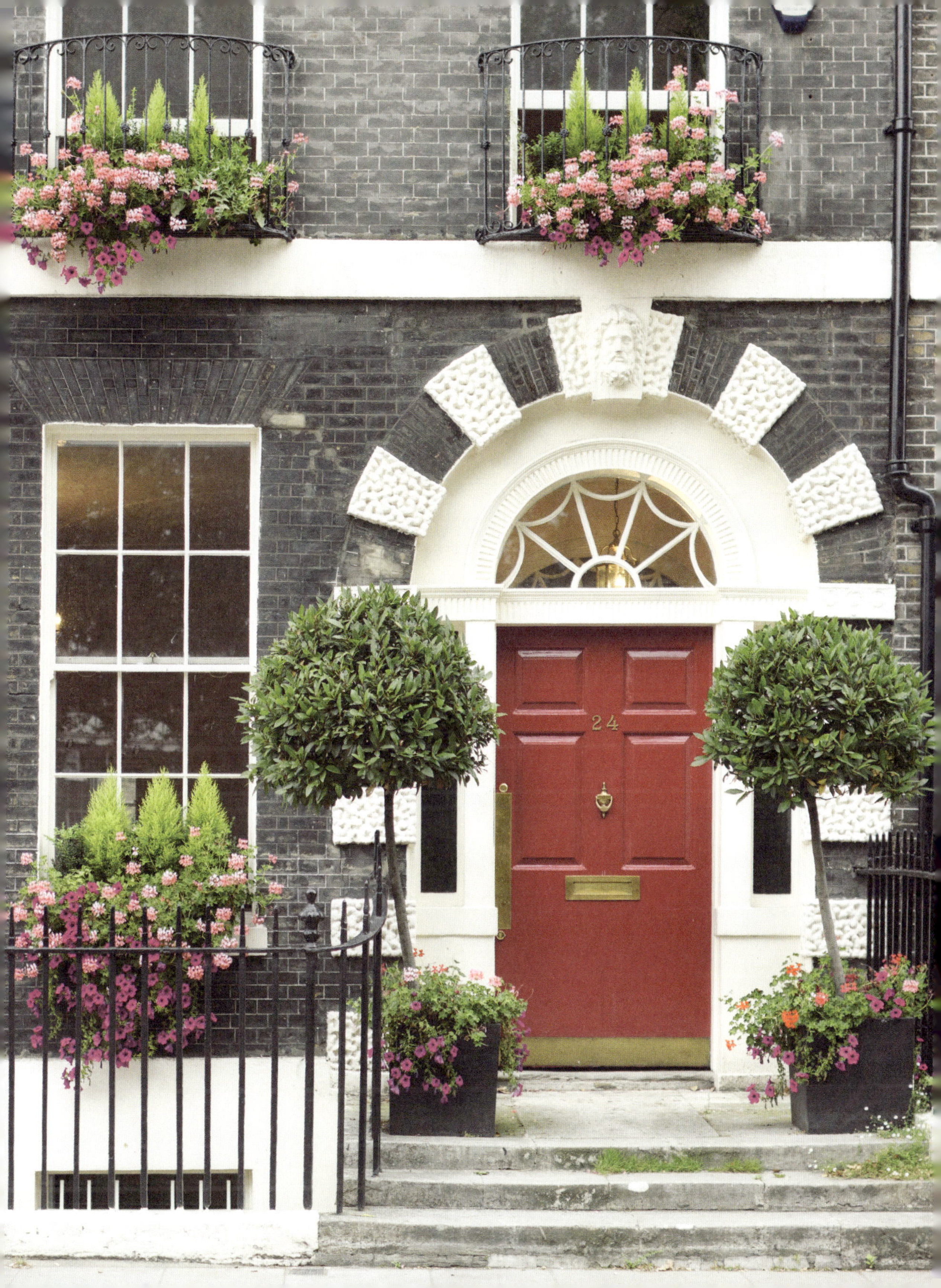

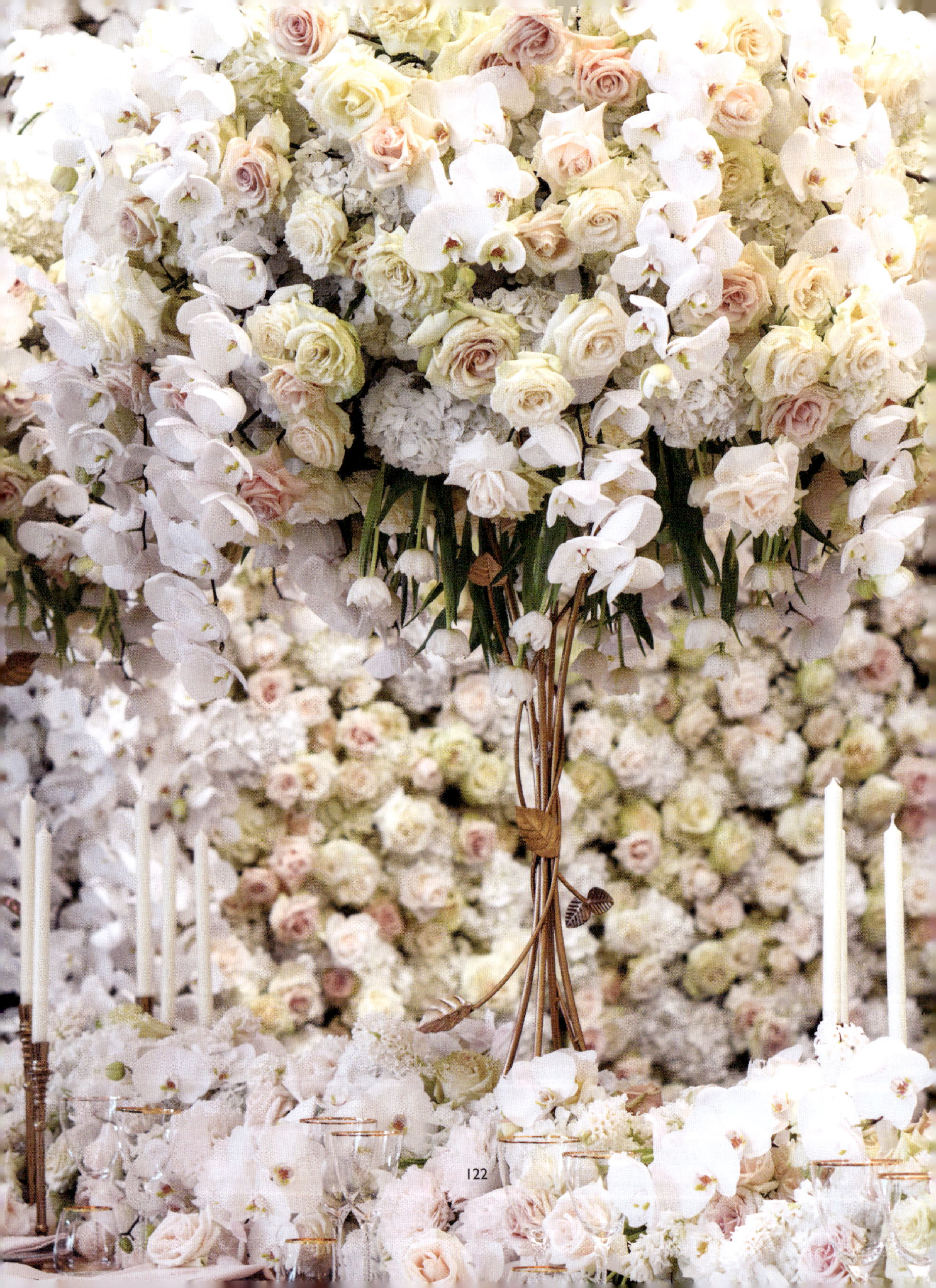

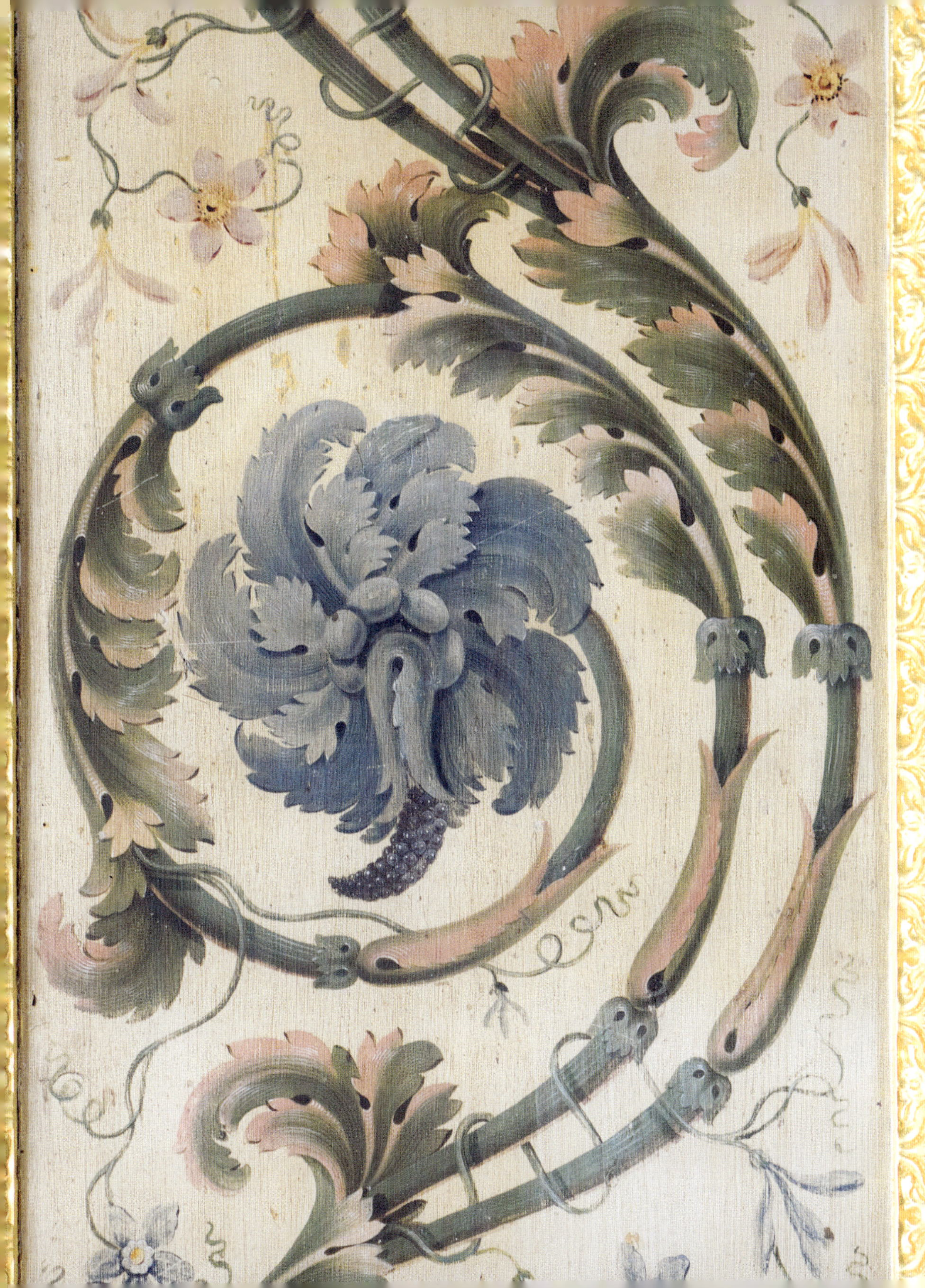

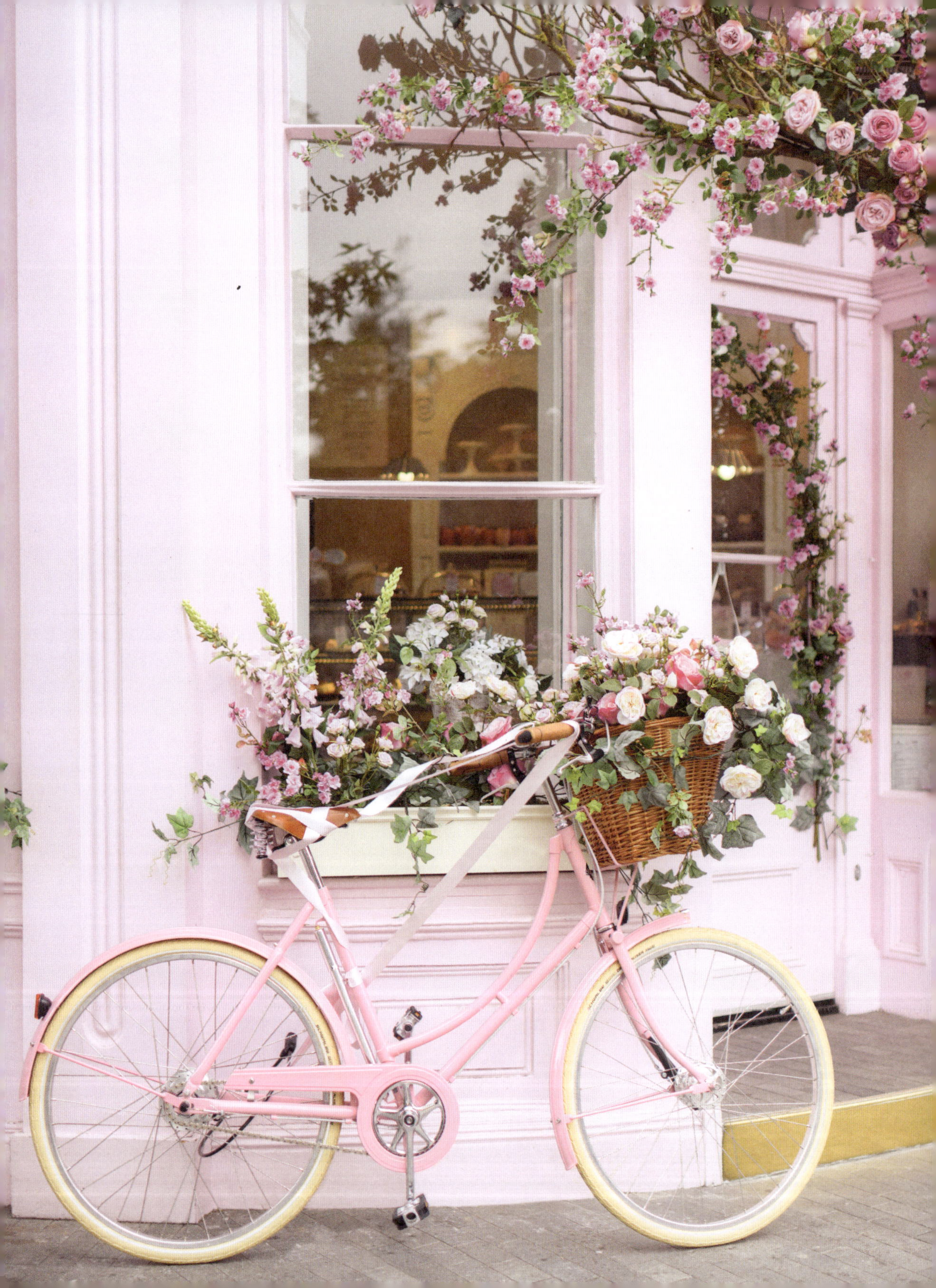

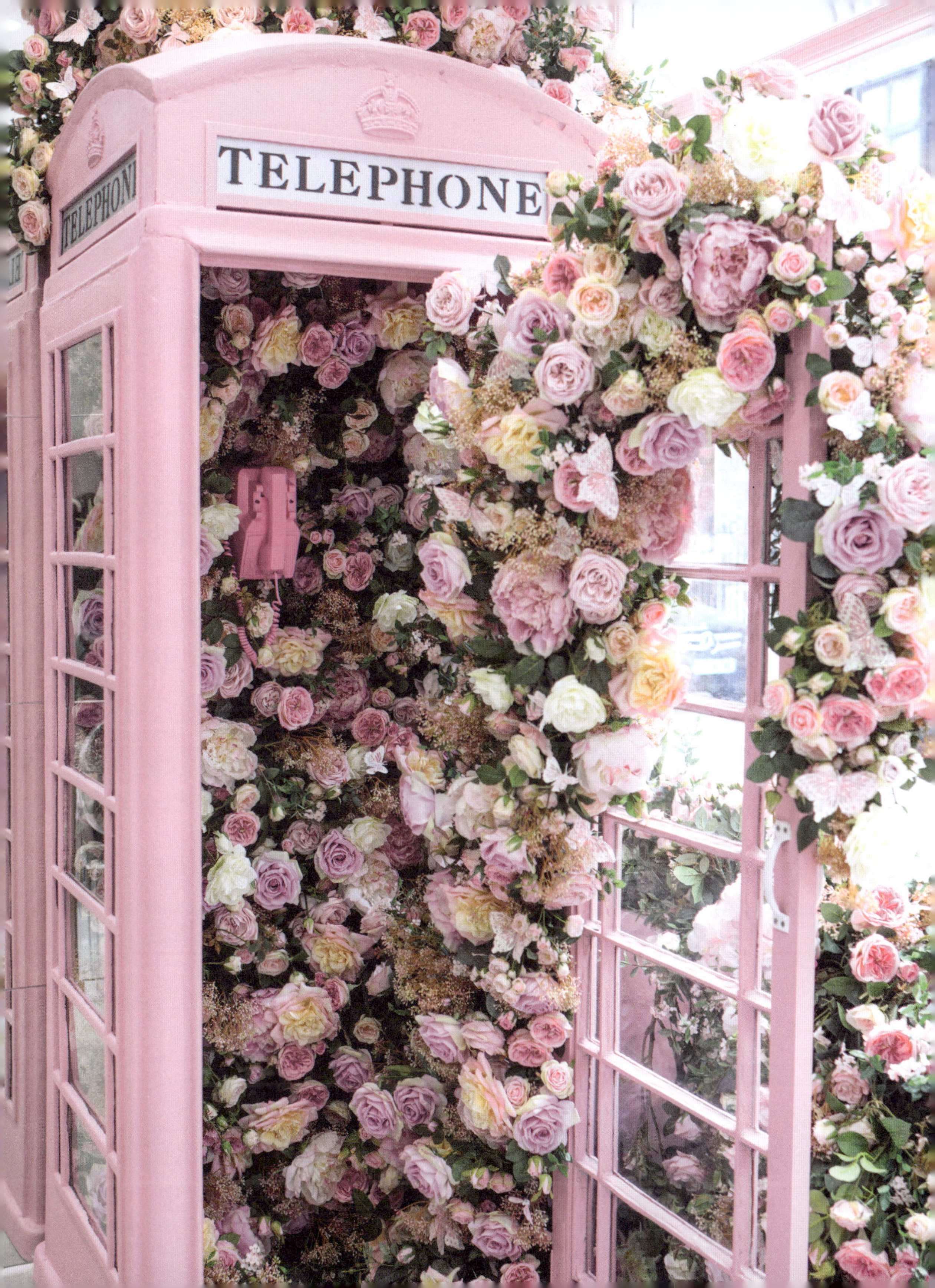

TELEPHONE
TELEPHONE

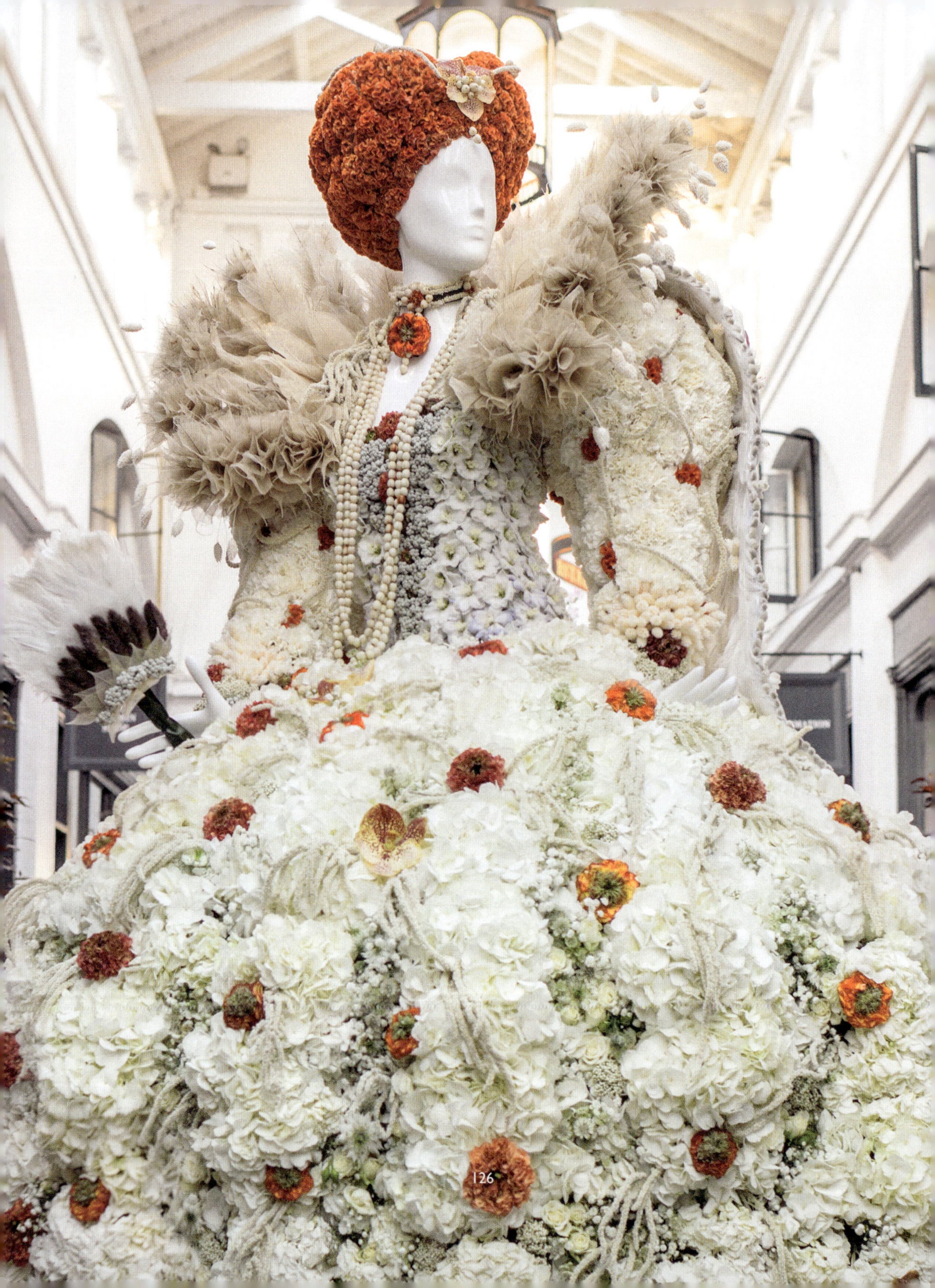

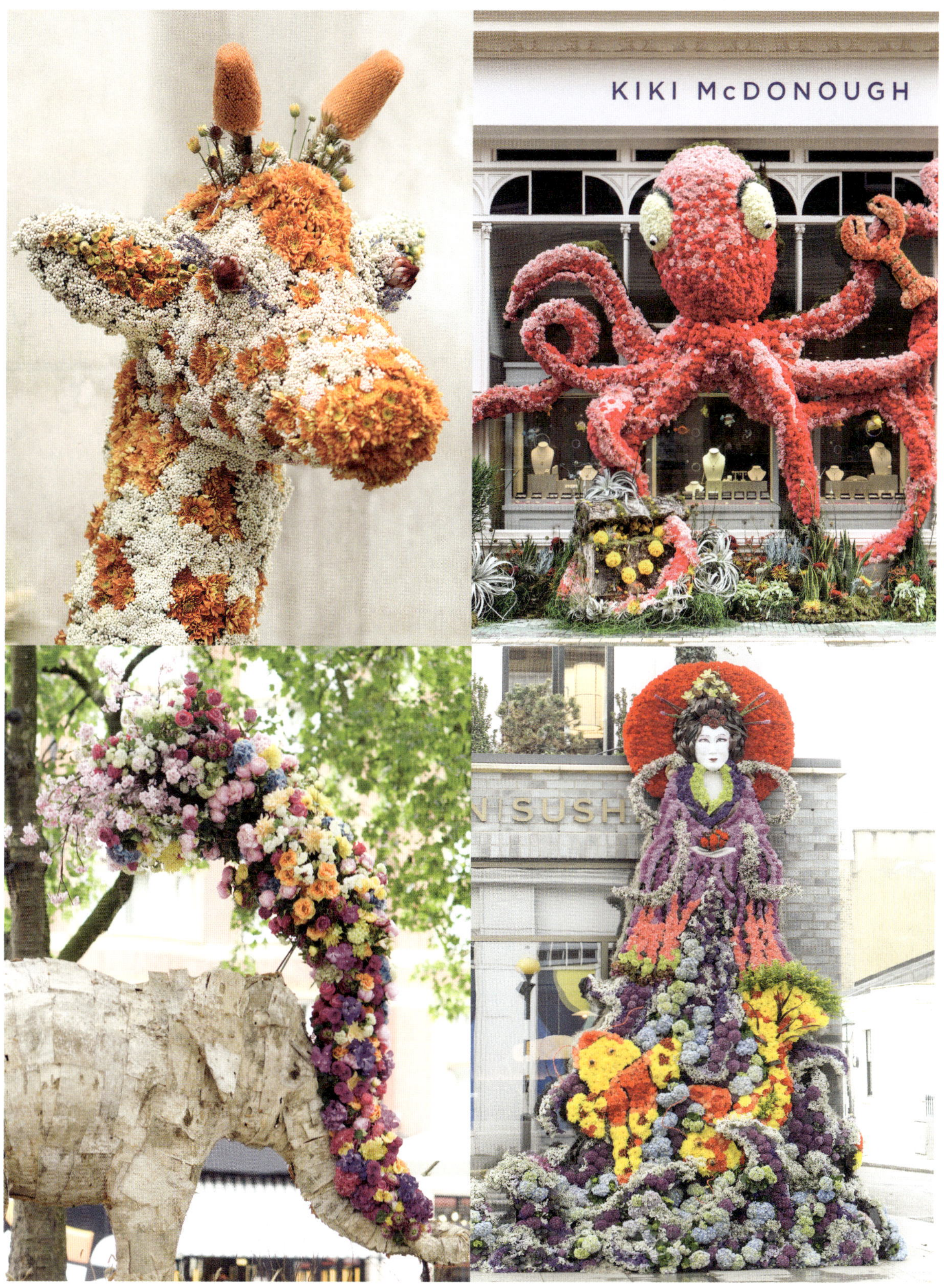
KIKI McDONOUGH

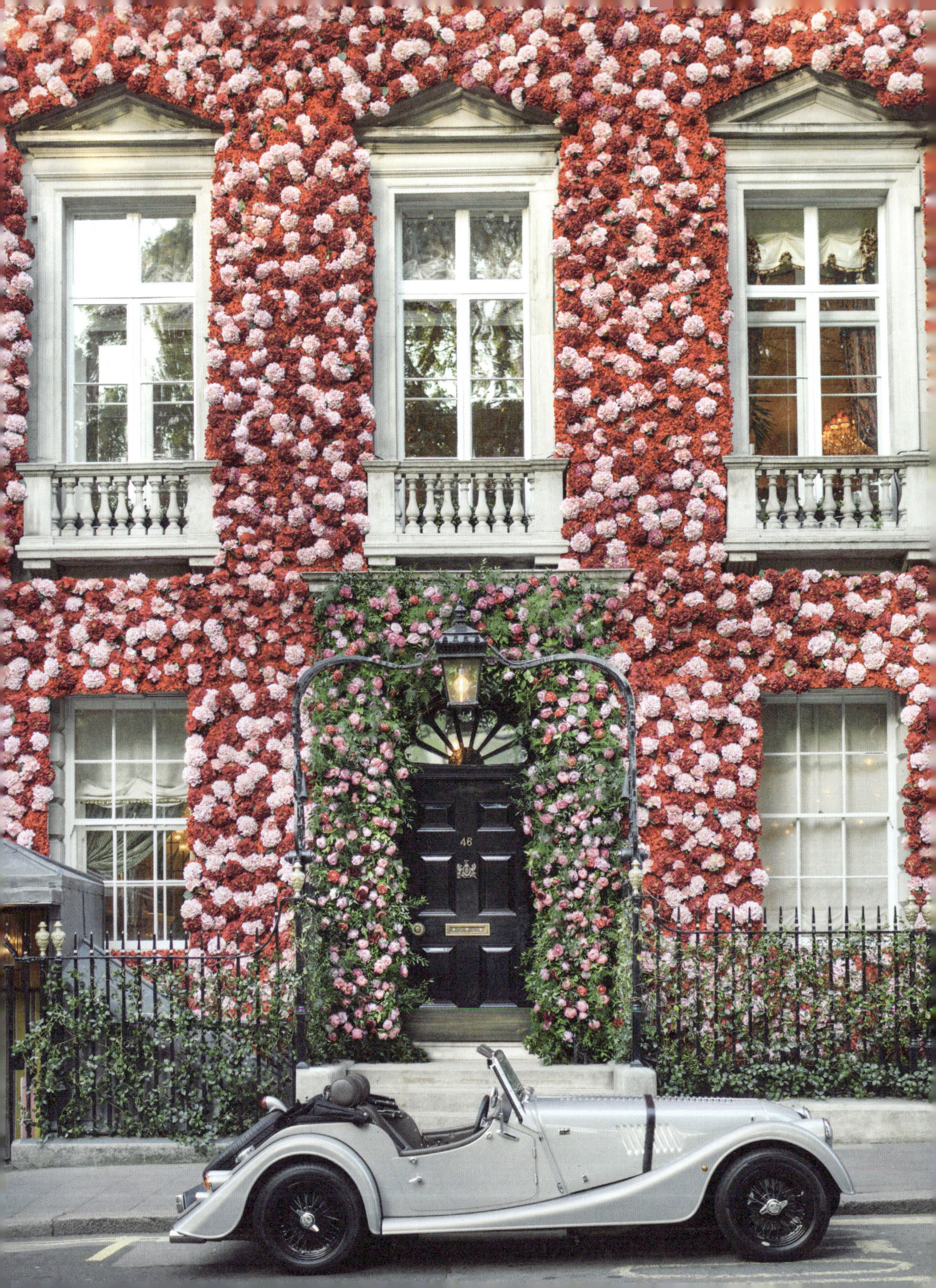

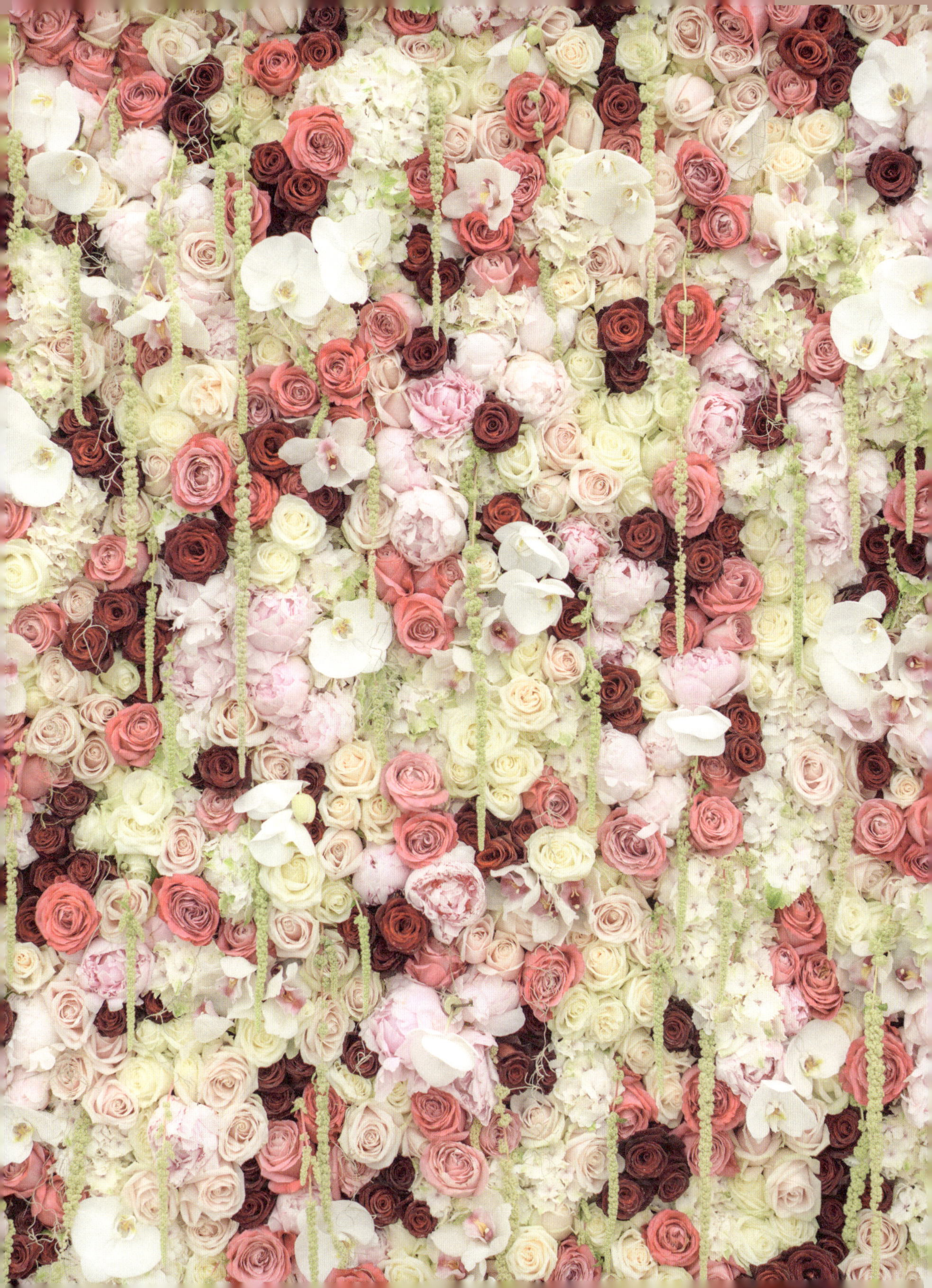

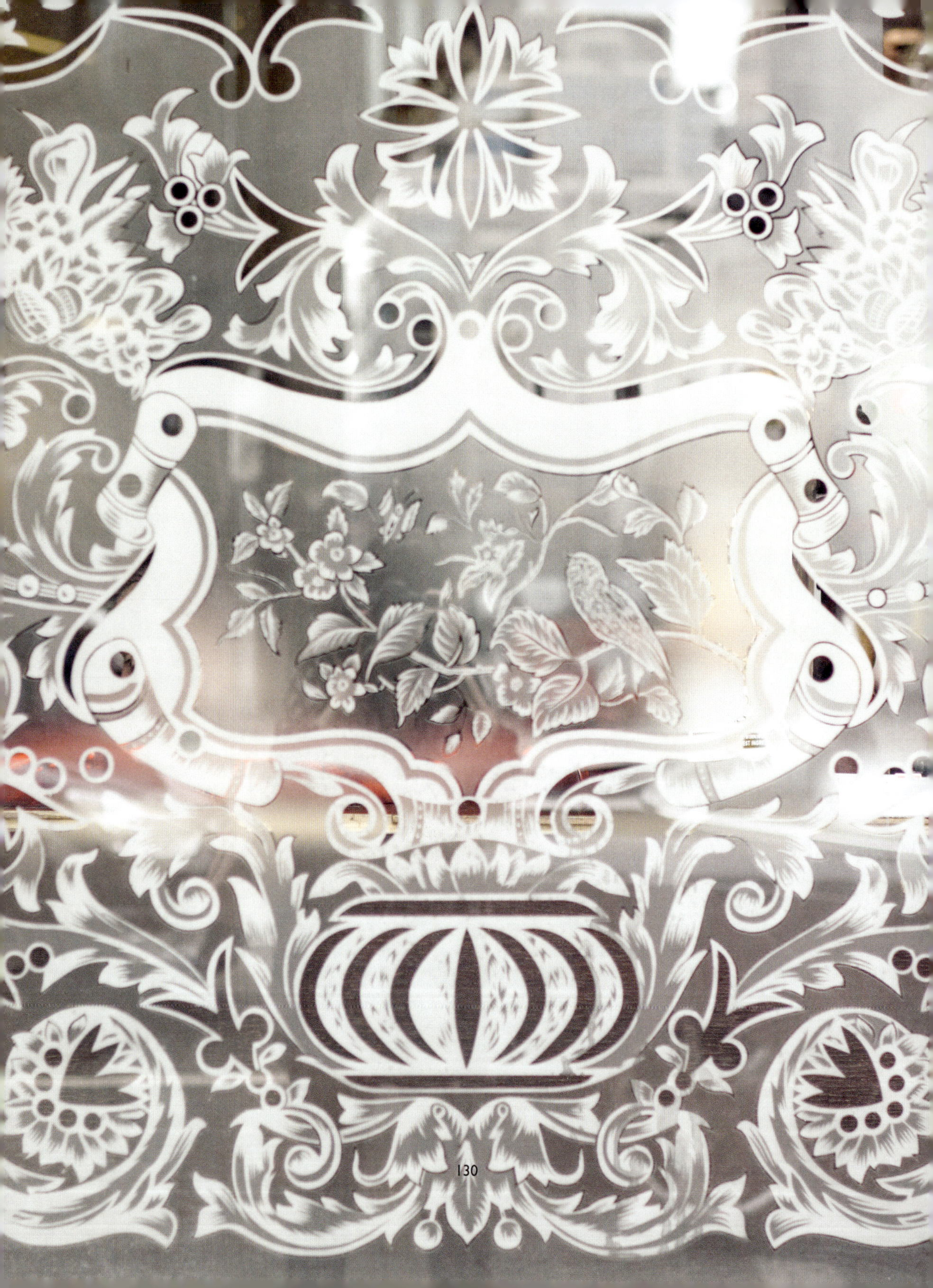

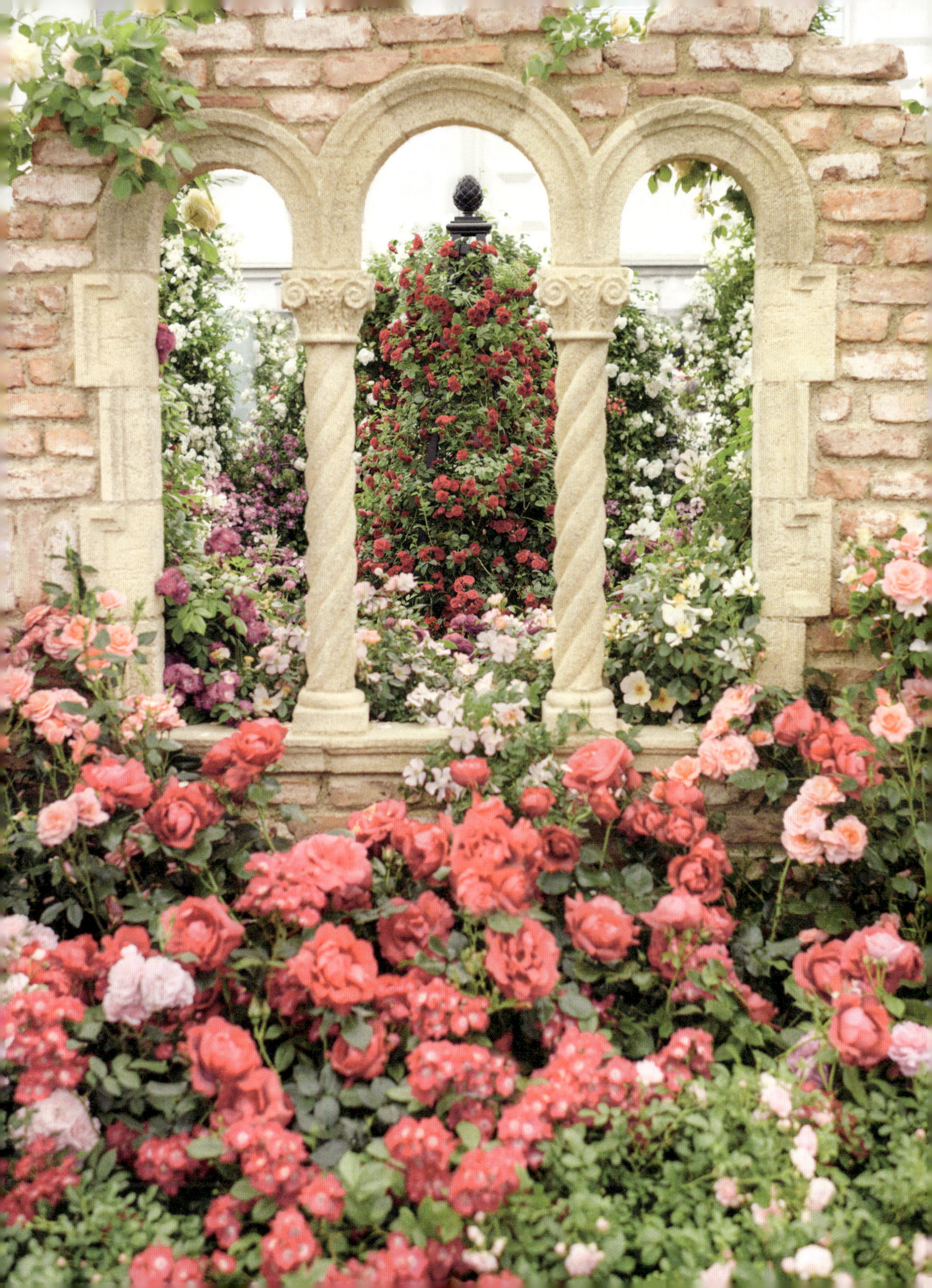

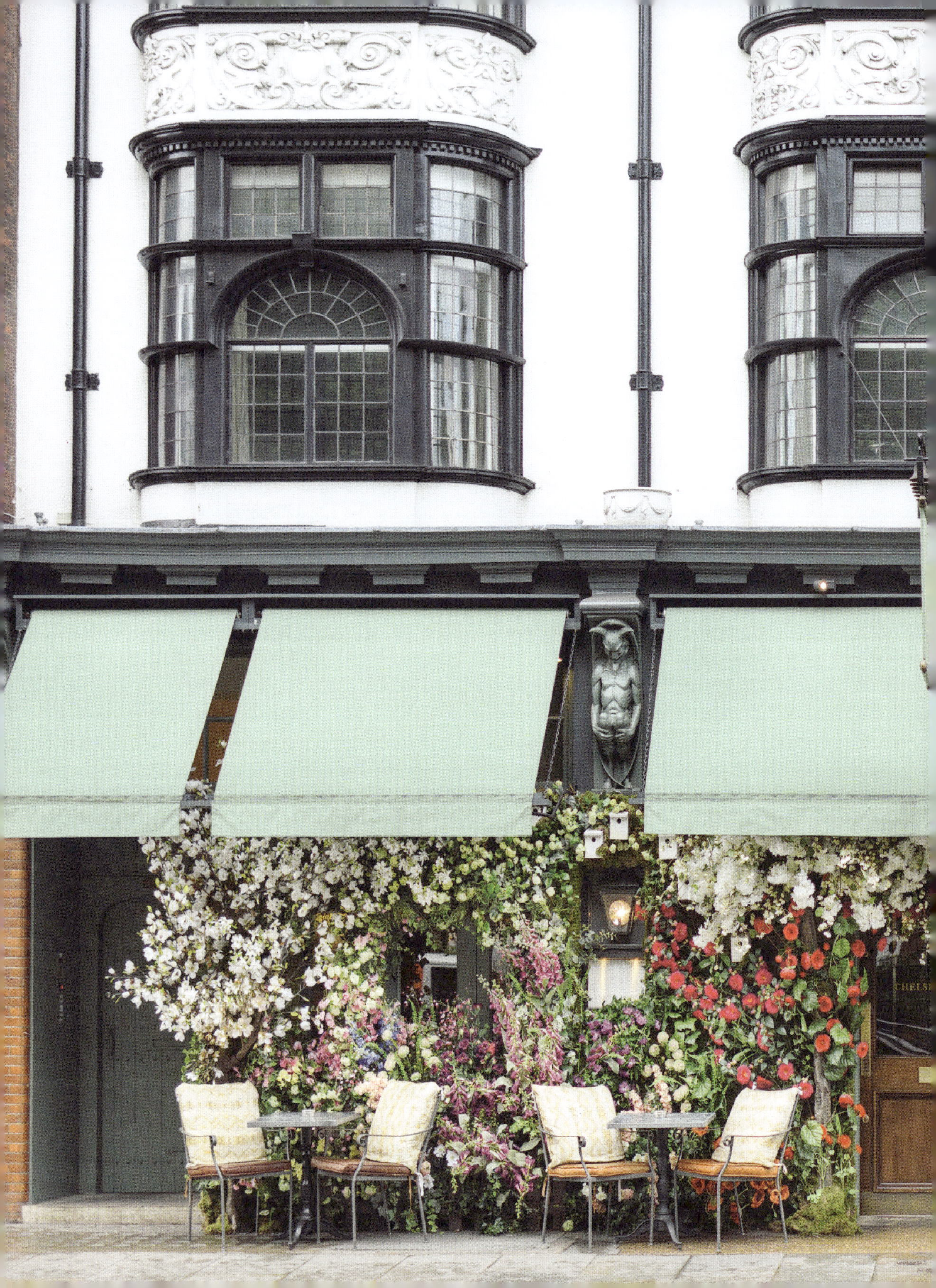

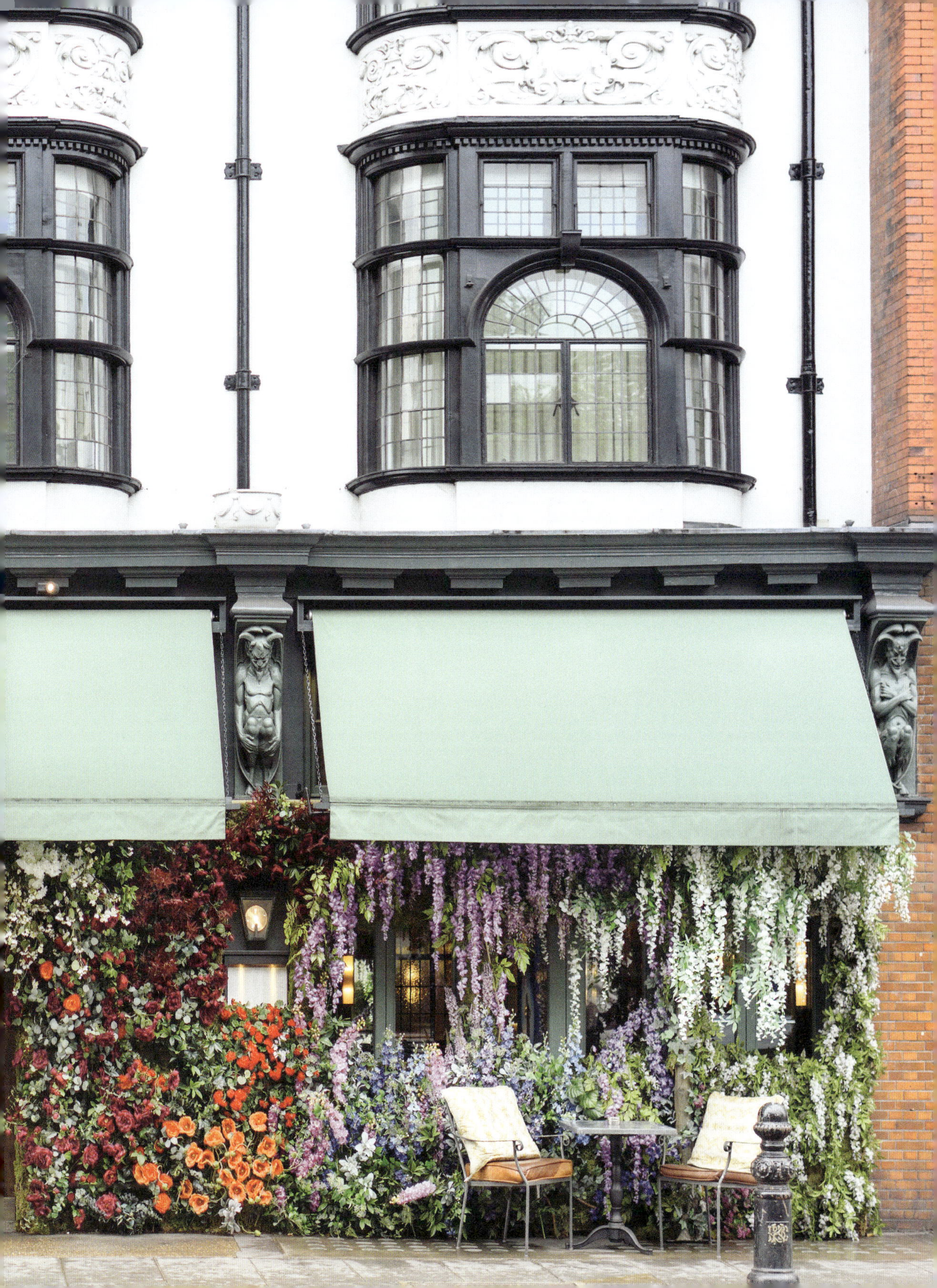

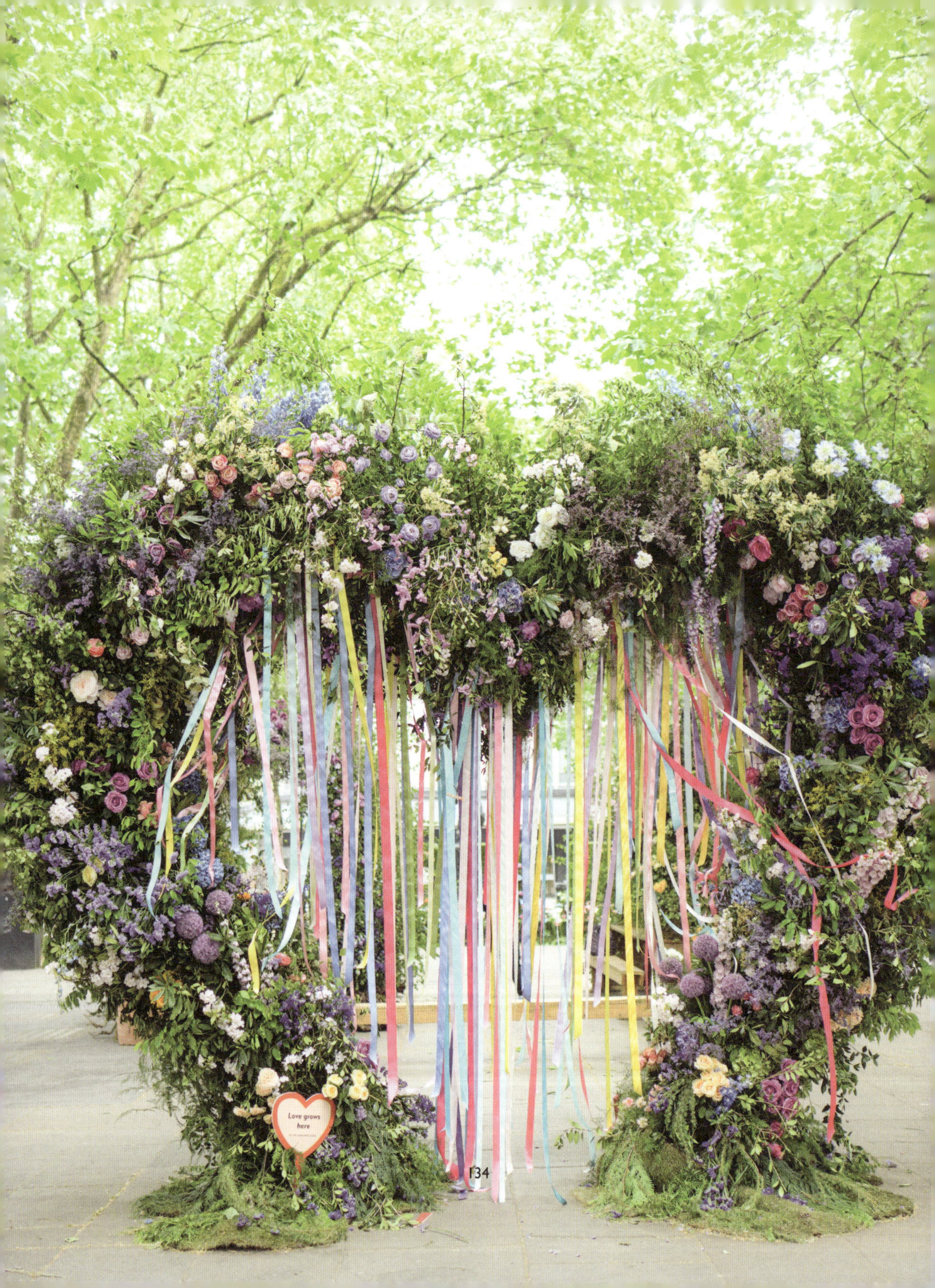
Love grows
here

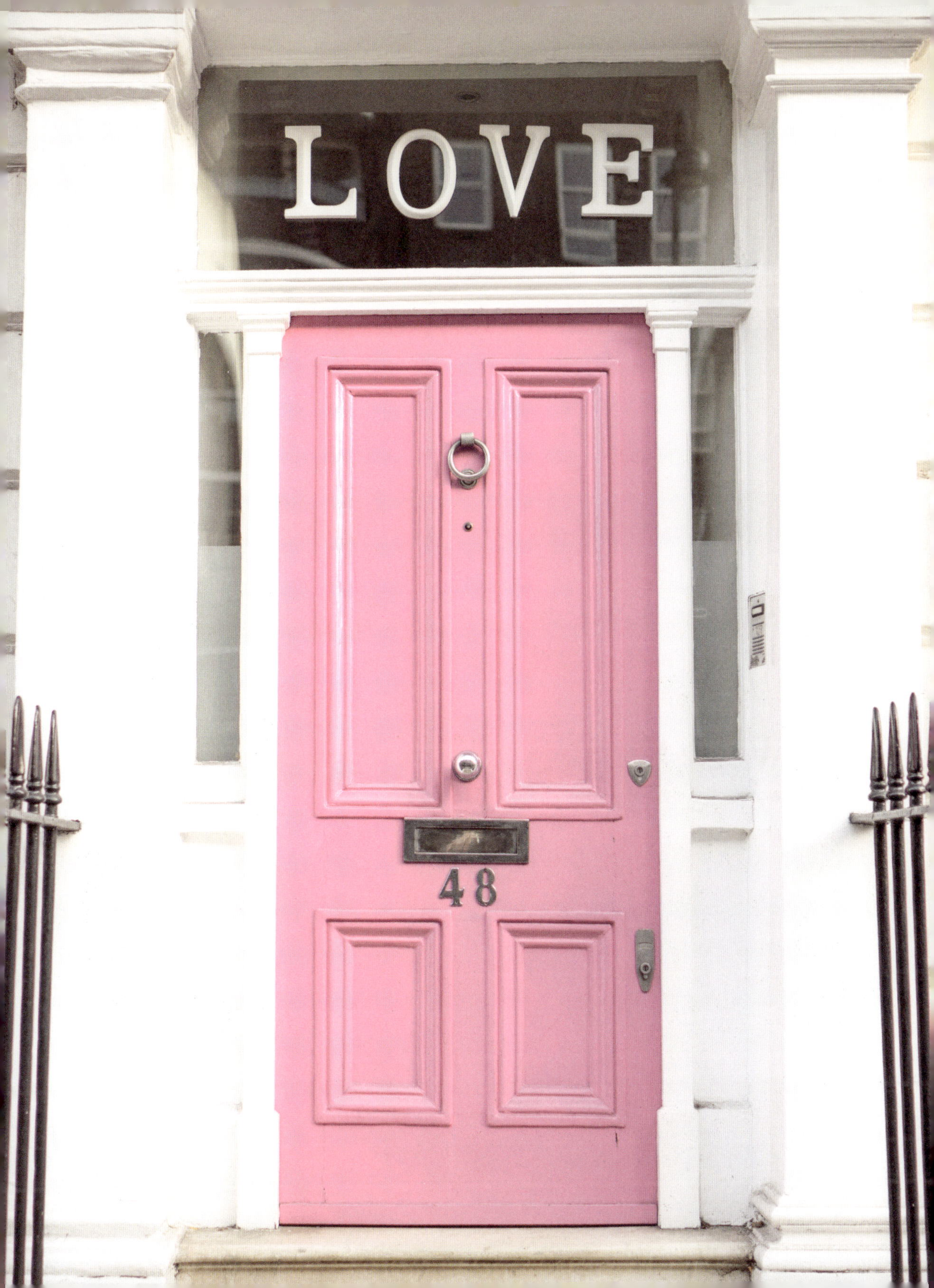

LOVE
48

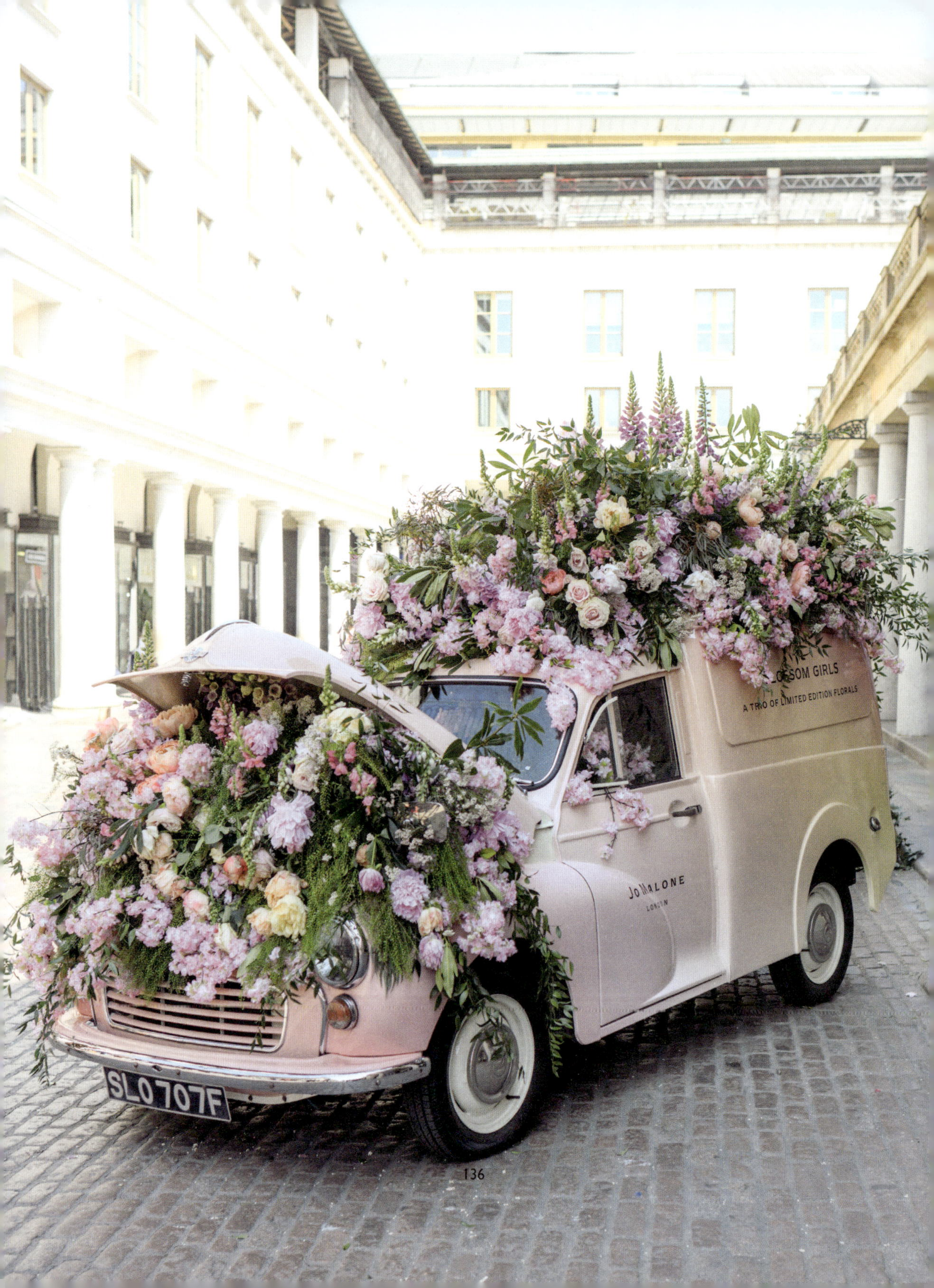
BLOSSOM GIRLS
A TRIO OF LIMITED EDITION FLORALS
Jo Malone
LONDON
SLO 707F

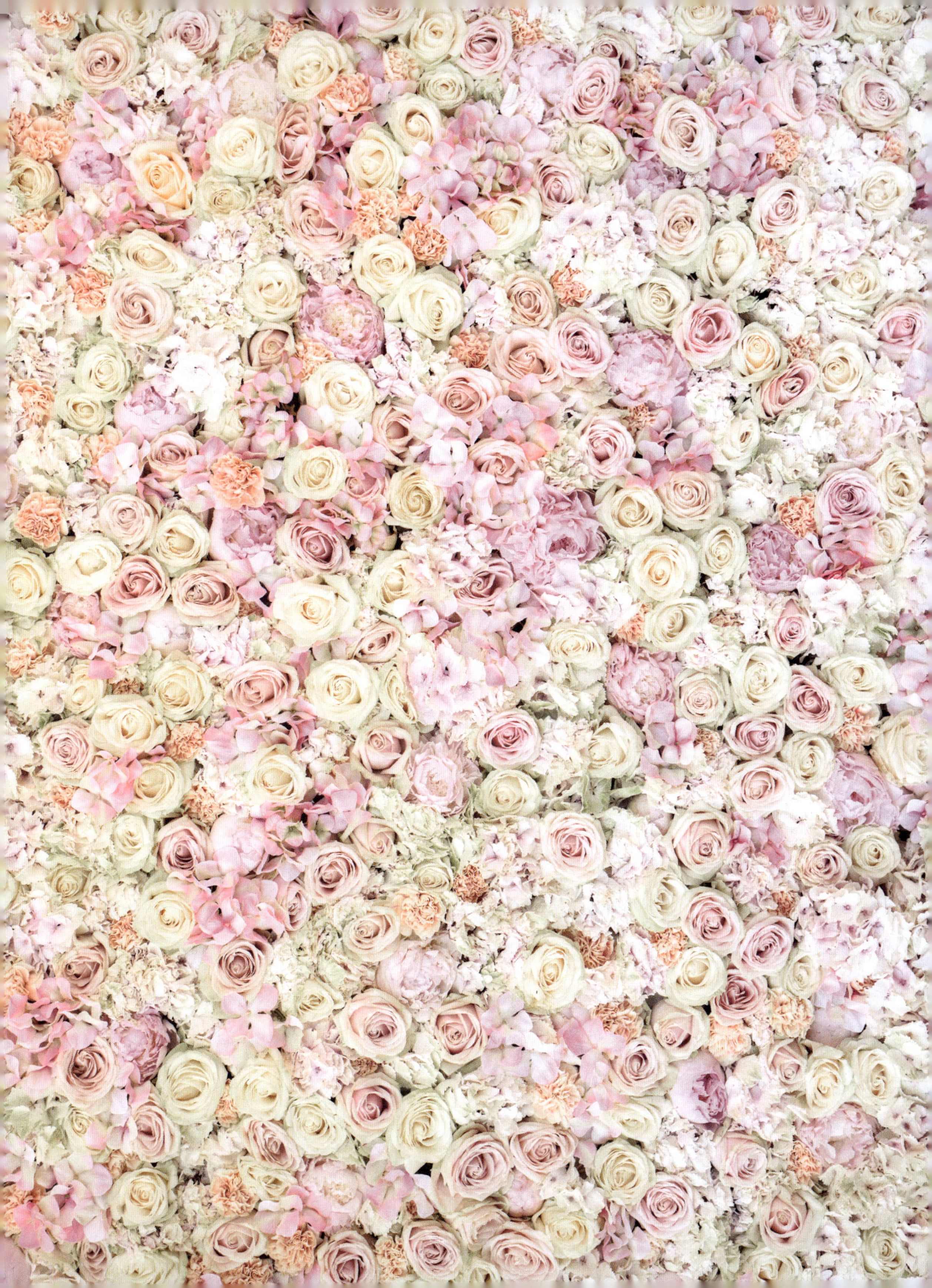

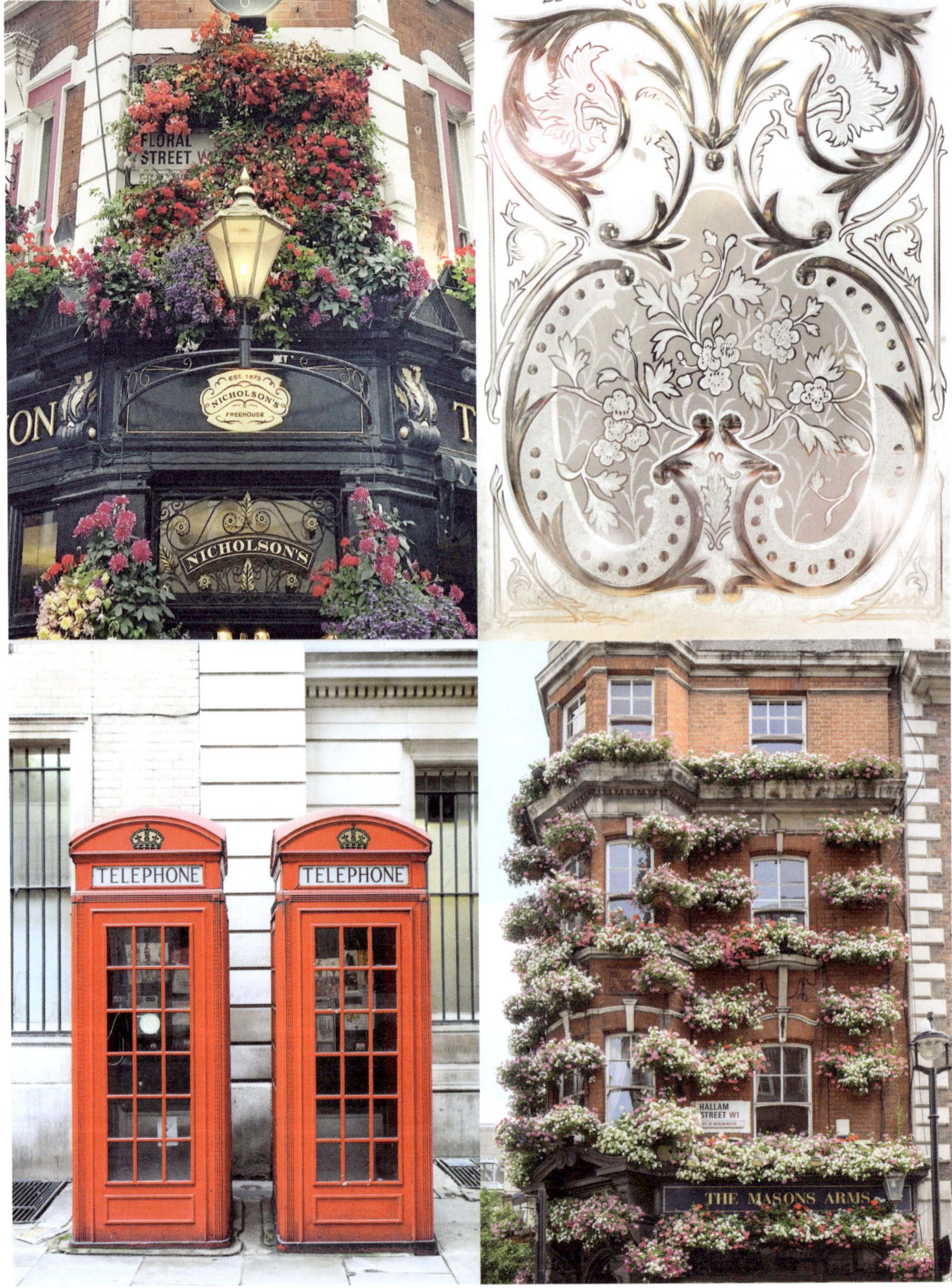

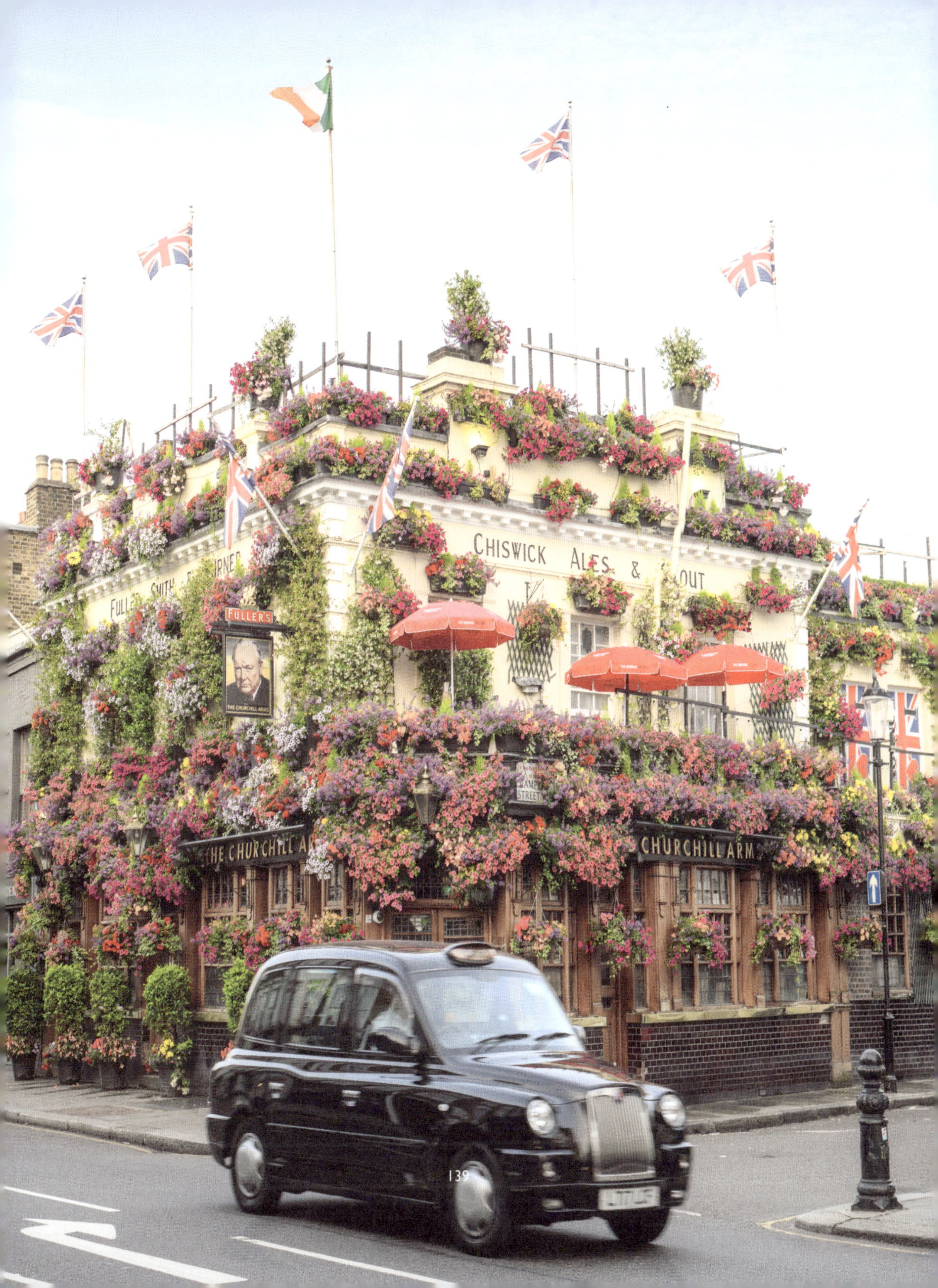

FULLER SMITH TURNER
CHISWICK ALES & STOUT
FULLERS
THE CHURCHILL ARMS
THE CHURCHILL AR
CHURCHILL ARM

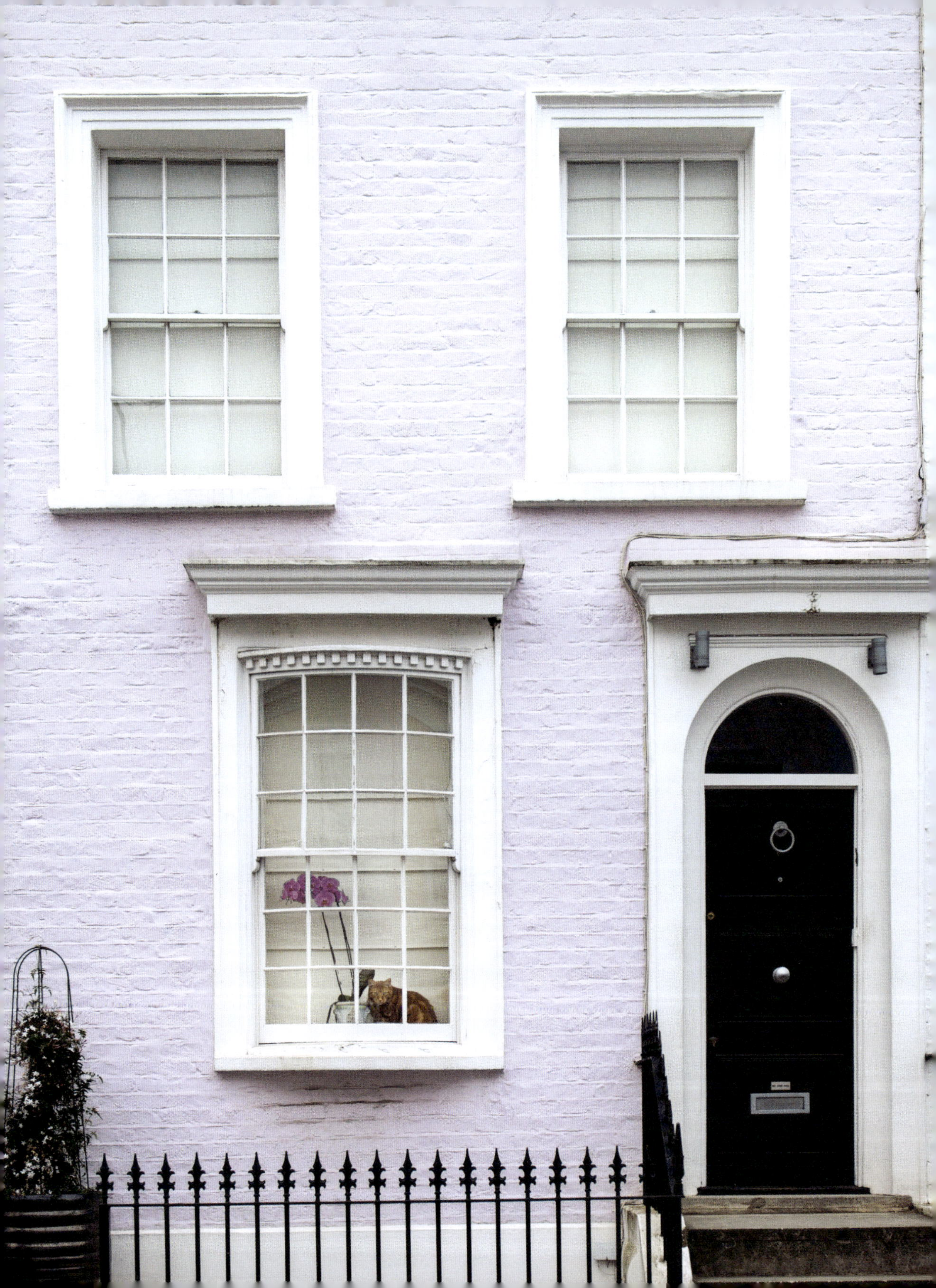

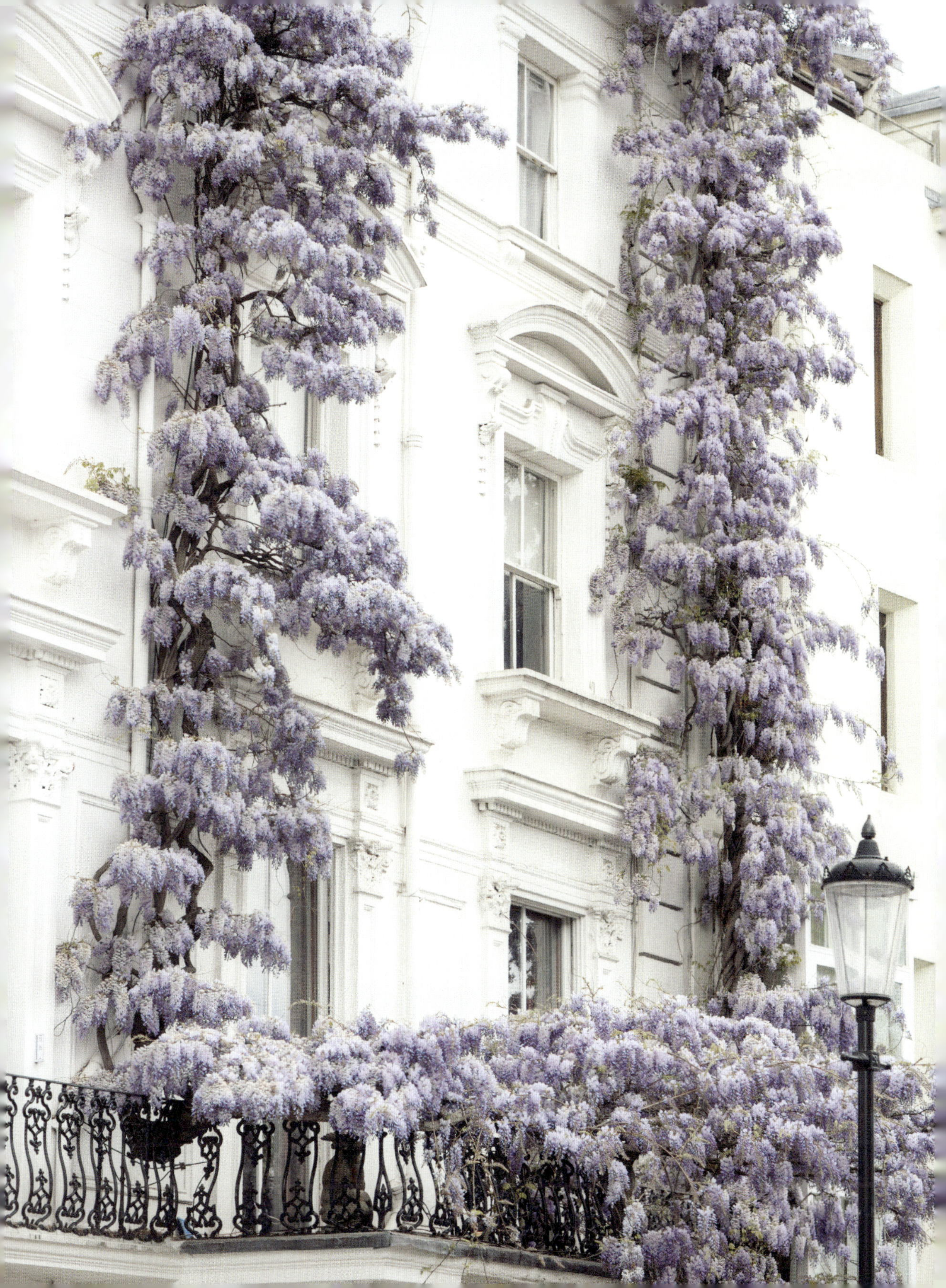

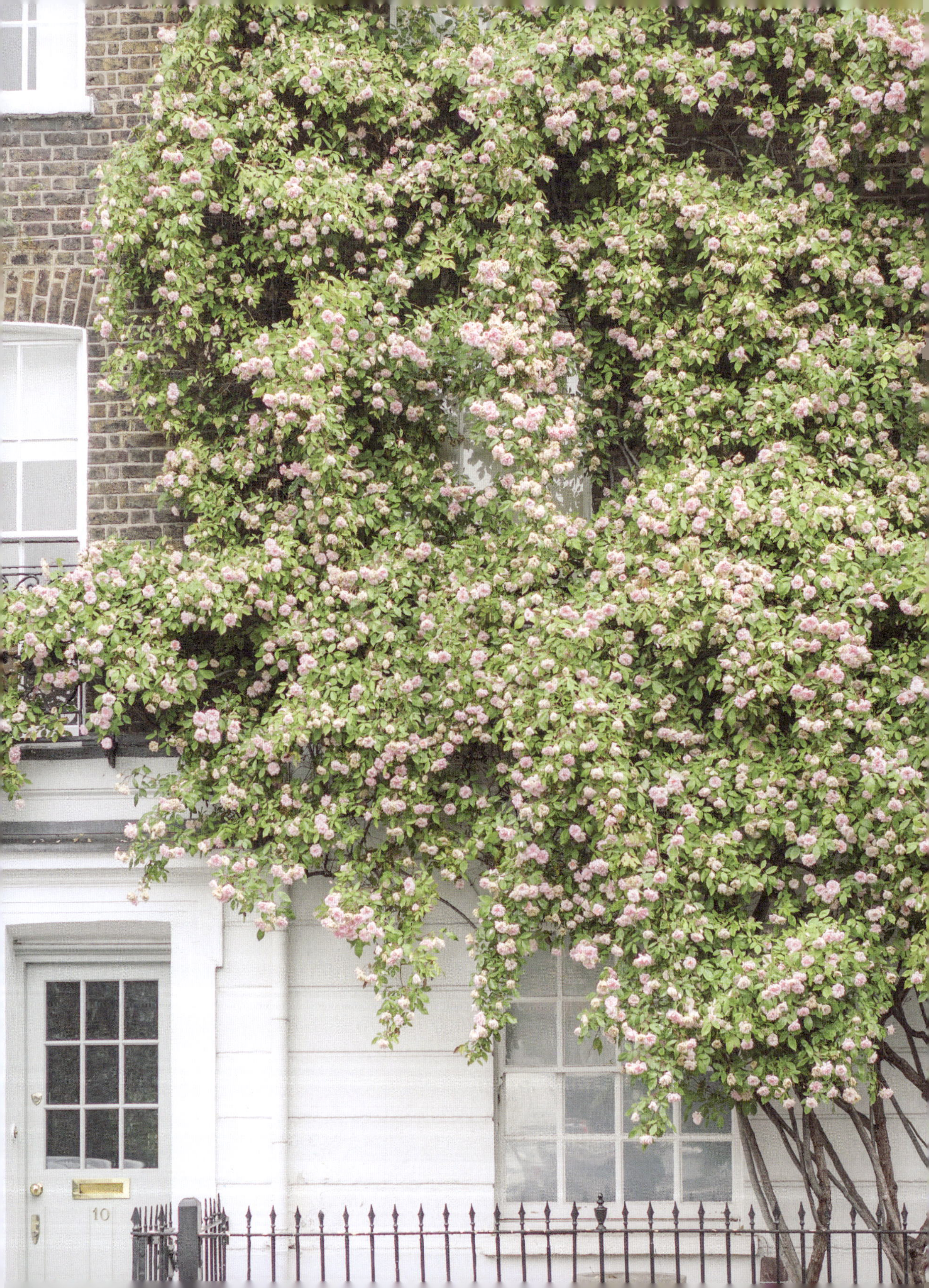

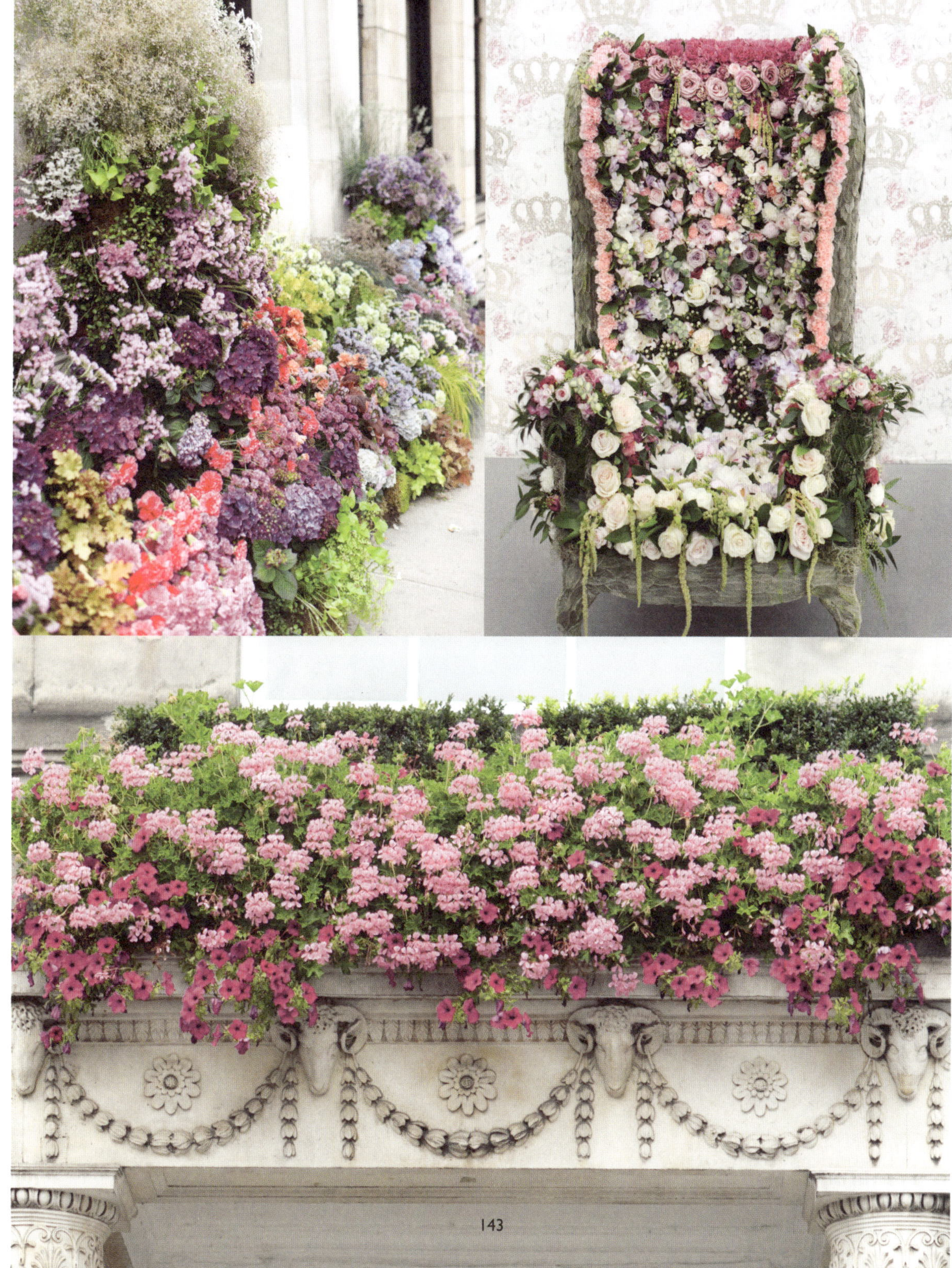

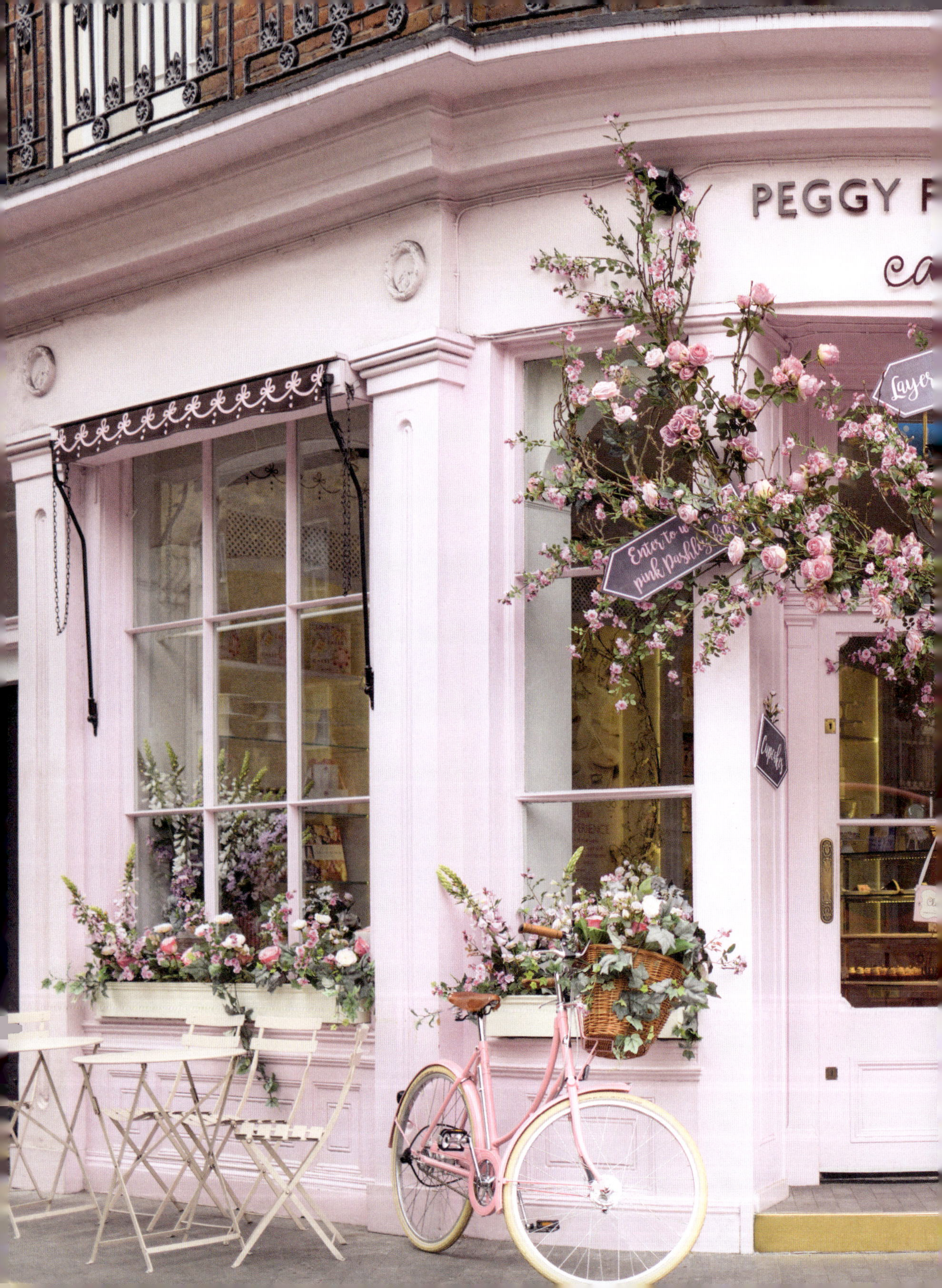

PEGGY P
ca
Layer
Enter to win a
pink pashley bike
Cupcakes

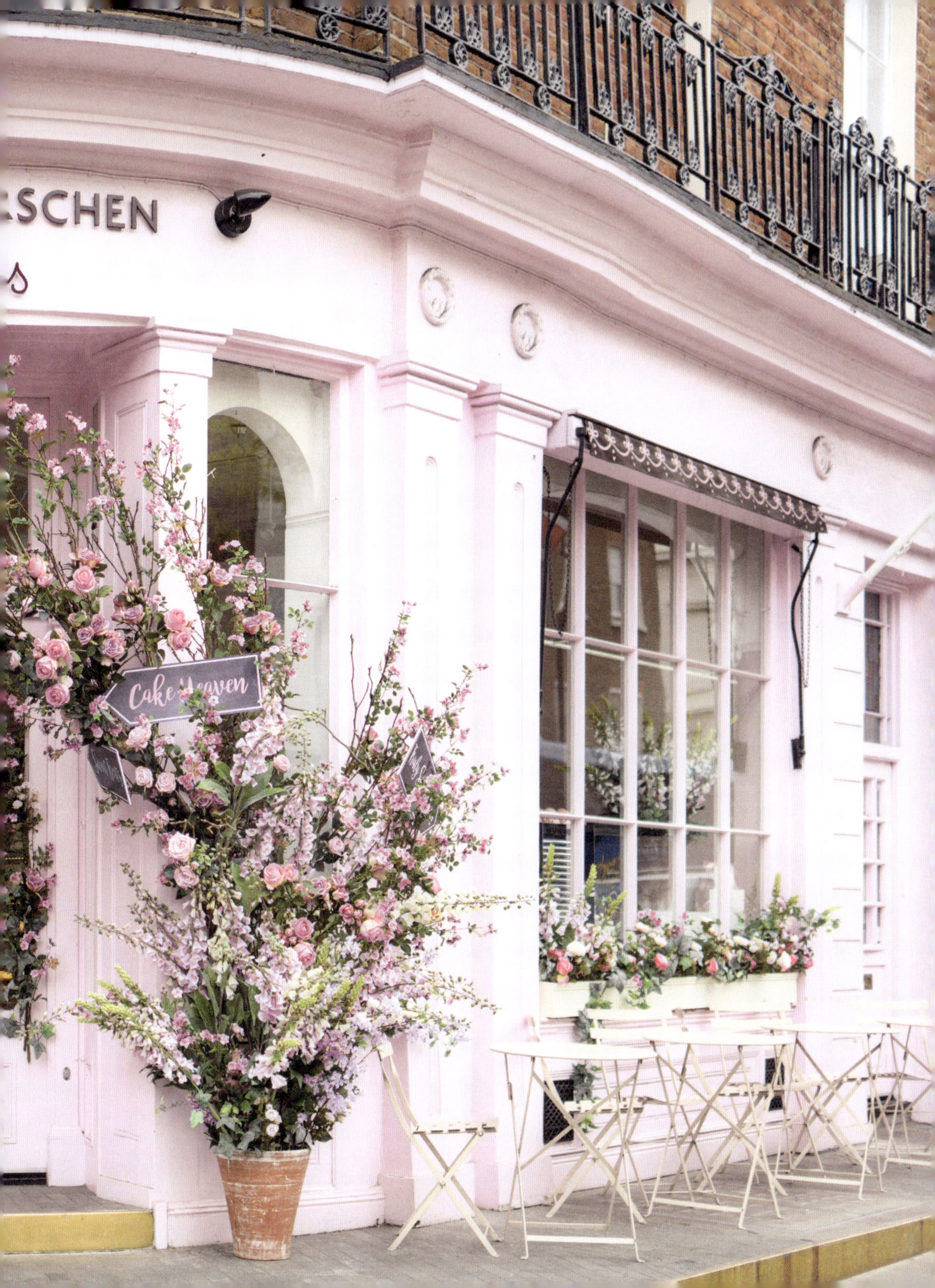
ESCHEN
Cake Heaven

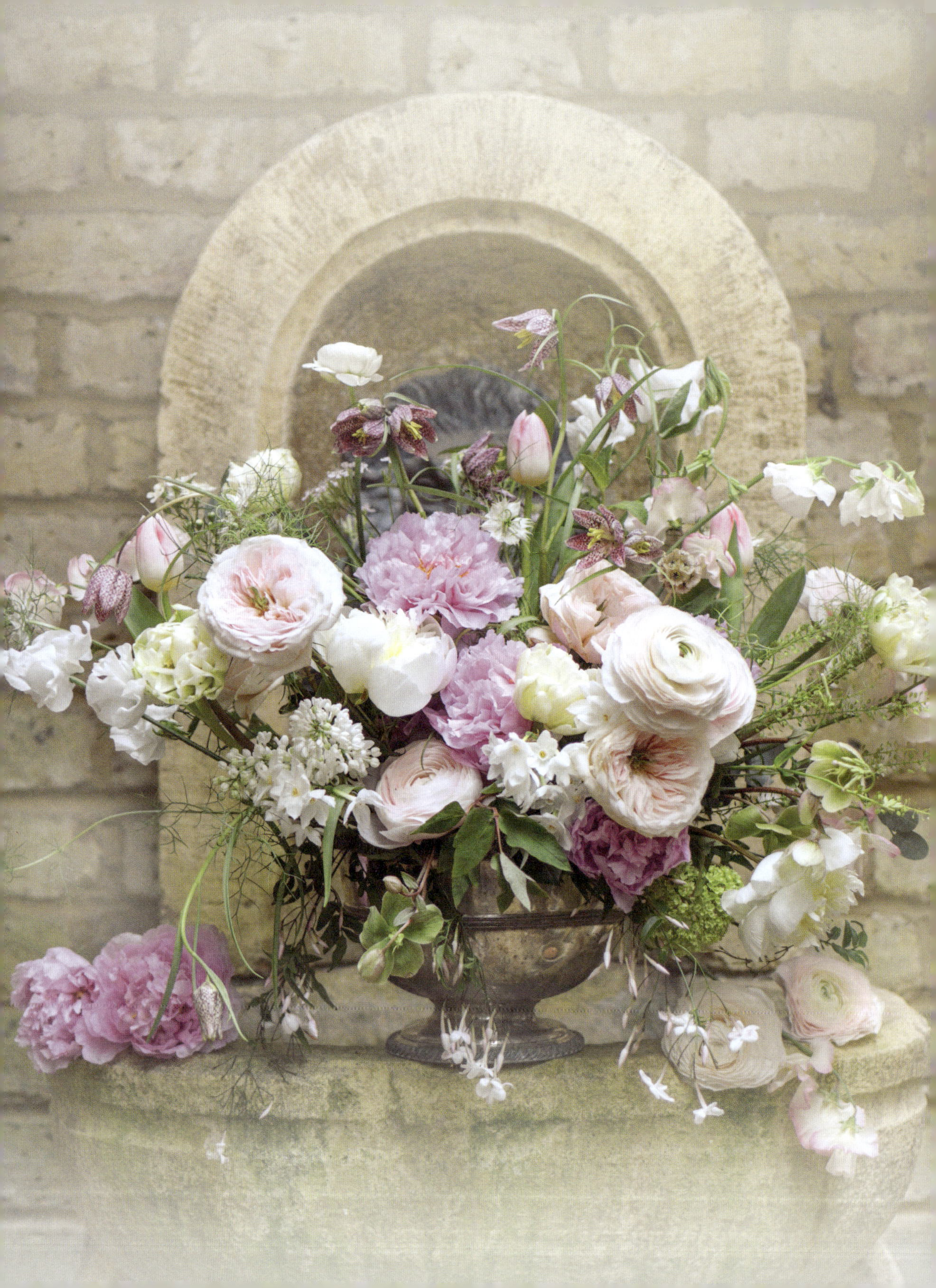

Creating Your Own London-Style Bouquet

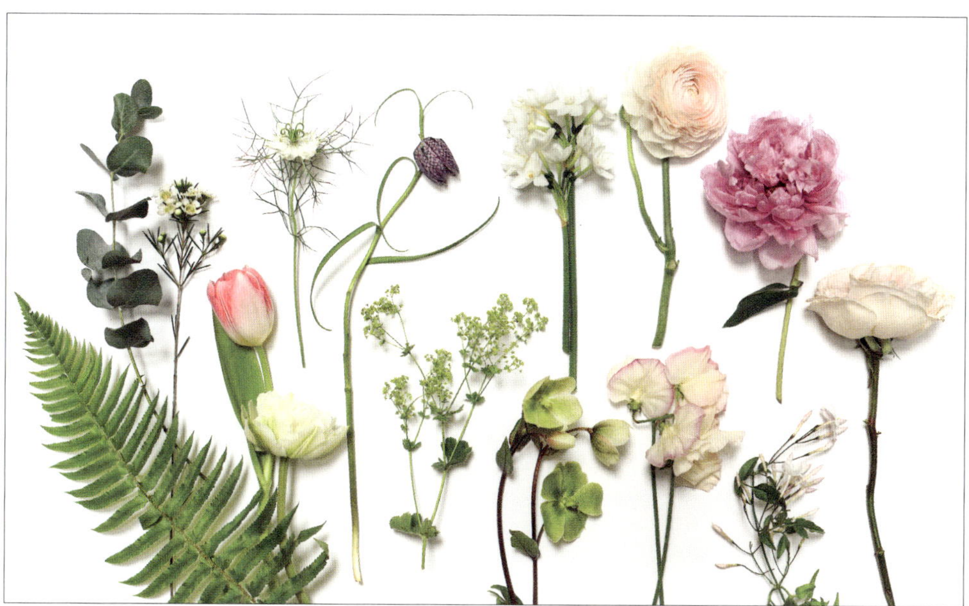

Following these simple steps, using readily available supplies, you can create your own beautiful flower arrangement, inspired by the work of popular London floral designers.

You will need:

1. A 12-inch (30-cm) square of chicken wire cut from a roll using tin snips. (**Tip:** Do not use gardening clippers to cut wire, as it will dull them.) Alternatively, you can substitute floral foam.
2. Thick gardening gloves to wear while shaping the chicken wire, if using.
3. Floral preservative and a suitable decorative container, such as an urn or shapely vase. Ensure that it will hold water.
4. Floral clippers strong enough to cut stems.
5. Flowers and foliage:
   a. Choose two or three varieties of flowers in complementary colors to feature. Here we've used blush ranunculus, pink peonies, and blush roses, all of which are available in season at almost any flower market or stand and many grocery stores, too.
   b. Choose several pretty secondary flowers. We've used pink tulips and sweet peas, hellebores, fritillaria, and white narcissus.
   c. Choose two or three feathery accent flowers. We've used nigella and jasmine.
   d. Choose three or four stiff flowers and foliage for structure. We've used eucalyptus, fern, and wax flower. These will form the foundation of your arrangement, so don't choose limp or flimsy varieties.

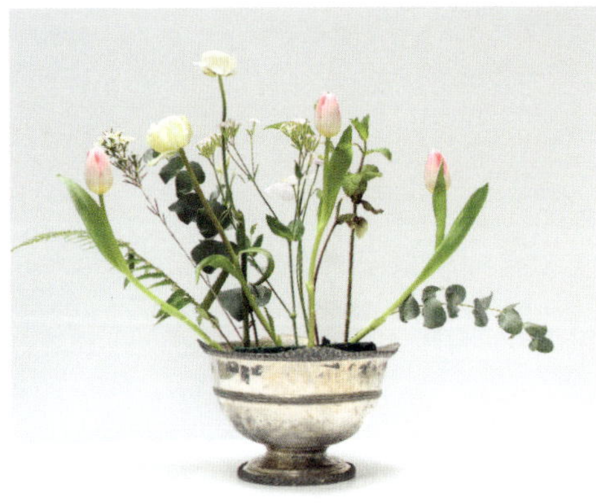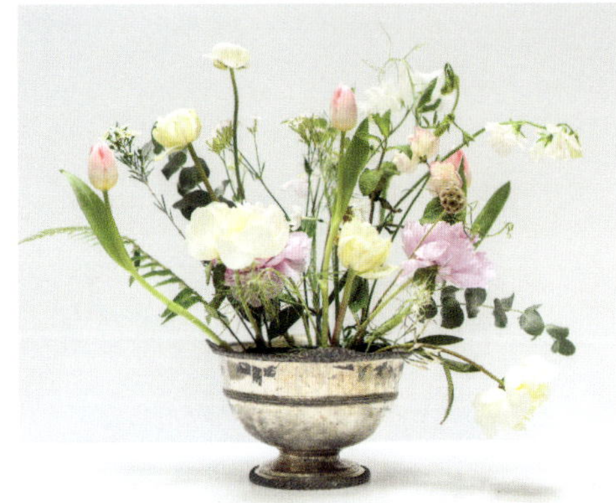

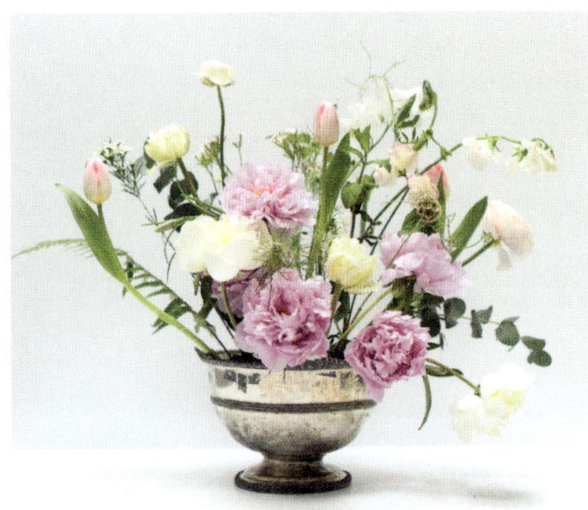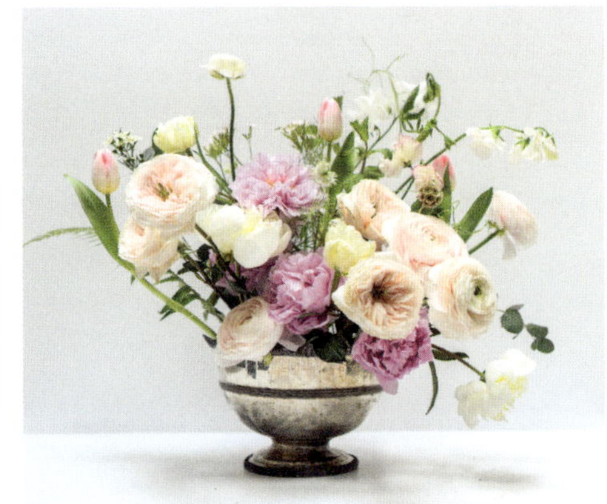

Steps:

1. Prepare all the flowers and foliage by stripping off the leaves that would sit below the water level in the container. Remove any thorns from the roses. Cut the stems at an angle and put them in fresh water.

2. Wearing gloves, crush the chicken wire, if using, into a loose ball, taking care not to poke yourself on the sharp edges.

3. Place the chicken wire (or floral foam) into the decorative container and fill with water. Add floral preservative to the water to help prolong the life and freshness of the flowers.

4. Choose a selection of nice-looking stems of each foliage plant. Cut to the length appropriate for the size and shape of the arrangement you envision. Hold them up before you place them in the container to ensure that they are not too long. Trim as needed.

5. Place the trimmed foliage in the container to create a good foundation for the flowers to come. Ensure all the stems are stable in the foam or wire and not easily moved. You can also add some of the stiffer secondary flowers, such as ranunculus and tulips, for structure.

6. Choose your first featured flowers, preferably round blossoms (ours are peonies and roses), and trim their stems to a length that will allow them to nestle in among the foliage.

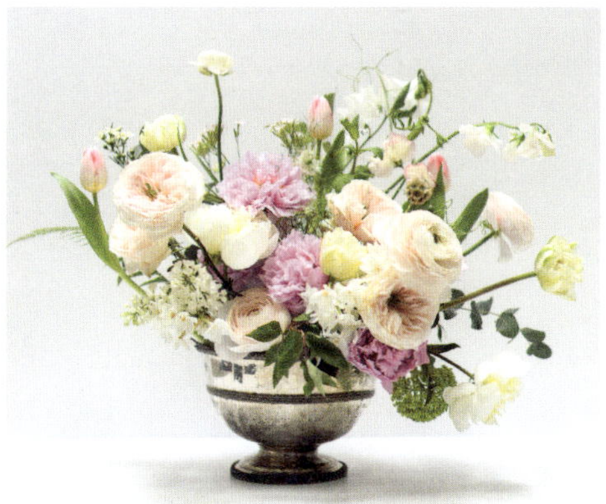 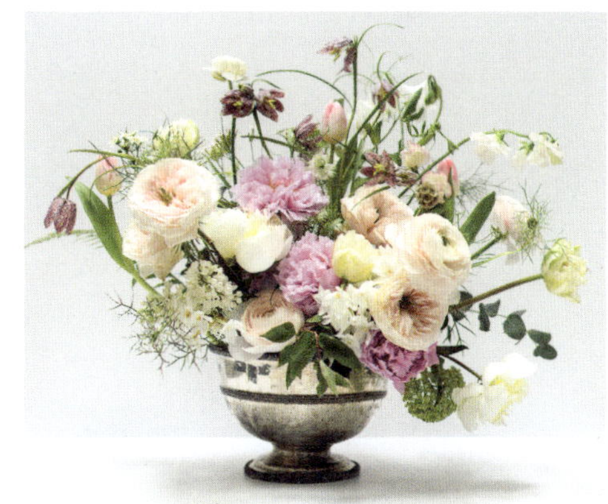

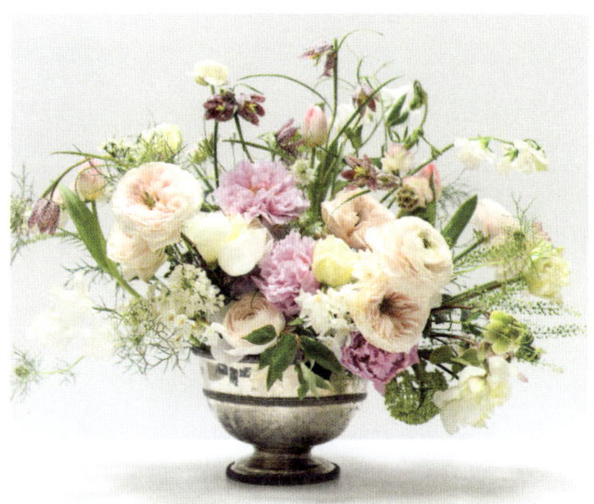 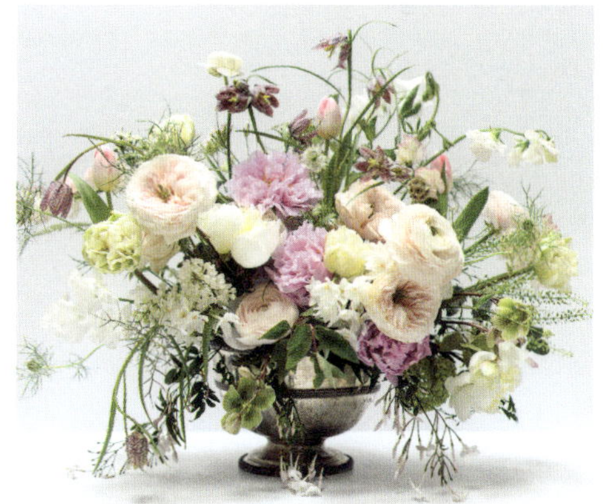

7. Place more featured flowers in prominent spots, clustering them together as shown. Ensure they are secured in position, with their stems firmly in the foam or wire so the flowers will not droop or fall out of the container.

8. Begin to add the secondary flowers to give color and more texture. Place them on the sides and behind the first featured flowers as you face the arrangement.

9. Add more of the secondary flowers to fill any gaps and make a lush presentation.

10. Add the feathery accent flowers (ours are jasmine and nigella) at varying heights, for interest and movement.

11. Trail the jasmine down the sides of the container (keeping the stem in water) for a soft, romantic look. Do a final adjustment. Look at your arrangement from all angles to check for gaps or holes. Fill any gaps with more flowers, trimming the stems as needed.

12. Display your arrangement in a location where it will bring you and others joy and be appreciated. Be sure to check the water level several times a day and refresh as needed.

FIELD GUIDE TO COMMON SPRING-BLOOMING TREES AND SHRUBS IN LONDON

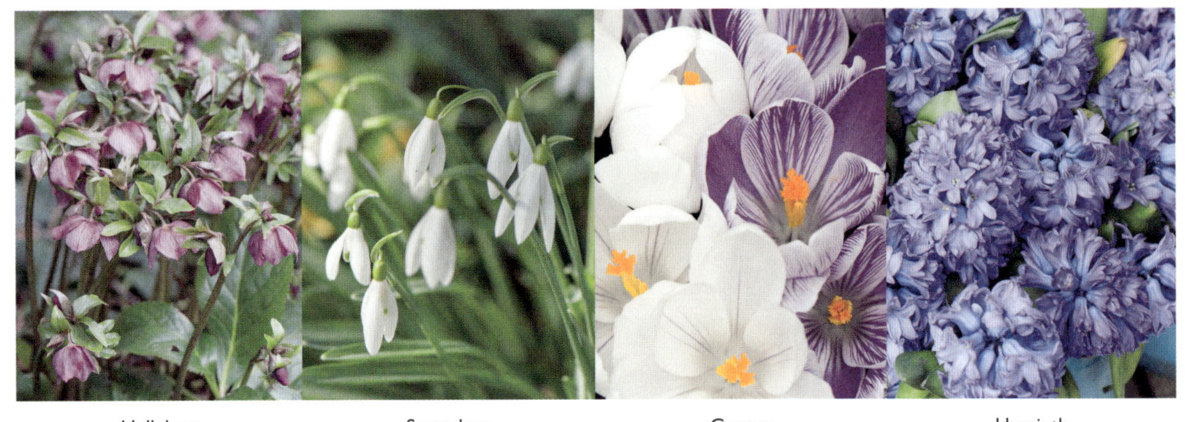

Hellebore
(*Helleborus*)

Snowdrop
(*Galanthus*)

Crocus
(*Crocus*)

Hyacinth
(*Hyacinthus orientalis*)

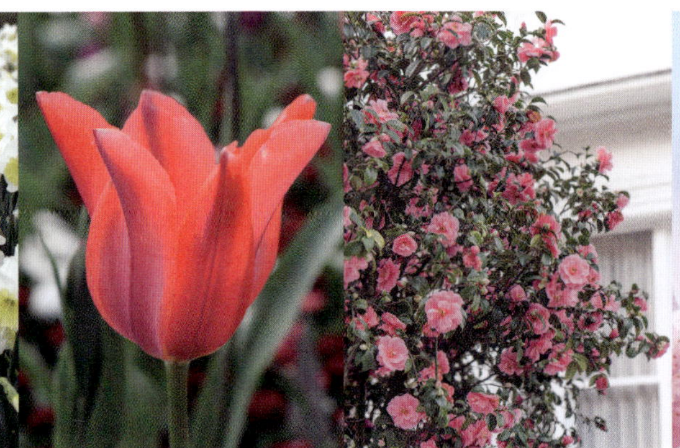

Daffodil
(*Narcissus*)

Tulip
(*Tulipa*)

Camellia
(*Camellia japonica*)

Blireiana plum
(*Prunus* × *blireiana*)

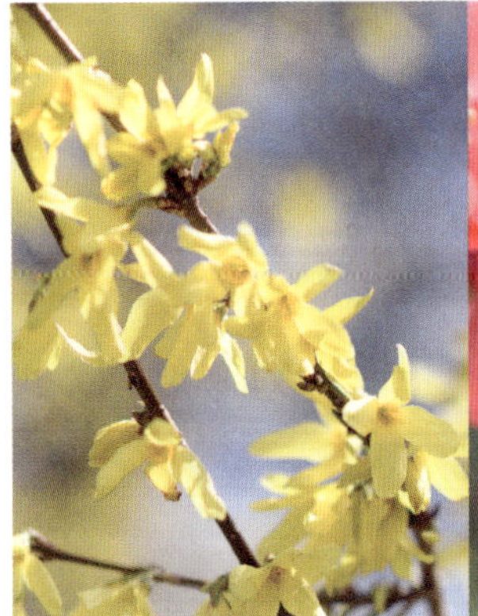
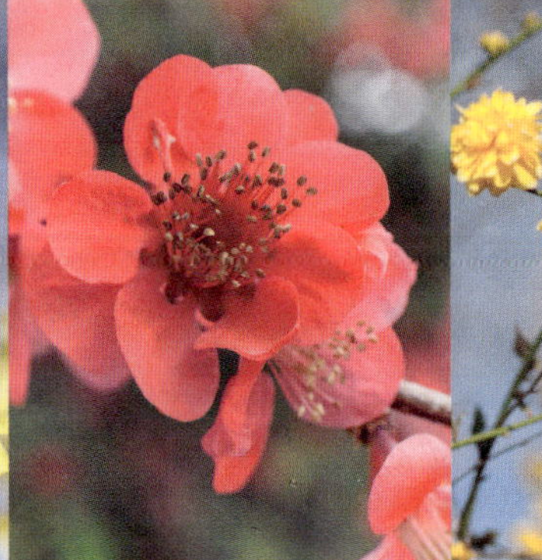
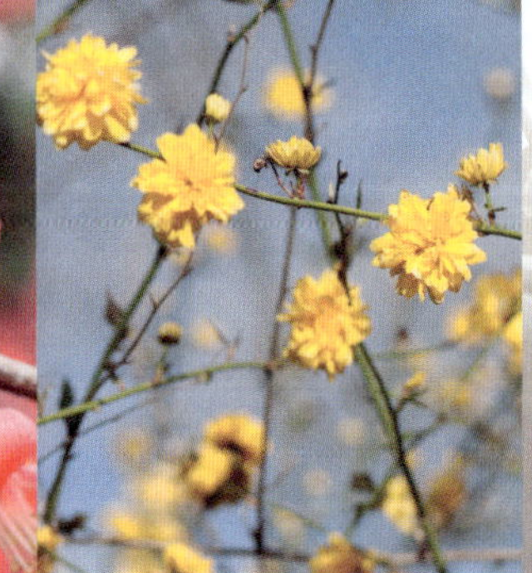
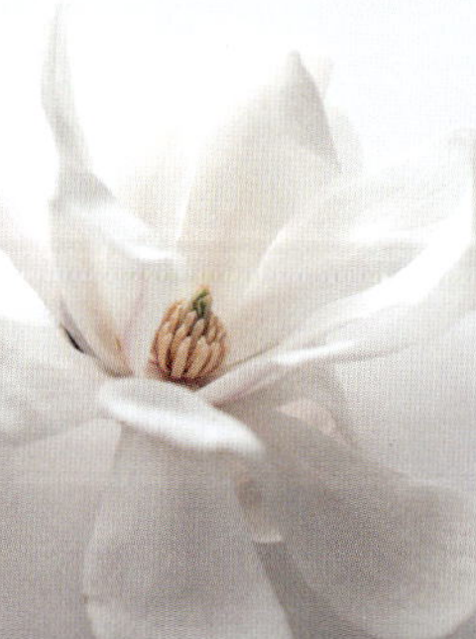

Forsythia
(*Forsythia* × *intermedia*)

Flowering quince
(*Chaenomeles*)

Kerria
(*Kerria japonica*)

Star magnolia
(*Magnolia stellata*)

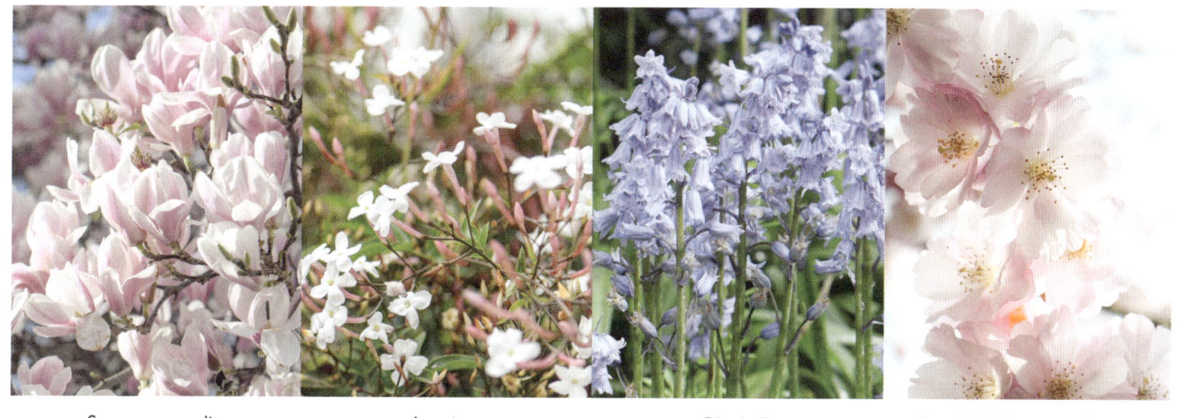

Saucer magnolia
(*Magnolia* × *soulangeana*)

Jasmine
(*Jasminum*)

Bluebell
(*Hyacinthoides non-scripta*)

Accolade flowering cherry
(*Prunus* 'Accolade')

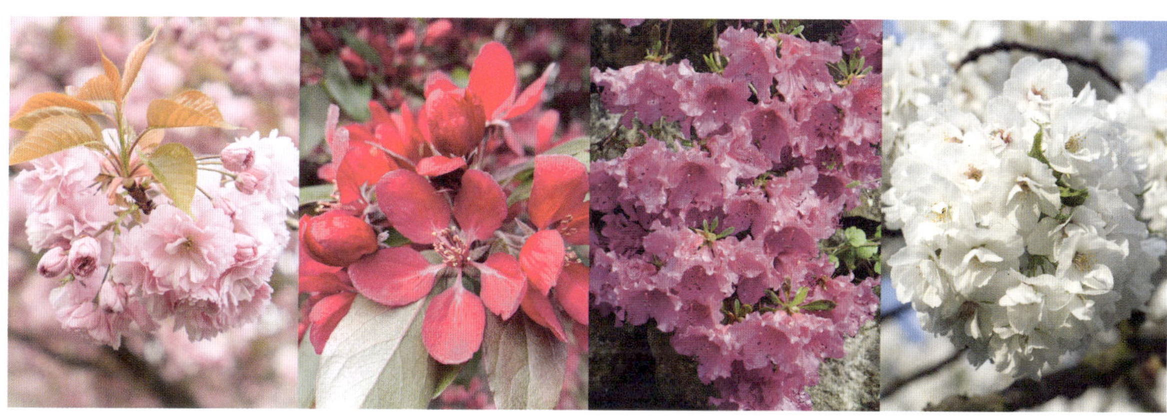

Kwanzan (or Kanzan) flowering cherry (*Prunus serrulata* 'Kwanzan' or 'Kanzan')

Flowering crabapple
(*Malus spectabilis*)

Azalea
(*Rhododendron*)

Mount Fuji flowering cherry
(*Prunus* 'Shirotae')

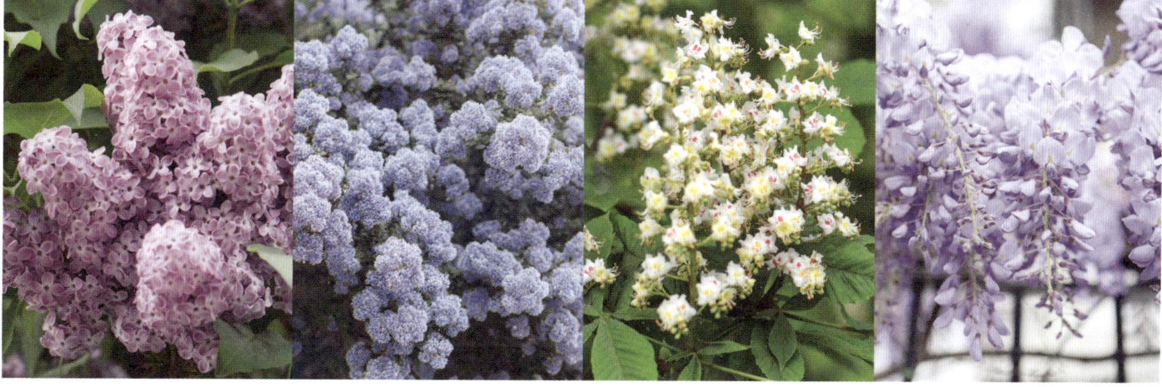

Lilac
(*Syringa vulgaris*)

California lilac
(*Ceanothus*)

European horse chestnut
(*Aesculus hippocastanum*)

Wisteria
(*Wisteria sinensis*)

SPRING TOUR OF BLOSSOMS AND BLOOMS

This introductory guide will lead the enthusiastic blossom hunter to many of my favorite springtime blooming scenes throughout London.

Where: St. James's Park
When: Late February to March. Daffodils in swathes of yellow and white fill the park along Birdcage Walk and the Mall.
Late March to early April. Cherry trees bloom along St. James's Park Lake and near Constitution Hill.

Where: The Green Park
When: Late February to March. Yellow and white daffodils line the paths from Constitution Hill and Piccadilly.

Where: Buckingham Palace flower beds, also known as the Memorial Gardens, St. James's Park
When: March to April. Red tulips and yellow wallflowers provide a bright carpet in front of Buckingham Palace.

Where: The Regent's Park
When: Early April. Cherry and crab apple trees bloom throughout the park. A particularly beautiful area is the path to the east of the Broad Walk, in the English Gardens, which features arched cherry trees in April, flanked by fountains and bedded tulips.
From mid-May throughout the summer. Roses bloom in abundance in Queen Mary's Gardens.

Where: Kensington Gardens
When: March through April. Numerous locations in this huge park offer spring-blossom viewing. In late February and early March, crocus and daffodils bloom in carpets throughout the garden. Near the Albert Memorial is a small grove of cherry trees that bloom in April, and other cherry and crab apple trees bloom throughout the spring. Also in April, the beds are filled with azaleas, bluebells, and tulips. The Sunken Garden is planted with bright tulips, as is the Orangery.

Where: Hyde Park
When: February through April. Crocus, daffodils, and tulips in succession fill the beds from February to March, while blooming trees dot the landscape in late March to April.
Mid-May through summer. The Rose Garden near Hyde Park Corner is a beautiful respite of winding paths and roses on hanging swags.

Where: Royal Botanic Gardens, Kew
When: March to April. Blooming plants and trees can always be found here in spring. In particular, narcissus surround the Palm House, and cherry trees can be found along Cherry Walk in mid-April.
Mid-May through summer. Roses bloom in the large garden behind the Palm House.

Where: Battersea Park
When: Late March to mid-April. Blooming cherry trees create a pink canopy in this large and lovely park.

Where: Holland Park
When: April. Tulips are planted in the boxwood-hedged garden near the Belvedere. Beautiful crab apple trees bloom at the same time near the tennis court.

Where: Potters Fields Park, at the base of Tower Bridge
When: Early to mid-April. White cherry trees bloom, framing Tower Bridge.

Where: Ravenscourt Park
When: Mid- to late March. A double row of cherry trees blooms near the north playground.

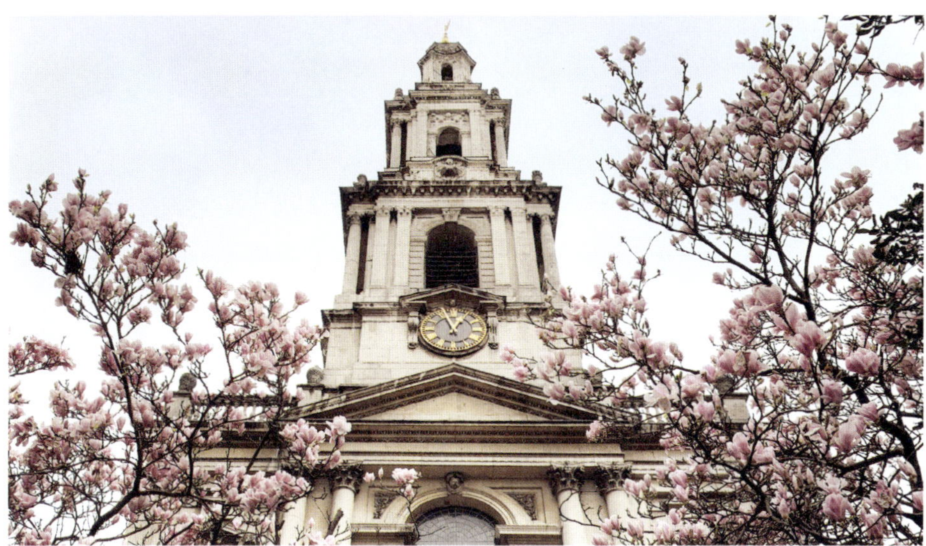

Where: Isabella Plantation, Richmond Park
When: Late April to early May. A large collection of azaleas and rhododendrons blooms in this 40-acre (16-ha.) woodland garden.

Where: Mount Street Gardens
When: Mid-April. One very large and beautiful Kwanzan cherry tree blooms, casting a pink glow over the gardens and row of benches.

Where: Constitution Hill at Buckingham Palace
When: Mid-April. Several enormous dark-pink crab apple trees and a number of white cherry trees bloom along Spur Road.

Where: Royal Borough of Kensington and Chelsea, Notting Hill
When: March and April. The residential neighborhoods of Kensington, Chelsea, and Notting Hill put on a spectacular show of blooming plum, magnolia, cherry, and crab apple trees and, in late April, wisteria.

Where: Chelsea, Mayfair, and Belgravia
When: During the third week of May, when the Chelsea Flower Show takes place, these three neighborhoods become outdoor floral art shows with numerous beautiful and impressive installations.

Where: St. Paul's Cathedral
When: During March, magnolia and cherry trees bloom in the Carter Lane and Festival Gardens adjacent to the cathedral.
May through the summer. Roses bloom in the same gardens, as well as along the fence in the Festival Gardens.

Where: St. Mary le Strand
When: March. Tall magnolia trees bloom, romantically framing the entrance to the church.

Where: Cromwell Gardens
When: Mid-April. A small grove of Kwanzan cherry trees blooms, directly opposite the Victoria and Albert Museum.

Where: Greenwich Park, near Ranger's House
When: Mid-April. A double row of Kwanzan cherry trees creates a magical view in this beautiful park.

SELECTED ADDRESSES

A complete listing of London's parks and floral resources is beyond the scope of this section, but these are my personal favorites.

PARKS AND GARDENS

Kensington Gardens and Hyde Park
London W2
Several gardens within these two expansive parks are regular destinations for me, including the Sunken Garden, also known as the Princess Diana Memorial Garden, the Italian Gardens, and the Rose Garden.

St. James's Park
London SW1A 2BJ
Daffodils in March and blossoming trees in April are among the main attractions here, as well as beautiful, long views across the lake, home to numerous swans.

The Green Park
London SW1A 1AA
A lovely place for a break from shopping or sightseeing, just off Piccadilly. The stunning Spencer House faces the park and is well worth a visit.

The Regent's Park
Chester Road
London NW1 4NR
This is definitely one of my top choices with so much to offer, including the Queen Mary's Gardens, the Open Air Theatre, formal garden beds, fountains, and many blooming trees in March and April.

Greenwich Park
Greenwich, London SE10 8QY
The historic area of Greenwich warrants a full day of exploration. The park is home to the Royal Observatory, the Prime Meridian, and, near Ranger's House, a double row of pink Kwanzan cherry trees that bloom around mid-April.

Richmond Park
Richmond upon Thames
This huge nature reserve is also the home of the Isabella Plantation, a woodland garden of azaleas and rhododendrons that explode into vibrant color in early May.

Royal Botanic Gardens, Kew
Richmond TW9 3AB
Visit this magnificent garden, a UNESCO World Heritage site, throughout the year to revel in the incredibly diverse botanical collections.

Chelsea Physic Garden
66 Royal Hospital Road
Chelsea, London SW3 4HS
The oldest botanical garden in London with a fascinating history and nearly five thousand herbal, medicinal, and edible plants, it has occupied the same location along the Thames since 1673.

OTHER RECOMMENDED PARKS

Ravenscourt Park
Paddenswick Road
Hammersmith, London W6 0UA

Battersea Park
Battersea, London SW11 4NJ

Holland Park
Ilchester Place
Kensington, London W8 6LU

Potters Fields Park
165 Tower Bridge Road
Bermondsey, London SE1 3LW

Mount Street Gardens
Mount Street
Mayfair, London W1K 2TH

Festival Gardens and Carter Lane Gardens
St. Paul's Churchyard
City of London, London EC4M 8AD

Cromwell Gardens
South Kensington, London SW7

FLORAL BOUTIQUES

Wild Things Flowers
47 Davies Street
Mayfair, London W1K 4LZ
Based in Mayfair since 1996, this shop specializes in luxury weddings, and other events, but it will happily create a luscious custom bouquet for anyone who stops in. Visit also to see its famous outdoor "ponds" filled with floating roses.

Nikki Tibbles Wild at Heart
30a Pimlico Road
Belgravia, London SW1 8LJ

222 Westbourne Grove
Notting Hill, London W11 2RH

32–34 Great Marlborough Street
Liberty
Soho, London W1B 5AH
All three locations of this celebrated company are visually arresting. The well-known location at the entrance of Liberty on Great Marlborough Street presents an ever-changing floral tableau.

Scarlet & Violet
76 Chamberlayne Road
Kensal Green, London NW10 3JJ
This well-known boutique makes breathtaking custom bouquets using seasonal flowers in its charming shop filled with vintage pottery and jars.

OTHER HIGHLY RECOMMENDED FLORISTS
Neill Strain Floral Couture
11 West Halkin Street
Belgravia, London SW1X 8JL

Harrods Food Halls
87–135 Brompton Road
Knightsbridge, London SW1X 7XL

Moyses Stevens
188 Pavilion Road
Chelsea, London SW3 2BF

53 Elizabeth Street
Belgravia, London SW1W 9PP

324 Regent Street
Marylebone, London W1B 3BJ

Zita Elze
287 Sandycombe Road
Richmond TW9 3LU

John & Jessie
131e Kensington Church Street
Kensington, London W8 7LP

Galton Flowers
13 Flask Walk
Hampstead, London NW3 1HJ

MARKET FLOWERS

Columbia Road Flower Market
Columbia Road
Bethnal Green, London E2 7RG
A must-visit destination for flower lovers. Sundays only, but go early, as it becomes very crowded by midmorning.

Petals at Bibendum
Michelin House
81 Fulham Road
Chelsea, London SW3 6RD
Housed in the historic Michelin building, the setting for this vendor is as appealing as its avalanche of cut flowers and pre-made bouquets, which often extends out to the pavement.

The Flower Stand Chelsea
243 Fulham Road at Old Church Street
Chelsea, London, SW3 6HY
For over a quarter of a century, this colorful stand has been located at the corner of Fulham Road and Old Church Street and is a beloved Chelsea landmark.

Kensington Flower Corner
80a Kensington High Street
Kensington, London W8 4SG
Established in 1977, this cheerful seller is located outside St. Mary Abbots Parish Church, which provides a magnificent backdrop for the buckets of blooms and bouquets.

Ronnie's Flowers
Berwick Street Market
Berwick Street
Soho, London W1F 0PH
Reportedly the oldest flower stall in London, Ronnie's is *the* place for cut flowers in the Soho area.

**New Covent Garden Market
and Floral Angels**
Nine Elms Lane
SW8 5BH
Tours through this massive wholesale market, which sells produce in addition to flowers, can be arranged through its website: newcoventgardenmarket.com.

OTHER RECOMMENDED SOURCES
Pink Pansy
Embankment Station
Embankment Place
Charing Cross, London WC2N 6NS

Flowers, Inc.
138 Gloucester Road
South Kensington, London SW7 4SF

Borough Market
8 Southwark Street
Southwark, London SE1 1TL

The Flower Station
Rossmore Court, Park Road
Marylebone, London NW1 6XU

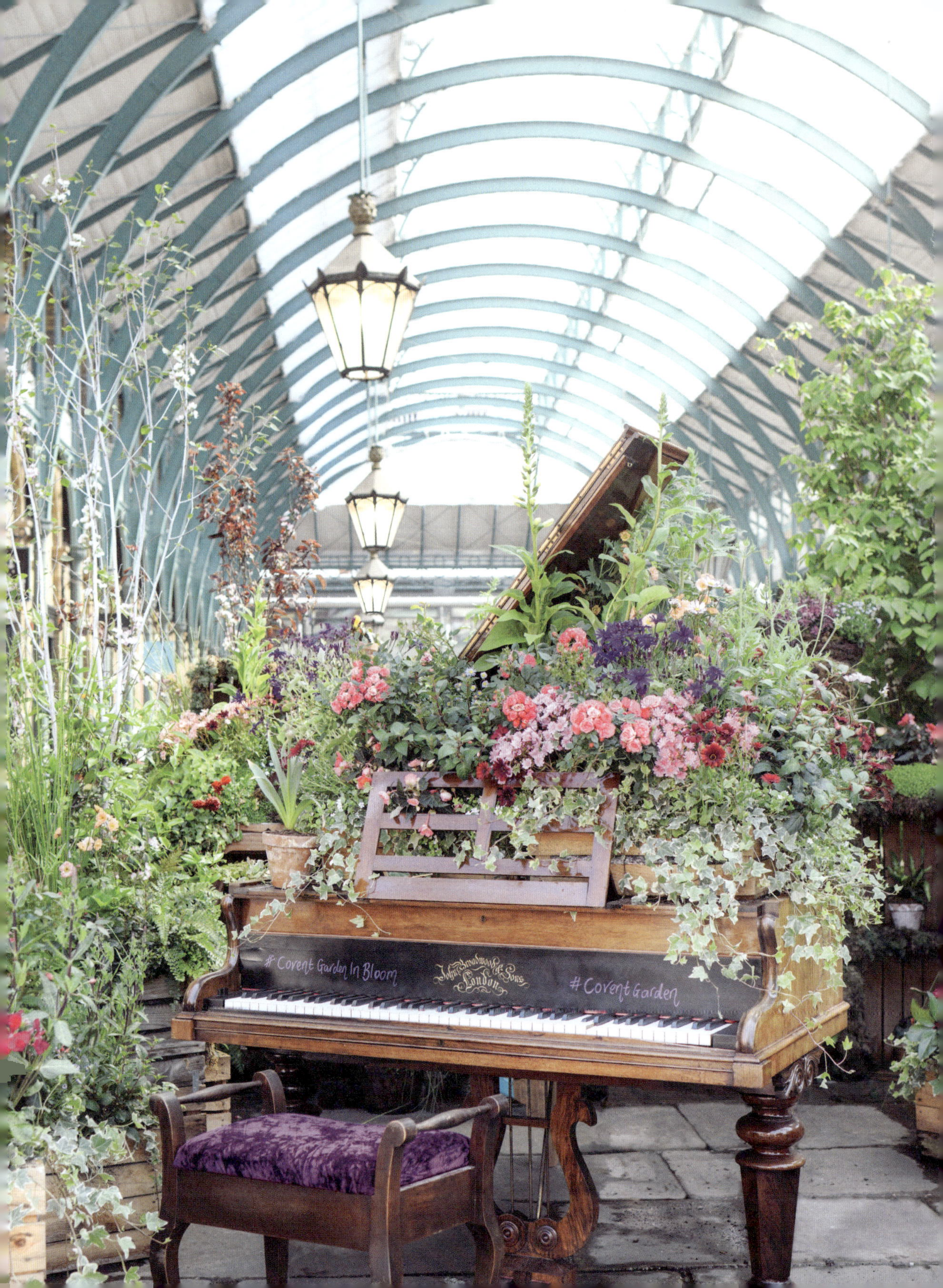
＃ Covent Garden In Bloom
John Broadwood & Sons
London
＃ Covent Garden

DEDICATION

To David, my English gentleman.

ACKNOWLEDGMENTS

Photographing the floral delights of London has been an unforgettable pleasure. I am very grateful for the generous support and contribution of many individuals and organizations:

My longtime agent Kate Woodrow for her invaluable guidance and support.

My patient and insightful editor, Laura Dozier, and my talented and creative designer Darilyn Carnes at Abrams.

Nim Ben-Reuven for the exquisite custom lettering on the cover and throughout the book.

The administrators of London's parks and gardens, including the Royal Parks (owned by the Crown, and maintained by the Royal Parks charity), the Chelsea Physic Garden, the Royal Botanic Gardens, Kew, and Holland Park.

The directors and staff of Spencer House, London, in particular Nathan Jones (property director) and Vicky Wilson (collections manager), for allowing me private access and permission to photograph and publish details from this treasured location.

The directors and staff of the museums, galleries, and historic buildings featured, including the Queen's House, Greenwich, the Royal Academy of Arts, the National Portrait Gallery, Host Café at St. Mary Aldermary, the Michelin House, and the Grange Langham Court Hotel.

My fellow author Siobhan Ferguson, founder and editor of @prettycitylondon, for her warm welcome, vital advice, and introductions to the London social community.

My London friends for their much-appreciated support, advice, inspiration, encouragement, and location assistance: Gray Levett and Gillian Greenwood of Grays of Westminster, Nathan Rollinson, Victoria Metaxas, Philippa Stanton, Miranda Mills, Gulshan Batool, Julie Taylor, Michelle Corbett, and Ana Linares.

The Royal Horticultural Society, the organizers of the Chelsea Flower Show, and Peter Beales Roses.

Peggy Porschen and Hannah Clifford for generous permission to feature the Peggy Porschen Belgravia and Chelsea Parlours, with floral displays by Dickinson & Doris, and pink bicycle by Pashley Cycles, on the front cover and interior pages.

Jo Malone and company for featuring their pink flower–bedecked Morris.

Louise Bermingham, founder and director of Wild Things Flowers, for her kindness and generosity in creating the luscious custom arrangements on page 85 and in the appendix.

Vic Brotherson for welcoming me to photograph her charming floral boutique, Scarlet & Violet.

Amie Bone and staff for featuring their award-winning Queen Elizabeth floral installation from Fleurs de Villes, Covent Garden.

Additional floral studios and markets featured: By Appointment Only Design, Neill Strain Floral Couture, Zita Elze, John & Jessie, Bramble & Moss, Moyses Stevens, Nikki Tibbles Wild at Heart, Petals at Bibendum, Kensington Flower Corner, the Flower Stand Chelsea, Pink Pansy, and Columbia Road Flower Market.

The designers of the featured spring outdoor floral installations: Harper and Tom's, Phillip Corps Flowers, In Water Flowers, Flowerbx, Early Hours, All for Love, Megan Ingram, and Kenny Raybould.

The owners of the classic London pubs whose facades and window glass details are featured: the Churchill Arms, the Masons Arms, the White Lion, the Salisbury, the Albert, and Angel in the Fields.

The owners of the featured homes of Kensington, Chelsea, Notting Hill, and Primrose Hill.

Tricia Guild and the Designers Guild for sharing their beautiful floral fabrics.

Laurence at Old Books London on Portobello Road for the rare botanical books and vintage china I purchased for pages 66, 104, 106, 108, and 109, and Alice's on Portobello Road for the floral Staffordshire pitchers on page 108.

Angels Coffee on Kensington Church Street for featuring their new café.

Karen Tran, Mwai Yeboah, and Jane Riddell for welcoming me to the magnificent Karen Tran Opulence Gala at the Savoy Hotel.

Nail'd It salon for featuring their fun floral phone booth.

Photographer Neil Emmerson for allowing me to photograph his setup shot of the 2018 Morgan Plus 4 in front of Annabel's.

Annabel's for graciously allowing the photograph of their facade and floral display by Flowerbx.

SJ Thomson of Covent Garden London (Capco) for welcoming me to the Covent Garden community and for her enthusiasm for this project.

Madelyn Byrne Willems and the exceptional team at London Perfect for once again providing me with a beautiful, quiet, and inspiring place to call home during the creation of this book.

My husband, David, and my family for always being supportive and enthusiastic about my work, despite my long absences and perpetual deadlines.

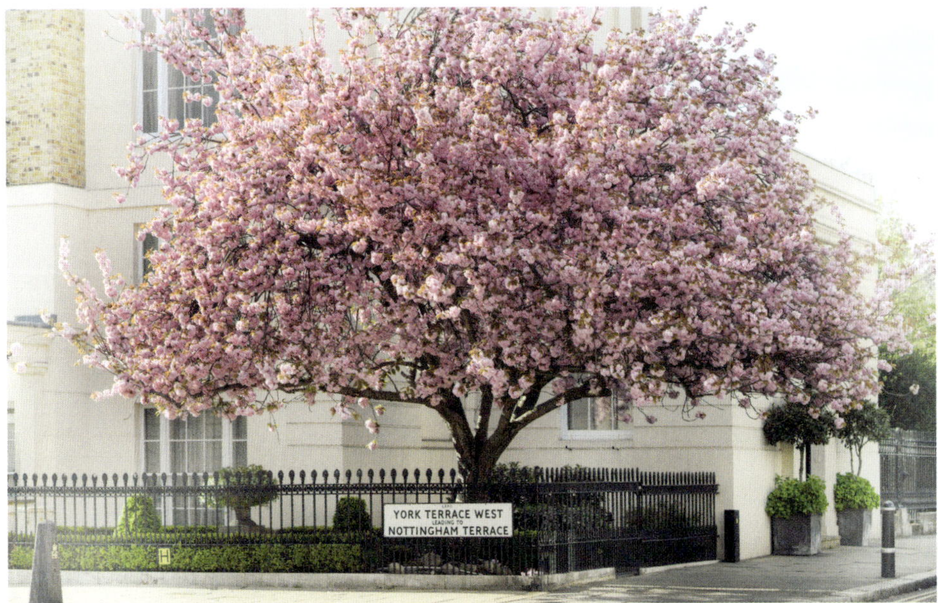

Editor: Laura Dozier
Designer: Darilyn Lowe Carnes
Production Manager: Kathleen Gaffney

Library of Congress Control Number: 2019939757

ISBN: 978-1-4197-3078-8
eISBN: 978-1-68335-886-2

Printed and bound in China
10 9 8 7 6

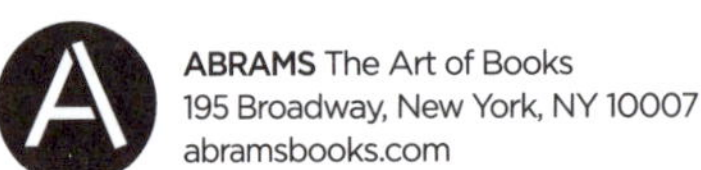

ABRAMS The Art of Books
195 Broadway, New York, NY 10007
abramsbooks.com